How to Research
Elections

How to Research Elections

Fenton S. Martin
Robert U. Goehlert

Indiana University

CQ PRESS

A Division of Congressional Quarterly Inc.
Washington, D.C.

A fully searchable electronic version of *How to Research Elections* is available online at http://research_elections.cqpress.com, for a limited time.

CQ Press
A Division of Congressional Quarterly Inc.
1414 22nd Street, N.W.
Washington, DC 20037

(202) 822-1475; (800) 638-1710

www.cqpress.com

Printed in the United States of America
04 03 02 01 00   5 4 3 2 1

Library of Congress Cataloging-in-Publication Data
In process.

ISBN 1-56802-597-1

Contents

Part II Selected Bibliography on Elections

Preface

In *How to Research Elections* we introduce the various types of resources available for studying elections. We also include information on materials that provide background data on elections. We have been selective in the resources included and have kept the annotations as simple as possible.

The first part of this book covers secondary and primary sources and the finding tools that can be used to locate them. Chapter 1 lists secondary sources and finding tools, including news sources, newspapers, newsmagazines, journals, statistics, polls, and Internet sites that provide current information on elections. It also describes pertinent indexes, abstracting services, online databases, and CD-ROM products. These publications and services are important not only in pinpointing specific information but also in simplifying the research process. Primary sources and finding tools include information on primaries and caucuses, conventions, campaign finance, interest groups and political action committees, electoral returns, district data, and other topics. Chapter 2 identifies primary sources for studying elections, including platforms, information on advocacy groups, and election returns. The primary research sources are grouped by categories: campaigns, primaries and caucuses, conventions, campaign finances, interest groups, political action committees, political consultants, the electoral system, political parties, election data, district data, voting and registration data, and party strength data. Short descriptions are provided for many of the sources. Some of the sources also provide background or historical information, thus helping to put the elections in perspective.

The second part of this book presents a selected bibliography of major books about elections. The books listed offer information on the nomination process, primaries, conventions, campaigning, candidates, presidential debates, campaign finance, media coverage of elections, political parties, the electoral system, redistricting, and voting participation. We were selective in our choice of materials, including only books that we believe are of lasting interest to election scholars. We did not include some books that were significant at the time of their publication but have been superseded by newer works, and not all areas are covered equally. The book concludes with title and author indexes covering material presented in the first part.

We are grateful to the manuscript editor, Sharon Lamberton, for skillfully editing the manuscript. We thank Tom Roche for his attention to detail while the book moved through production. We owe much to the executive editor at CQ Press, David Tarr, for his advice, support, and friendship. He has made our association with CQ Press a pleasurable one. We wish to extend our appreciation to Richard L. Pacelle Jr. for his expert counsel. We appreciate the love and patience that Virginia and Amanda Goehlert have given their father, Robert Goehlert, and the love and patience Russell and Craig have given their mother, Fenton Martin, through the years of our producing guides and bibliographies in political science. We thank the Political Science Department at Indiana University for its support of our research.

Introduction
Designing a Research Strategy

Outlining a research strategy ahead of time will make your information search more efficient and productive. The research strategy you develop can determine the kinds of materials you seek. This introduction presents basic guidelines for developing a topic and designing a research strategy for finding material about elections.

Developing a topic that is sufficiently narrow, manageable, and original is not an easy task. Most topics grow from some unanswered question that may warrant further analysis and explanation. If you have not yet identified or defined a topic for your research, browse through current newspapers, books, bibliographies, a periodical index, and the Web to see what is being written about elections. Preliminary research and reading can help you develop a topic. Then do some initial research to see what books and articles have been written about that particular topic.

Make a list of questions regarding elections. As you develop your topic, keep in mind that eventually you will need to define a proposition or thesis to prove or disprove. Think of questions that can help you describe the topic: When did an event take place? Who was involved? Why was an event or issue considered a problem? Who was affected? The more you think about a topic and outline the details, the easier it will be to search thoroughly and systematically for material later on. Remember that secondary sources, such as encyclopedias, dictionaries, or journal articles, can provide a starting point for your research and direct you to important primary sources.

Once you have a topic, but before you begin to search for additional materials, you should think through a basic research design. This process will help you organize your research strategy and clarify the topic by revealing, for example, if the topic is too broad to be manageable. If a thesis cannot be argued effectively, you will have to take another approach. A research design should include a statement of the topic, a review of the literature, a definition of the thesis to be argued, a description of the operational design, and the methods of analysis and interpretation.

As part of the research design, develop a checklist of the kinds of materials you are looking for and the specific finding tools necessary to gain access to those materials. Identify which disciplines, such as law, history, or political science, you might explore for materials, as well as the time period you will cover, such as one year, a decade, or some other time period. Identifying significant facts and issues that need to be researched helps you create a logical outline of issues and subissues, which can be extremely useful as you refine your research strategy. As your outline changes, so will your research strategy.

List the information sources you will consult. Your plan should include the following steps:

1. Search libraries' subject catalogs.
2. Search research guides to identify any special compilations, bibliographies, and other finding tools germane to the topic.
3. Search periodical indexes and abstracting services in print, CD-ROM, and online formats.
4. Search online information services, such as LEXIS/NEXIS Academic Universe or CQ.COM ON CONGRESS, for primary sources and background information.
5. Search the Internet for pertinent primary sources, background information, and government documents.
6. Search encyclopedias and dictionaries for background information and citations to primary sources.
7. Search newspaper indexes for information on the topic.
8. Search for bibliographies on the topic.
9. Check bibliographies and footnotes in books, articles, dissertations, and other materials you will use to begin your research. Such references can lead you to important primary and secondary sources.
10. Search the appropriate finding tools for identifying government documents.
11. Search appropriate indexes and Internet sources for data.

Make a checklist of all of the possible terms, concepts, and names that you will consult as subject headings. Such a list may include a dozen or more possible subject headings. Because subject headings vary in subject catalogs, encyclopedias, and other finding tools, think of synonyms to try as you move from one finding tool to another. As you conduct your research you will discover which subject headings are most useful; however, it is better to begin by searching under a variety of subject headings rather than just using one or two. A common mistake researchers make is to look under only one or two subject headings, find only a few citations, and assume that little has been written about a topic. Although that may be the case, often the materials simply are indexed under other subject headings. If you use tools that allow you to perform key word searching, track the terms you use. If your tools allow both subject and key word searching, try each approach.

Record which finding tools you have checked and the subject headings and key words you have used. Keeping a record of your research makes it easier to revise your strategy and remember which finding tools are available, especially if you need to refer back to a source to get additional citations or information. The most important thing to do when conducting a search is to take notes that record where you find a particular citation. A record of the finding tools you have searched, listing, for example, which volumes or years or which subject headings you have consulted, will save you time and facilitate the writing of your research paper.

How to Research
Elections

Part I

Secondary Sources, Primary Sources, and Finding Tools

1

Secondary Sources and Finding Tools

This chapter lists secondary sources and finding tools, including news sources, newspapers, newsmagazines, journals, statistics, polls, Internet sites, pertinent indexes, abstracting services, online databases, and CD-ROM products.

Indexes

Indexes and abstracting services are crucial tools for finding journal articles on elections. Using the many indexes now available on CD-ROM or online can save you time and effort. The following indexes are the most useful for finding journal articles pertaining to elections:

ABC POL SCI: A Bibliography of Contents: Political Science and Government. Santa Barbara, CA: ABC-Clio, 1969–.

The tables of contents of U.S. and foreign journals appear six times a year in this index. Because it is published in advance of the journals' publication dates, the index is especially useful for finding very recent articles on elections. It is available on CD-ROM as ABC POL SCI ON DISC and as an online database.

America: History and Life. Santa Barbara, CA: ABC-Clio, 1964–.

This serial bibliography and abstracting service provides excellent coverage of articles, book and film reviews, and dissertations in history, political science, and the social sciences. Always include this index when doing historical research on elections. It is available on CD-ROM and as an online database.

Humanities Index. New York: H. W. Wilson, 1974–.

This quarterly index to English-language journals in the humanities organizes entries by author and subject. This index covers the major history journals and is best used in searches for citations related to the history of elections. It is available on CD-ROM and as an online database.

Index to Legal Periodicals. New York: H. W. Wilson, 1908–.

This work indexes articles appearing in legal periodicals of the United States, Canada, Great Britain, Northern Ireland, Australia, and New Zealand. Indexes are provided for authors, subjects, book reviews, and cases. This index should be used in almost every literature search on elections. Because the *Index to Legal Periodicals* is one of the oldest legal indexes, it also can be used for historical research. It is available on CD-ROM and as an online database.

International Political Science Abstracts. Paris: International Political Science Association, 1951–.

This index abstracts articles from English-language and foreign-language political science journals. The abstracts of the English-language articles appear in English, and the abstracts of the foreign-language articles appear in French. *International Political Science Abstracts* is a reliable source of information on foreign-language articles about elections. Even if you are not interested in foreign-language material, check to see if this index contains citations on elections that have not appeared in other indexes. *International Political Science Abstracts* is available on CD-ROM and as an online database.

PAIS International in Print. New York: PAIS, 1915–.

This monthly subject guide to American public policy and public affairs continues the *PAIS Bulletin,* formerly the *Public Affairs Information Service Bulletin.* It indexes government publications, books, and periodical literature, including the *National Journal* and *CQ Researcher.* It is available on CD-ROM and as an online database called PAIS International. A full-text version, called PAIS Select, is issued as a CD-ROM.

Psychological Abstracts. Washington, DC: American Psychological Association, 1927–.

This index covers almost one thousand journals, as well as books, dissertations, and research reports. The author and subject indexes are cumulated quarterly and annually. It also is available on CD-ROM and as an online database.

Reader's Guide to Periodical Literature. New York: H. W. Wilson, 1905–.

This semimonthly guide indexes articles in popular periodicals published in he United States. The entries are indexed by author and by subject. The *Reader's Guide* is a vital reference tool for researching campaigns and elections. It is available on CD-ROM and as an online database.

Social Sciences Citation Index. Philadelphia: Institute for Science Information, 1973–.

The *Social Sciences Citation Index* indexes more journals than any other index in the social sciences. Works cited include books, journal articles, dissertations, reports, and proceedings. It includes four separate indexes: a source (author) index, a corporate index, a key word subject index, and a citation index. Items appearing in the citation index have been cited in footnotes or bibliographies in the social sciences. The *Social Sciences Citation Index* has several unique features that are helpful for studying elections. The corporate index allows the user to identify publications issued by particular organizations, such as the Brookings Institution. The source and citation indexes can be used to identify the writings of a particular scholar who has written extensively on elections, and to identify other researchers who have cited these writings. The *Social Sciences Citation Index* is published three times a year and cumulated annually and quinquennially. It is available on CD-ROM and as an online database. The online database is available through the Web of Science.

Social Sciences Index. New York: H. W. Wilson, 1975–.

This quarterly index covers articles that are found in the major English-language political science and other social science journals. Every literature search on elections, regardless of the topic, should include this index. It is available on CD-ROM and as an online database.

Sociological Abstracts. San Diego, CA: Sociological Abstracts, 1952–.

Sociological Abstracts is the major abstracting service in the field of sociology. It indexes journals, conference papers, dissertations, and book reviews. The author and subject indexes are cumulated annually. It is available on CD-ROM and as an online database.

Databases

Scholars of elections will find the following online services especially helpful. These services allow the researcher to obtain information on candidates, campaign contributions and financing, government documents, and information on campaigns and elections. The major online databases providing information on elections are listed below:

CONGRESSIONAL UNIVERSE. Washington, DC: Congressional Information Service.

This online database provides a section called Inside Washington, where the *National Journal* is indexed. The database provides information on campaign contributions and a member directory. A section called List of Links contains information on political parties. An abstracting service for congressional committee hearings, committee prints, reports, documents, and public laws, CONGRESSIONAL UNIVERSE includes the full texts of bills and regulations. This database is by subscription only, so check to see if your library subscribes.

CQ.COM ON CONGRESS. Washington, DC: Congressional Quarterly.

This database provides coverage of daily events in Congress and current political news. Information on politics and elections can be found in a section named the News and Analysis Area. The full texts of the *CQ Weekly, CQ Monitor News,* and Newsmaker Transcripts also are provided in this section. Newspapers from around the country and broadcast news from more than fifty cities are indexed in a section called the Bulletin News Network. This database is available by subscription only, so check to see if your library subscribes.

DOW JONES INTERACTIVE. New York: Dow Jones Company.

Dow Jones Interactive on the Web includes a section, Business Newsstand, which provides newswires from major newspapers and magazines including the *Wall Street Journal, New York Times,* and *Washington Post.* The Publications Library section contains more than 6,000 newswires, newspapers, and magazines and can be used for in-depth research. The Web Center section provides links to news, corporate, industry, and government sites. This database is available by subscription only, so check to see if your library subscribes.

LEXIS/NEXIS Academic Universe. Dayton, OH: Reed Elsevier Inc.

This database can be used for finding information about elections, as it provides full text to news, biographical information, Roper Center for Public Opinion Research polls and surveys, business, legal and reference materials. It includes data from the Federal Election Commission and analyses from news transcripts from CNN, ABC, and NPR. LEXIS/NEXIS includes the full texts of the *National Journal, Congressional Record,* and the *Almanac of American Politics.* Numerous legal journals also can be accessed. This database is available by subscription only, so check to see if your library subscribes.

STATISTICAL UNIVERSE. Washington, DC: Congressional Information Service.

This database indexes more than 100,000 statistical publications by subject, title, issuing agency, and author. The *Statistical Abstract of the United States* also is provided, in a format searchable for statistics on elections. This database is available by subscription only, so check to see if your library subscribes. The *Statistical Abstract of the United States* is available online for the years 1995 to 1999 in PDF format. It is available for free on the Web site for CenStore at http://www.census.gov/mp/www/censtore.html.

THOMAS. Washington, DC: Library of Congress.

The Library of Congress provides THOMAS, an electronic tool for accessing government information on the Web. THOMAS gathers several government resources into one place. THOMAS is accessible at http://thomas.loc.gov. It contains the full text of legislation, the full text of the *Congressional Record*, Senate and House information, and C-SPAN and hypertext links.

Journals

Many print and online journals regularly publish articles about some aspect of elections. *Campaigns & Elections* is devoted exclusively to elections. This journal is available both in print form and online at http://www. campaignline.com. The *American Political Science Review*, *Journal of Politics*, and the *American Journal of Political Science* are on the Web from the Journal Storage Project (JSTOR), which is available by subscription only. JSTOR archives full-text versions of scholarly journals. *CQ Weekly* is available online from CQ.COM ON CONGRESS News and Analysis and in *CQ Library*. The *National Journal* is available online from CONGRESSIONAL UNIVERSE and LEXIS/NEXIS Academic Universe. Abstracts and sometimes the full texts of journal articles can be found in indexes and databases cited previously. The following journals contain articles on elections:

American Journal of Political Science. Madison, WI: Midwest Political Science Association, University of Wisconsin Press, 1973–.

American Political Science Review. Washington, DC: American Political Science Association, 1906–.

American Politics Quarterly. Beverly Hills, CA: Sage, 1973–.

Campaigns & Elections. Washington, DC: Congressional Quarterly, 1980–.

Congress and the Presidency: A Journal of Capitol Studies. Washington, DC: Center for Congressional and Presidential Studies, American University, 1983–.

CQ Weekly. Washington, DC: Congressional Quarterly, 1945–.

Electoral Studies. Guildford, England, Butterworths, 1982–.

Journal of Politics. Austin, TX: Southern Political Science Association, University of Texas Press, 1939–.

Journalism and Mass Communication Quarterly. Columbia, SC: Association for Education in Journalism and Mass Communication, 1928–.

Legislative Studies Quarterly. Iowa City: Comparative Legislative Research Center, University of Iowa, 1976–.

National Journal. Washington, DC: National Journal, 1969–.

Political Research Quarterly. Salt Lake City, UT: University of Utah, Western Political Science Association, 1993–.

Polity. Amherst, MA: Northeastern Political Science Association, 1968–.

Presidential Studies Quarterly. New York: Center for the Study of the Presidency, 1972–.

Public Choice. Norwell, MA: Kluwer Academic Publishers, 1968–.

Public Opinion Quarterly. Chicago: University of Chicago Press, 1937–.

Social Science Quarterly. Austin, TX: Southwestern Social Science Association, University of Texas, 1968–.

Newsmagazines

Newsmagazines are an excellent source of current information about elections in their news stories, editorials, and feature articles. One of the best indexes for finding articles for newsmagazines, the *Reader's Guide to Periodical Literature,* is available in print, on CD-ROM, and online. Several vendors provide other online indexes to general newsmagazines. One example is Academic Search Elite. The magazines listed below regularly carry election-related articles written from a variety of political viewpoints. Many of these magazines are available through online services such as LEXIS/NEXIS Academic Universe. Determine to which online indexes your library subscribes. The online services change what they carry, so the best way to determine what magazines they include is to check online.

Several of the newsmagazines, including *Time, CQ Researcher, National Review,* and *U.S. News and World Report* have Web versions. *CQ Researcher* also is available online in CQ Library. A weekly faxed newsletter, *Campaign Insider,* published by Congressional Quarterly, also provides information on elections.

The following newsmagazines are most useful for keeping up on current events and as a record of public opinion via their editorials and opinion articles:

Atlantic Monthly. Boston: Atlantic Monthly Company, 1857–.

Commentary. New York: American Jewish Committee, 1945–.

CQ Researcher. Washington, DC: Congressional Quarterly, 1991–.

Current. Washington, DC: Heldref Publications, 1960–.

Harper's Magazine. New York: Harper's Magazine Company, 1851–.

National Review. New York: National Review, 1955–.

New Republic: A Journal of Opinion. Washington, DC: New Republic, 1914–.

Newsweek. New York: Newsweek, 1933–.

Progressive. Madison, WI: Progressive, 1909–.

Society. New Brunswick, NJ: Transactions Periodicals Consortium, Rutgers University, 1963–.

Time: The Weekly Newsmagazine. New York: Time-Life, 1923–.

U.S. News and World Report. Washington, DC: U.S. News and World Report, 1933–.

Washington Monthly. Washington, DC: Washington Monthly, 1969–.

News Sources

The two best newspapers for following elections are the *New York Times* and *Washington Post*. Several vendors, such as Proquest Direct or Newspaper Source, provide indexes to and full texts of a variety of newspapers either on CD-ROM or online. Check with your library to find out the vendors to which they subscribe. The *National Newspaper Index* indexes the *New York Times*, *Washington Post*, and other major newspapers. *Roll Call: The Newspaper of Capitol Hill* also deserves mention. Published twice weekly, except for August and two weeks in December, *Roll Call* reports on candidates and campaigns and offers regular guest columns and editorials. *Roll Call* is available in full text on LEXIS/NEXIS Academic Universe. A Web version, *Roll Call Online*, is available at http://www.rollcall.com. Also check the online services, such as LEXIS/NEXIS Academic Universe and CQ.COM ON CONGRESS, to see what newspapers they provide. For example, LEXIS/NEXIS Academic Universe and DOW JONES INTERACTIVE both provide the *New York Times*, the *Washington Post*, and numerous other newspapers.

Many newspapers are available on the Web either at no cost or by subscription. NewsDirectory.com at http://newsdirectory.com, E&P Media Links Online, Media Directory at http://emedia1.mediainfo.com/emedia, and NewspaperLinks.com at http://newspaperlinks.com can help you find newspapers on the Web. The *New York Times* is available online as New York Times on the Web at http://www.nytimes.com. The *Washington Post* is available online as WashingtonPost.com at http://www.washingtonpost.com.

Television Coverage

Television news coverage is available to the public through television news archives at various locations in the United States. Because newscasts devote a major portion of each program to governmental issues, they can be of considerable value to scholars of elections.

The Television News Archives at Vanderbilt University is the most complete television news archive in the United States. The collection holds more than 30,000 individual network evening news broadcasts and more than 9,000 hours of special news-related programming. There are three Television News Archive Indexes: Network Television News Abstracts offers summaries of network evening news programs; Special Reports and Periodic News Broadcasts contains summaries of other news shows collected at the Archives; and Specialized News Collections contains summaries of collections of news materials on major events. The Archives can be searched online at http://tvnews.vanderbilt.edu. Videotapes of the news programs are available for a fee.

The Cable Satellite Public Affairs Network (C-SPAN), available on cable

TV, is a valuable asset to students of American politics. Started in 1979, this live broadcast of congressional proceedings provides gavel-to-gavel coverage of the House and Senate plus other public affairs programming, such as National Press Club speeches, policy addresses, debates, and public policy forums and call-in programs. While C-SPAN focuses on the Congress, a considerable amount of programming is related to the presidency, including coverage of presidential candidates and campaigns. C-SPAN broadcasts on two twenty-four-hour channels: C-SPAN and C-SPAN 2. The C-SPAN homepage on the Web includes information about programs and other activities. A section called Campaign 2000 carries information on the presidential election, campaign advertising, campaign events, and the campaign in 1998. The C-SPAN Web address is http://www.c-span.org.

Keep in mind that the online databases, CQ.COM ON CONGRESS, DOW JONES INTERACTIVE, and LEXIS/NEXIS Academic Universe, are especially useful for finding current information, including the previous day's events. In addition to newspaper sources, these online services include the transcripts of television and radio news broadcasts, as well as many other sources of up-to-date news and analyses.

Television networks also have individual sites on the Internet. ABC News is found at http://www.abc.go.com. Cable News Network (CNN) maintains http://www.cnn.com/ALLPOLITICS online, with information on politics including a section on Election 2000. CBS maintains http://www.cbs.com, with a section for CBC News. The Microsoft/NBC online address is http://msnbc/news.com. PBS news and views can be found at http://www.pbs.org. Research Publications International publishes *Broadcast News on CD-ROM*, which includes transcripts of more than seventy television and radio news broadcasts found on ABC, CNN, PBS, and NPR, among other news stations. *Broadcast News on CD-ROM* is updated monthly and can be tailored to include only specific stations.

Statistics

Students and researchers can use statistical indexes to locate data about voting and election returns. The best index to statistics is STATISTICAL UNIVERSE, which indexes and abstracts government statistics since 1974, business association and state statistics since 1980, and international agency statistics since 1983. This database indexes more than 100,000 statistical publications by subject, title, issuing agency, or author. The *Statistical Abstract of the United States* also is searchable online as part of STATISTICAL UNIVERSE. Paper and CD-ROM versions of STATISTICAL UNIVERSE also are available. STATISTICAL UNIVERSE is available by subscription only, so check to see if your library subscribes.

The *American Statistical Index: A Comprehensive Index to the Statistical Publications of the U.S. Government* (Washington, DC: Congressional Information Service, 1974–) is the most inclusive index to statistics published by the federal government. It provides abstracts of the documents it indexes. The index covers the publication of all major statistical agencies as well as statistics reported in committee hearings and prints. The *American Statistical Index* is available online as part of STATISTICAL UNIVERSE.

The Census Bureau offers a free version of the *Statistical Abstract of the United States* for the years 1995 to 1999 in PDF format at http://www.census.gov/mp/www/censtore.html. Fedstats also provides accessibility to statistics produced by more than seventy agencies in the federal government. Fedstats can be found online at http://www.Fedstats.gov.

The following publications are useful for finding tables on elections:

Vital Statistics on American Politics. Washington, DC: Congressional Quarterly, 1988–.

This publication includes information on campaigns and elections, legislative term limits, public opinion, interest groups, political parties, and the mass media. The volume includes more than 200 tables and charts. It is also available on CD-ROM.

Vital Statistics on Congress. Washington, DC: Congressional Quarterly, 1980–.

This handbook contains statistical data on Congress, including elections and campaign financing. The data are historical, with most going back two decades and some even further.

Vital Statistics on the Presidency. Washington, DC: CQ Press, 1996–.

This statistical handbook covers the personal backgrounds of the presidents, presidential selection and elections, and public opinion. More than 150 tables and figures summarize and illustrate aspects of both the individual presidents and the presidency as an institution.

Public Opinion Polls

There are several ways to find information about polls that focus on elections. Summary results of current Gallup polls are available at the Gallup Organization Web site at http://www.gallup.com. The texts of weekly Time, CNN and Gallup opinion polls can be found at http://cnn.com/ALLPOLITICS. Two other important Web sites are the Roper Center for Public Opinion Research, found at http://www.ropercenter.

uconn.edu, and the Pew Research Center, found at http://www.people-press.org.

PollingReport.com, at http://pollingreport.com, is an online service of The Polling Report, an independent, nonpartisan resource on public opinion. It supplies the results of various polls taken on elections. Roper polls can be searched in LEXIS NEXIS Academic Universe in the reference section. STATISTICAL UNIVERSE indexes public opinion polls by private organizations. Hundreds of other organizations also conduct polls. The annual *American Public Opinion Index,* published by Opinion Research Services, covers major polls done throughout the United States at the national, state, and local levels since 1981. An excellent source of information on polls, the *American Public Opinion Index* provides a topical index to questions and a list of the polls at the back of the volume, including the name and address of the organization that took each poll. The index covers more than fifty-five national, state, and local polls and includes more than 7,500 entries. For Gallup Polls consult the following sources:

The Gallup Poll Cumulative Index: Public Opinion, 1935–1997. Wilmington, DE: Scholarly Resources, 1999.

This volume is a comprehensive index to the twenty-five-volume Gallup Poll annual series. The CD-ROM version of the *Cumulative Index* is titled the *Gallup Poll Public Opinion, 1935–1997: The CD-ROM Edition.* In either format, the index includes all the results for polls conducted between 1935 and 1997. It is searchable by topic or year.

The Gallup Poll: Public Opinion, 1935–1971. 3 vols. New York: Random House, 1972.

These three volumes provide a complete collection of the Gallup Polls from 1935 to 1971. An index in the third volume provides easy subject access to the polls. Supplementary volumes have been published covering the next six years, then annual volumes starting with 1978.

The Gallup Poll: Public Opinion, 1972–1977. Wilmington, DE: Scholarly Resources, 1978.

This set covers the Gallup Poll from 1972 to 1977.

The Gallup Poll: Public Opinion, 1978–. Wilmington, DE: Scholarly Resources, 1979–.

Scholarly Resources of Wilmington, DE publishes individual years of the Gallup Poll annual series beginning with 1978 and continuing up to the present.

Gallup Opinion Index Report: Political, Social and Economic Trends. Princeton, NJ: Gallup International, 1965–.

The *Report* is published monthly, with special issues appearing from time to time. The surveys are based on a population of at least 1,500 respondents, who are selected according to scientific protocol. The surveys include findings on a variety of campaign and election issues.

Finally, many of the ABC/*Washington Post*, CBS/*New York Times*, and Harris surveys are available as data sets. The Inter-University Consortium for Political and Social Research has many of these data sets in its archival holdings.

Data Archives

Many data archives throughout the country maintain holdings that include quantitative data on elections. The major social science data archive is the Inter-University Consortium for Political and Social Research at the University of Michigan. For more information about the archive's holdings, consult the consortium's latest *Guide to Resources and Services* or its Web site at http://www.icpsr.umich.edu. There you will find a catalog and index to ICPSR's holdings of machine-readable data tapes. Many of the codebooks and data sets are available online with links to other U.S., international, and foreign data archives. The *Guide to Resources and Services* and the Web site also include information about training programs, classes, remote access computer assistance, and how to obtain data and codebooks from the consortium. The listing of archival holdings provides the name of the data collector, the title and detailed description of the data file, and related publications that have used the data. In addition to election data, the consortium also holds many other data files relevant to elections. Many of the statistical sources mentioned throughout the guide, such as Census Bureau publications, the *Congressional District Data Book,* and public opinion polls, are available on tape. Additional data sets contain demographic, economic, social, and other kinds of political data.

Bibliographies

When studying elections it is always useful to get as much background information as possible. Ever since the first election, people have been analyzing the results and writing commentaries. An effective way to begin a literature search is to use the following bibliographies:

Agranoff, Robert. *Elections and Electoral Behavior: A Bibliography.* DeKalb: Center for Governmental Studies, Northern Illinois University, 1972.

This annotated bibliography is a listing of more than 300 items dealing with theoretical and practical issues of elections. The bibliography is divided into four sections: (1) electoral system and voting rights, (2) candidate selection, nominations and party conventions, (3) voting behavior, and (4) electoral interpretation.

The American Electorate: A Historical Bibliography. Santa Barbara, CA: ABC-Clio, 1983.

This bibliography contains more than 1,300 abstracts of articles on electoral history and politics, voting patterns, and individual elections. The bibliography includes periodical literature published since 1963. It is organized by chapter according to subject, with entries arranged by author, and provides a subject index.

Goehlert, Robert U., and Fenton S. Martin. *CQ's Guide to Modern Elections: An Annotated Bibliography 1960–1996.* Washington, DC: CQ Press, 1999.

This annotated bibliography includes more than 3,300 entries to scholarly books and articles. It includes entries on topics such as primaries, conventions, campaigning, debates, financing, media coverage, voting participation, and elections.

Mauer, David J. *United States Politics and Elections: Guide to Information Sources.* Detroit, MI: Gale Research, 1978.

This annotated bibliography includes citations to articles and books on electoral politics in general, elections, and candidates. It is arranged by chapter according to historical periods and contains a wealth of biographical materials on candidates. It also includes citations to important political issues and trends for each historical period.

Miles, William. *The Image Makers: A Bibliography of American Presidential Campaign Biographies.* Metuchen, NJ: Scarecrow Press, 1979.

This bibliography includes books, pamphlets, magazines, almanacs, speeches, and miscellaneous political compendia on candidates of official parties. It includes citations to both successful and unsuccessful candidates and many vice presidential contenders. The materials cited include both favorable and unfavorable accounts. Many of the citations in this bibliography are to publications not widely owned by most libraries, such as pamphlets and party documents.

Smith, Dwight L., and Lloyd W. Garrison, eds. *The American Political Process: Selected Abstracts of Periodical Literature (1954–1971).* Santa Barbara, CA: ABC-Clio, 1974.

This work contains a lengthy section on American elections. The abstracts in the work were taken from *Historical Abstracts* and *America: History and Life.*

Szekely, Kalman S., comp. *Electoral College: A Selected Annotated Bibliography.* Littleton, CO: Libraries Unlimited, 1970.

While this bibliography is selective, it is the most comprehensive compilation on the subject. It contains 794 items covering periodicals, books, pamphlets, and unpublished dissertations. The sources span the time from the Constitutional Convention to 1970. The work is arranged according to a subject outline in the following categories: (1) Historical Background and Organization; (2) Arguments in Favor of Retaining Present System; (3) Arguments Against Present System; (4) Proposals to Reform Present System; (5) Popular Interest in Reform; and (6) Reapportionment of Electoral System. Unfortunately, the only subject access to entries is through the table of contents, because the work lacks a subject index.

Wynar, Lubomyr R., comp. *American Political Parties: A Selective Guide to Parties and Movements of the 20th Century.* Littleton, CO: Libraries Unlimited, 1969.

This work is a compilation of more than 3,000 books, monographs, and unpublished dissertations on significant twentieth-century American parties and movements. The arrangement is by subject and party. The book is helpful in providing general background material related to elections, public opinion, parties, and political behavior.

Documentary Histories

The following four documentary collections and histories relate to elections:

Jensen, Merrill, and Robert A. Becker, eds. *The Documentary History of the First Federal Elections 1788–1790.* 3 vols. Madison: University of Wisconsin Press, 1976–1982.

This set focuses on a time period for which there was previously little documentary material. Because the first elections are important both historically and politically, this material is extremely useful for researchers interested in electoral history.

Nelson, Michael, ed. *Historical Documents on Presidential Elections, 1787–1988.* Washington, DC: Congressional Quarterly, 1991.

This volume contains speeches and documents on U.S. presidential elections, including campaign speeches, public letters, and candidate debates. Each document begins with an introduction providing the historical context.

Schlesinger, Arthur M., Jr., ed. *History of Presidential Elections, 1789–1968.* 4 vols. New York: Chelsea House, 1971.

This comprehensive history of presidential elections, written by prominent historians and political scientists, covers the particular social and political climate of each election. The forty-five contributors were asked to analyze a presidential election and to select relevant documents illustrating their theses. An appendix in the fourth volume includes the popular and electoral vote by states, as well as all the party elections. Of special interest is an annotated bibliography, arranged by election, contained in the appendix. A supplemental volume, *History of Presidential Elections, 1972–1984,* was published in 1986.

Silbey, Joel H., ed. *The American Party Battle: Election Campaign Pamphlets, 1828–1876.* 2 vols. Cambridge: Harvard University Press, 1999.

   This two-volume work samples political party pamphlets in the nineteenth century. These pamphlets reflect the political issues and controversies of the time and reflect the ideological and electoral themes of the political parties.

Internet Sources

   Internet users have access to library catalogs, databases, documents, electronic mail, images and sound, and electronic discussion groups. Internet users can access all kinds of federal government information, including Supreme Court decisions, census data, White House briefings, committee assignments, congressional directories and biographies, and legislation. Congress, the White House, and government departments all have Web sites. This is just a sample of what is available on the Internet, which expands daily. Most individual electoral candidates have campaign Web pages that provide biographical background and issue positions.

   One of the best Web sites for identifying various issues dealing with campaigns and elections is the University of Michigan Documents Center's Political Science Resources, United States Politics at http://www.lib. umich.edu/libhome/Documents.center/psusp.html. This site provides links to sites about campaign finances, consultants, elections, lobbyists, political parties, public opinion, news sources, and other topics. The following books also are useful for finding sources on the Web:

> Androit, Laurie. *Internet Blue Pages: The Guide to Federal Government Web Sites: 1999.* Internet Blue Pages, 1999.
>
> Maxwell, Bruce. *How to Access the Federal Government on the Internet: Washington Online.* Washington, DC: Congressional Quarterly, 1998.
>
> Maxwell, Bruce. *How to Track Politics on the Internet.* Washington, DC: CQ Press, 2000.
>
> Notess, Greg R. *Government Information on the Internet.* 3d ed. Lanham, MD: Bernan Press, 2000.

Some of the best Web sites for studying campaigns and elections are:

Campaign 2000 (C-Span) at http://www.c-span.org/campaign2000.
This site includes links to campaign Web sites and contains video clips of candidate speeches and interviews, archival campaign advertising, a campaign calendar, campaign events, and the searchable archive of the *Road to the White House* program.

Democracy Network at http://www.democracynet.org.
This site is a project of the League of Women Voters Education Fund and the Center for Governmental Studies. Enter a zip code to find candidates running for office in elections in that area. The site provides the candidate's position on various issues and provides information on presidential candidate events and news on elections.

Elections U.S.A. at http://www.geocities.com/CapitolHill/6228.
This site provides news information about presidential, congressional, gubernatorial, mayoral, and minor elections. It offers voting results from current primaries and elections, and includes past election results. In addition to news about current elections, the site provides stories by newspaper columnists.

ElectNet at http://www.electnet.org.
This site provides national and state news updates on elections. They offer essays on the elections, give the 1998 congressional election results, and give links to other Web sites dealing with elections.

The Hill Campaign 2000 at http://www.hillnews.com/campaign.html.
This site provides links to state-by-state candidate and campaign links, presidential candidate links, political party links, and Leadership PAC links. It also offers back issues of Campaign 2000, information about open congressional seats, and who is up for reelection.

National Election Studies at http://www.umich.edu/~nes.
This site provides data on voting, public opinion, and political participation. It includes information about data sets, study resources, a NES bibliography, reports and papers, and a Guide to Public Opinion and Electoral Behavior, which provides summary data from 1952 to the present.

National Political Index at http://www.politicalindex.com.
This Web site provides an index to political information. It offers links to political news headlines, federal, state, and local candidates, and political parties. It indexes and links 3,500 political Web sites and 200 political science departments.

OpenSecrets.Org at http://www.opensecrets.org/home.

This site from the Center for Responsive Politics provides information about money in presidential and congressional elections. It lists information about campaign contributions and contributors. It profiles every political action committee registered with the Federal Election Commission and lists who gave and who received campaign contributions. It has a searchable database of individual contributors of $200 or more to federal candidates, PACs, and political parties. It offers background on lobbyists and their political issues and spending patterns. It provides links to organizations with money and politics data.

Politics1.com at http://www.politics1.com.

This site provides information on presidential election 2000, state races and links, political parties, campaign issues and debates, campaign consultants, a primary calendar and results, and news links.

Politics.com at http://www.politics.com.

This site provides information on candidates, campaign finance, political polls, and news events concerning elections

Project Vote Smart at http://www.vote-smart.org.

This site provides information on presidential, congressional, gubernatorial, and state elections. Search full-text copies of speeches, issue statements, and position statements by individual candidates, or search by issue. This site provides information on campaign finance, special interest groups, and voting records.

U.S. Census Bureau. Voting and Registration at http://www.census.gov/population/www/socdemo/voting.html.

This site provides information on reported voting and registration by various demographic and socioeconomic characteristics collected in November of congressional and presidential election years in the Current Population Survey (CPS), at http://www.bls.census.gov/cps/cpsmain.htm. The site offers information from recent surveys and historical trends in selected areas. Projections of the voting-age population by age, race, Hispanic origin, and gender derived from administrative data also are produced every other year in anticipation of the elections.

Web White and Blue at http://www.webwhiteblue.org.

This site provides access to online election directories and voter information sites on the Internet. It provides information on voting, candidate positions, election news, and issues.

Welcome to USElections.com at http://www.uselections.com.

This site provides information on federal, state, and local elections. It offers information on campaign finance, Federal Election Commission records, campaign media, election news, and political parties.

2

Primary Sources and Finding Tools

This chapter lists primary sources and finding tools for locating data about primaries and caucuses; conventions and platforms; campaign finance; advocacy groups, interest groups, and political action committees; district data; and election returns. These sources and finding tools are grouped by category.

Campaigns

Binning William C., Larry E. Esterly, and Paul A. Sracic. *Encyclopedia of American Parties, Campaigns, and Elections.* Westport, CT: Greenwood Press, 1999.

This book consists of easy-to-understand definitions and explanations of common and complex political terms. It includes short biographies of major political figures, descriptions of parties and movements, and explanations of important cases about elections and campaign finance. The entries are arranged alphabetically, with cross-references and a list of helpful books.

Havel, James T. *U.S. Presidential Candidates and the Elections: A Biographical and Historical Guide.* New York: Macmillan Library Reference, 1996.

This two-volume set provides information about candidates and elections. The first volume includes biographical information about all candidates for presidential elections. The second volume is arranged chronologically by election. It includes a brief description of the election of candidates and platform highlights for each party, primary data, and a summary of the general and Electoral College data.

Schlesinger, Arthur M., Jr., ed. *Running for President: The Candidates and Their Images.* New York: Simon and Schuster, 1994.

This two-volume reference work covers the years 1789 to 1992. Essays focus on the style, tactics, and techniques used in presidential campaigns and cover the rise of television in campaigns, the role of consultants, and the use of public opinion polls. The work also includes 1,304 illustrations of political paraphernalia, including posters, buttons, and bumper stickers. Complementing the essays, the illustrations provide a visual history of presidential campaigns.

Shields-West, Eileen. *World Almanac of Presidential Campaigns.* New York: World Almanac, 1992.

This publication describes the character of each campaign from 1789 to 1989, providing an abundance of information regarding the candidates' credentials, the party conventions, campaign notes, symbols, slogans, songs, paraphernalia, popular labels, and name-calling.

Southwick, Leslie H. *Presidential Also-Rans and Running Mates, 1788 through 1996.* 2d ed. Jefferson, NC: McFarland, 1998.

This volume provides biographical portraits of presidential also-rans and their running mates for each presidential election. The book is arranged in chronological order by election. Each biographical entry includes a bibliography about the candidate.

Utter, Glenn H., and Ruth Ann Strickland. *Campaign and Election Reform: A Reference Handbook.* Santa Barbara, CA: ABC-CLIO, 1997.

This reference guide includes a chronology of campaign reform, biographical information, survey data and quotations, a directory of organizations and agencies, and a biography of print and nonprint sources.

Primaries and Caucuses

The best sources for primary and caucus information are the following volumes:

Cook, Rhodes. *Race for the Presidency: Winning the 2000 Nomination.* Washington, DC: CQ Press, 2000.

This book provides detailed information on the 2000 presidential nomination process, including state-by-state delegate selection and political party rules. State-by-state sections are arranged by the date when the states hold their primaries or caucuses. Each state section includes a county outline map of the state, primary results since 1968 including major county data, and demographic and historical highlights of the state's presidential primaries or caucuses.

Davis, James W. *U.S. Presidential Primaries and the Convention System: A Sourcebook.* Westport, CT: Greenwood, 1997.

This book provides a comprehensive overview of the presidential primary system and the caucus-convention system that the fifty states use to send candidates to the national nominating conventions. The volume includes statistical tables, documents, and commentary.

The following volumes are the sources to use for finding primary and caucus data:

Cook, Rhodes. *U.S. Presidential Primary Elections, 1968–1996: A Handbook of Election Statistics.* Washington, DC: CQ Press, 2000.

This volume provides state-by-state primary election data, maps, and tables.

Cook, Rhodes, and Alice V. McGillivray, comps. *U.S. Primary Elections, 1995–1996: President, Congress, Governors: A Handbook of Election Statistics.* Washington, DC: Congressional Quarterly, 1997.

This election reference handbook provides official county-by-county results for presidential, congressional, and gubernatorial primaries in the 1995–1996 election cycle. All returns are gathered from the final, official results from each state authority.

Cook, Rhodes, and Alice V. McGillivray, comps. *U.S. Primary Elections, 1997–1998: Congress and Governors: A Handbook of Election Statistics.* Washington, DC: CQ Press, 1999.

This election reference handbook provides official county-by-county results for congressional and gubernatorial primaries in the 1997–1998 election cycle. All returns are gathered from the final, official results from each state authority.

McGillivray, Alice V., comp. *Congressional and Gubernatorial Primaries, 1991–1992: A Handbook of Election Statistics.* Washington, DC: Congressional Quarterly, 1993.

This election reference handbook provides official county-by-county results for congressional and gubernatorial primaries in the 1991–1992 election cycle. All returns are gathered from the final, official results from each state authority.

McGillivray, Alice V., comp. *Congressional and Gubernatorial Primaries, 1993–1994: A Handbook of Election Statistics.* Washington, DC: Congressional Quarterly, 1995.

This election reference handbook provides official county-by-county results for congressional and gubernatorial primaries in the 1993–1994 election cycle. All returns are gathered from the final, official results from each state authority.

McGillivray, Alice V. *Presidential Primaries and Caucuses: 1992: A Handbook of Election Statistics.* Washington, DC: Congressional Quarterly, 1992.

This election reference handbook provides official county-by-county results for every presidential primary held in 1992. All returns are gathered from the final, official results from each state authority.

Conventions

Long before an election takes place, presidential candidates must undergo the tedious and enduring campaign trail leading to their party's national nominating conventions. They must compete in primaries and contend with state political caucuses. In essence this process is the fight for convention delegates. The works presented in this section will help you become familiar with the entire nominating process.

Newspapers are an invaluable resource for anyone interested in researching national conventions. Newspapers are useful not only for their reporting of convention proceedings but also as a record of journalists' perceptions of the convention, issues, and public interest. The *New York Times,* the *Washington Post,* and other major newspapers cover conventions extensively. Also check the newspapers of the city and state where each convention was held. *Time, Newsweek,* and other newsmagazines also provide extensive coverage of national conventions.

Look in appropriate indexes for relevant news stories. Again, you may find the online database services useful, as they contain the full texts of newspapers, magazines, television news transcripts, and other news sources. The Internet also can provide information about party positions, platforms, and convention information.

The first set of sources in this section focuses on the nomination of presidential candidates and how delegates to the national conventions are chosen, followed by a guide to voting at the conventions. The last set of sources in this section includes guides to the platforms.

Procedures

U.S. Congress. Senate. *Nomination and Election of the President and Vice President of the United States including the Manner of Selecting Delegates to National Political Conventions.* Washington, DC: U.S. Government Printing Office, 1956–1992.

This series analyzes the procedure of the nomination and election of the president and vice president. It examines the rules of the major political parties, federal and state laws, and constitutional clauses governing the procedure. The document describes the manner in which delegates to the national conventions are selected, the number of delegates to be selected, and the dates on which the selection are made. It lists the states in which presidential preference primaries are held, the dates of such primaries, and the filing deadlines for candidates or delegates. Some statistical data also is included, such as the popular and electoral vote of presidential elections, campaign costs, and expenditures for political broadcasts.

Other useful tools for finding information about election laws and procedures include:

Ahlers, Glen-Peter, ed. *Election Laws of the United States.* New York: Oceana, 1995–.

Kimberling, William C., and Peggy Sims. *Federal Election Law 96: A Summary of Federal Laws Pertaining to Registration, Voting, and Public Employee Participation.* Washington, DC: Office of Election Administration, Federal Election Commission, 1996.

Voting

Bain, Richard C., and Judith H. Parris. *Convention Decisions and Voting Records.* 2d ed. Washington, DC: Brookings Institution, 1973.

This volume provides a narrative account of the convention proceedings of the two major parties between 1832 and 1972. Each convention is prefaced by a brief summary of the political situation. Appendixes list the nominees of the major parties, convention officers, and voting records, arranged chronologically within each convention and giving roll call votes of important motions. This volume is undoubtedly the best source for convention roll call votes. To update this volume, the researcher should consult the *CQ Weekly, National Journal, New York Times, Washington Post,* online databases, and the Internet.

Platforms

Both the Democratic and Republican parties publish written records of their convention proceedings. Information about party platforms and some recent political party platforms also are found in online databases and on the Internet. The best guides for past platforms are:

Johnson, Donald B. *National Party Platforms.* 6th ed. 2 vols. Champaign: University of Illinois Press, 1978.

Johnson, Donald B. *National Party Platforms of 1980.* Champaign: University of Illinois Press, 1982.

The two standard reference works listed above offer a comprehensive collection of party platforms for all major and minor parties competing at the national level. They present authenticated copies of platforms for all major and principal minor parties. They include the names of all presidential and vice presidential candidates, as well as the distribution of popular and electoral votes. The material is arranged in chronological order, and comprehensive indexes to the platforms are provided.

National Party Conventions, 1831–1996. Washington, DC: Congressional Quarterly, 1997.

This concise reference work is the best ready-reference guide to conventions. While it does not reprint platforms in their entirety, it includes excerpts and provides a chronology of all the nomination conventions, a list of nominees from all political parties, and a biographical directory of presidential and vice presidential candidates.

Third Party Presidential Nominating Conventions, Proceedings, Records, etc. 8 reels. LaCrosse, WI: Northern Micrographics, 1974.

With coverage of third party conventions so sparse, this microfilm collection is extremely useful, for it brings together various sources of information on the conventions, official proceedings, newspaper reports, parties' campaign books, and miscellaneous reports, minutes, and statements. The collection contains more than fifteen minor parties. A softbound index provides easy access to the various publications in the collection.

In addition to the volumes by Johnson, two similar volumes contain platforms, secondary analysis, and information:

> Chester, Edward W. *A Guide to Political Platforms.* Hamden, CT: Shoe String Press, 1977.
> McKee, Thomas H. *National Conventions and Platforms of All Political Parties, 1789–1905: Convention, Popular, and Electoral Vote.* 3d ed. St. Clair Shore, MI: Scholarly Press, 1970.

Campaign Finance

The Federal Election Commission (FEC) publishes two series that contain information on contributors and spending in elections. The first series is the FEC's *Annual Report,* which began in 1976. The second series is the *Report on Financial Activity,* which began in 1980. A third series, the FEC Disclosure series, uses information based on financial disclosure provisions of the 1977 House and Senate ethics codes. The FEC Web site can be found at http://www.fec.gov. The Campaign Finance Reports and Data section of the Web site presents 2000 campaign data, party fundraising data, political action committee data, and historical campaign data. The Campaign Finance Law Resources section presents legal documents, campaign guides, the FEC's *Annual Report,* and the FEC's monthly newsletter, *The Record.* The Elections and Voting section presents data about the voting-age population, voter results in presidential and congressional elections, the history and a description of the Electoral College, and voting systems. The Web site also provides news releases from 1997 to the present in a section titled News Releases.

CQ Weekly and the *National Journal* also publish articles based on federal campaign data. *Vital Statistics on American Politics, Vital Statistics on Congress,* and *Vital Statistics on the Presidency* have excellent sections on campaign finance, including information on expenditures, political action committees, and election returns. Newspapers also can be an important source for information about campaign finances. *The Political Finance and Lobby Reporter* (Ashburn, VA: Amward Publications) is a semimonthly newsletter concerning the financing of political campaigns and lobbying activities.

Several Web sites provide data on campaign financing. The Web site for the Center for Responsive Politics at http://www.opensecrets.org/home provides information on congressional campaign finance filings as well as lobby group campaign contributions. FECInfo at http://www.tray.com/fecinfo provides presidential and congressional campaign contributions searchable by name, state, or political action committee.

The most recent research guides to campaign spending have been published by Congressional Quarterly:

Makinson, Larry, and Joshua F. Goldstein. *Open Secrets: The Encyclopedia of Congressional Money and Politics.* 4th ed. Washington, DC: Congressional Quarterly, 1996.

This edition identifies, classifies, and catalogs the sources and recipients of congressional campaign contributions in the 1994 elections. It analyzes contributions from political action committees (PACs) and contribution from individuals and includes the campaign finance profiles of all members of Congress.

Fritz, Sara, and Dwight Morris. *Handbook of Campaign Spending: Money in the 1990 Congressional Races.* Washington, DC: Congressional Quarterly, 1992.

Morris, Dwight, and Murielle Gamache. *Handbook of Campaign Spending: Money in the 1992 Congressional Races.* Washington, DC: Congressional Quarterly, 1994.

Morris, Dwight, and Murielle Gamache. *Handbook of Campaign Spending: Money in the 1994 Congressional Races.* Washington, DC: Congressional Quarterly, 1996.

The three volumes listed above present an examination of campaign spending plus a race-by-race analysis of the House and Senate elections in 1990, 1992, and 1994. The volumes use data gathered from Federal Election Commission (FEC) reports and interviews with candidates, staffers, and consultants.

The following materials contain older data about campaign financing but remain valuable for historical research:

Alexander, Herbert E., and Caroline D. Jones, eds. *CRF Listing of Contributors of National Level Political Committees to Incumbents and Candidates for Public Office.* Princeton, NJ: Citizens' Research Foundation, 1968–1972.

This work provides data on contributions given to candidates by national-level political committees of the Republican and Democratic parties, and by committees representing labor, business, and professional interests.

Alexander, Herbert E., and Caroline D. Jones, eds. *CRF Listing of Political Contributors of $500 or More.* Princeton, NJ: Citizens' Research Foundation, 1968–1974.

This volume provides a list of contributors, arranged alphabetically, who gave to candidates both at the national and state levels. The publication lists the address of the contributor, the amount of the contribution, and the candidate and party to which the funds were given.

Common Cause. The Campaign Finance Monitoring Project. *1972 Congressional Campaign Finances.* 10 vols. Washington, DC: Common Cause, 1974.

This work provides a summary of the campaign finances of every major candidate for Congress in the 1972 election. The study is organized into ten volumes divided by regional area: (1) Border states, (2) Great Lakes states, (3) Mid-Atlantic states, (4) Mountain states, (5) New England states, (6) Plains states, (7) Southeastern states, (8) Southern states, (9) Southwestern states, and (10) West coast states. Each volume contains data on three areas of a candidate's campaign finances: (1) a summary of campaign financial data, (2) a list of registered special interest and national political party committees and their contributions, and (3) a list of large contributions from individuals.

Common Cause. The Campaign Finance Monitoring Project. *1974 Congressional Campaign Finances.* 5 vols. Washington, DC: Common Cause, 1976.

This five-volume work provides a summary of the campaign finances of every major candidate for Congress in the 1974 election. The first four volumes provide summaries of Senate and House races as follows: (1) Senate, (2) House races, Alabama–Iowa, (3) House races, Kansas–New York, and (4) House races, North Carolina–Wyoming. Volume 5 contains a summary of interest groups and political parties.

Common Cause. The Campaign Finance Monitoring Project. *1972 Federal Campaign Finances, Interest Groups and Political Parties.* 3 vols. Washington, DC: Common Cause, 1974.

This work provides the finances of all nationally registered political committees that contributed $5,000 or more to federal candidates in 1972. The lists of political committees have been arranged into three volumes: (1) Business, Agriculture and

Dairy, Health; (2) Labor; and (3) Miscellaneous, Democratic, Republican. Each volume contains a detailed table of contents that covers the interest groups for that volume; a financial summary for each interest committee, including a brief description of the group or interest that the committee represents and its activities in the 1972 elections; a complete list of every individual and group that received contributions from the committee and the amount received; and an index that lists the name and affiliation of all political committees registered during 1972.

Common Cause. The Campaign Finance Monitoring Project. *1976 Federal Campaign Finances.* 3 vols. Washington, DC: Common Cause, 1977.

This work provides a summary of the campaign finances of every major candidate for Congress in the 1972 election and presidential primary candidates in 1972. Volume 1 contains interest group and political party contributions to congressional candidates arranged by interest group and political party. Volume 2 contains interest group and political party contributions to congressional candidates arranged by candidates in Alabama through Mississippi. Volume 3 contains interest group and political party contributions to congressional candidates arranged by candidates in Missouri through Wyoming, and interest group contributions to 1976 presidential primary candidates.

Paul, Barbara D., et al., eds. *CRF Listing of Contributors and Lenders of $10,000 or More in 1972.* Princeton, NJ: Citizens' Research Foundation, 1975.

This work compiles campaign contributions to presidential, congressional, state, and local committees and candidates from more than 1,300 contributors. The volume lists each contributor's home address, business address, profession, and business affiliation. CRF has gathered data on individuals who made contributions of more than $10,000 in presidential election years since 1960. The same data have been published in Herbert E. Alexander's quadrennial series, *Financing the . . . Election.* Ten volumes have been published to date, covering the 1960, 1964, 1968, 1972, 1976, 1980, 1984, 1988, 1992, and 1996 elections.

U.S. Congress. House. *The Annual Statistical Report of Contributions and Expenditures Made during the 1972 Election Campaigns for the U.S. House of Representatives,* W. Pat Jennings, comp. Washington, DC: U.S. Government Printing Office, 1974.

This volume contains information on receipts and expenditures for candidates and political committees supporting a single candidate, arranged alphabetically by state and by district number; information on receipts and expenditures for political committees supporting two or more candidates, arranged alphabetically by committee; and information on individual contributions in excess of $100, arranged alphabetically by contributor or committee, including the address of the contributor and date of the contribution. Appendix A presents an alphabetical list of candidates and supporting political committees. Appendix B provides an alphabetical list of political committees and the candidates they supported.

U.S. Congress. Senate. *The Annual Statistical Report of Receipts and Expenditures Made in Connection with Elections for the U.S. Senate in 1972.* Washington, DC: U.S. Government Printing Office, 1975.

This report is divided into five sections. The first section, arranged by state, includes amounts reported by all Senate candidates and associated committees that support one candidate. Within-state breakdowns are listed according to party and candidate. The next section records amounts reported by all political committees supporting more than one candidate. This section is arranged alphabetically by committee. (The list of candidates supported appears in Appendix B.) The third section, arranged alphabetically by contributor, presents itemized receipts more than $100 received by committees and candidates as reported to the secretary of the Senate for 1972. Receipts are coded according to (1) individual contributions, (2) sales and collections, (3) loans received, (4) other receipts, and (5) transfers. Appendix A cross-indexes the committees to the candidates. Appendix B cross-indexes the candidates to committees. The last two sections provide cross-indexing of sections 1, 2, and 3. The report also provides a cross-index by state and party. The House and Senate volumes use the same format, which makes it easy to use the two together for comparative purposes.

Interest Groups

This section lists directories that identify and provide information on lobbyists and other associations and organizations involved in the political process. Both *CQ Weekly* and the *National Journal* offer extensive coverage of interest groups. Newspaper and magazine literature supply important information, too, for their coverage goes behind the scenes to detail the efforts of various political groups. Trade, industrial, and professional journals have regular columns or sections on national politics. Indexes and online database services provide a wealth of information on interest groups and lobbyists. Several Web sites are extremely useful. Political Advocacy Groups, a directory of advocacy groups by name and subject, is found at http://www.csuchico.edu/~kcfount. This site includes links to specific groups. The Center for Responsive Politics' online lobbyist report, Influence, Inc, is searchable by the name of the lobby group, client, and subject interest at http://www.opensecrets.org/lobbyists/index.htm. The report includes information about the dollar amounts devoted to lobbying. Many individual lobbyists have their own Web sites.

Directory of Federal Lobbyists. Lanham, MD: Bernan, 2000–.

This annual directory includes information about registered lobbyists who work with Congress. The information given includes name, address, telephone and fax numbers, email addresses, areas of practice, and reported income. An index lists lobbyists alphabetically and another index lists organizations represented by the lobbyists.

Directory of Washington Representatives of American Associations and Industry. Washington, DC: Columbia Books, 1977–.

This directory lists lobbyists, legal advisors, information collectors, and consultants representing public interest groups, corporations, labor unions, trade and professional associations, state and local governments, political action committees, and foreign governments. The information is arranged in two alphabetically cross-referenced lists. The first list provides representatives' names, addresses, and dates of registration. The second list provides organizations by the addresses, names, and titles of their representatives and includes brief descriptions of the organizations' activities. The directory also provides subject and country indexes.

Public Interest Profiles. Washington, DC: Congressional Quarterly, 1977–.

This volume provides detailed information on about 250 public interest and public policy organizations. For each organization it notes budget and funding services, the board of directors, major publications, methods of operation, and information on political action committees.

Washington Representatives. Washington, DC: Columbia Books, 1979–.

This annual directory contains a list of representatives, a list of organizations, a subject index, and a country index. It also offers a list of the congressional committees, along with their membership, and regulatory agencies that are the focus of lobbying efforts.

Political Action Committees

The following volumes are directories that provide lists of political action committees (PACs) and their interests. Because the number of PACs grows with each election, keeping up with the number and affiliation of PACs is difficult. Consequently, for current research you should always be sure to use *CQ Weekly* and the *National Journal,* as well as search online databases and the Internet.

Almanac of Federal PACs. Ashburn, VA: Amward Publications, 1986–.

Published every other year, this almanac provides campaign finance information on more than 2,300 PACs. It also is available online at http://PACfinder.com.

CQ's Federal PACs Directory. Washington, DC: Congressional Quarterly, 1998–.

This directory provides contact information for more than 2,300 PACs and includes background information, descriptions of each PAC's ideology and special interests, and a detailed analysis of each PAC's contributions. Each PAC is indexed by name, important personnel, and sponsoring organization.

The directories listed below were not specifically designed to identify lobbyists and interest groups but may be useful as sources of additional information about particular associations, organizations, or groups represented by registered lobbyists:

Encyclopedia of Associations. Detroit, MI: Gale Research Company, 1956–.

Greenwood Encyclopedia of American Institutions. Westport, CT: Greenwood Press, 1977–.

National Directory of Corporate Public Affairs. 17th ed. Washington, DC: Columbia Books, 1999.

National Trade and Professional Associations of the United States and Canada. Washington, DC: Columbia Books, 1975–.

Campaign Communication

In the age of electronic media, image-makers are becoming perhaps more important than the candidates themselves. Sophisticated public relations firms work extremely hard to package and sell their candidates. An obvious connection exists between a candidate's financial resources and his or her ability to maximize television exposure. One source of information on political communication is the literature in the fields of communication and journalism. Journals such as *Journalism and Mass Communication Quarterly, Quarterly Journal of Speech, Public Opinion Quarterly, Columbia Journalism Quarterly,* and *Journal of Communication* are rich sources of information dealing with politics and the media.

Communication Abstracts and *Journalism Abstracts* can help you identify materials in this research area. These two tools also can be used to research other topics, such as the role of the media in covering campaigns, elections, and congressional politics, or the use of public relations techniques in campaigning or by a standing member of congress. ComAbstracts is an online service that contains articles published in forty-two journals in the fields of journalism and communication. ComAbstracts can be found at http://www/cios.org.www/abstract/htm. These abstracting services can be used to research any aspect of elections that are related to the media or mass communication.

The Political Communication Center at the Department of Communication, University of Oklahoma publishes the *Political Advertising Research Reports.* The Political Commercial Archive at the Political Communications Center also is helpful. In 1996 Lynda Lee Kaid, Kathleen J. M. Haynes and Charles E. Rand published a guide to the Archive titled *Political Communication Center:*

A Catalog and Guide to the Archival Collections. The following bibliographies and dictionary also are useful for studying campaign communication:

Kaid, Lynda L., Keith R. Sanders, and Robert O. Hirsch. *Political Campaign Communication: A Bibliography and Guide to the Literature.* Metuchen, NJ: Scarecrow Press, 1974.

This general bibliography on the communication process in political campaigns covers the period from 1950 to 1972. Included in the bibliography are books, articles, government documents, pamphlets, and dissertations covering analysis and evaluation, public opinion polling, media use and expenditures, and all aspects of the communication process. The volume has a subject index.

Kaid, Lynda L., and Anne Wadsworth. *Political Campaign Communication: A Bibliography and Guide to the Literature, 1973–1982.* Metuchen, NJ: Scarecrow Press, 1985.

This bibliography is a continuation of the 1974 work. Together the two bibliographies cover the period from 1950 to 1982.

Stempel, Guido H., III, and Jacqueline N. Gifford. *Historical Dictionary of Political Communication in the United States.* Westport, CT: Greenwood Press, 1999.

This dictionary includes entries on people, organizations, and events in political communication.

Political Consultants

Two Web sites provide information about and links to a variety of consultants, pollsters, and other commercial firms that work in the area of political campaigning. *Campaigns & Elections* offers a section, Political Consultant Web Site Links, found at http://www.campaignline.com/links/index.cfm. Political Resources On-Line provides lists of political consultants and has links to consulting services. It is found at http://www.politicalresources.com/new-top.htm and also in print as *Political Resource Directory.* In addition to these Web sites, two print sources provide information about political consultants:

Kurian, George T., and Jeffery D. Schultz. *Political Market Place USA.* Phoenix, AZ: Oryx Press, 1999–.

This annual publication provides information about political groups and resources. It is organized into twenty-four sections that offer directories by types of groups related to the political industry. For example, there are directories of political parties, political action committees, political consultants, and political associations.

Rosenbloom, David, ed. *The Political Marketplace*. New York: Quadrangle Books, 1972.

Intended as a guide to campaign information for political candidates, this directory also serves as an excellent reference work. Even though it was written solely for the 1972 elections, it continues to be a valuable source of historical information. It includes lists of campaign management and counseling firms, political advertising and public relations firms, computer-list and direct-mail houses, TV and radio time buyers, media outlets and film producers, telephone consultants, demographic and audience research firms, and numerous other types of entities related to aspects of campaign management.

Electoral Systems

Because the laws regulating campaign finances and electoral procedures affect party competition and the nature of the electoral process, it is important to know where to find information on rules and legislation governing elections and party activities.

Goldstein, Michael L. *Guide to the 2000 Presidential Election*. Washington, DC: CQ Press, 1999.

This is a clear and precise guide to the presidential election process. The author discusses the entire process, including the preliminaries leading up to the nomination, the actual nomination, the complete campaign, and the issues. He also discusses campaign financing, the use of advertising, the role of the media, and other topics. The *Guide to the 2000 Presidential Election* is an excellent basic guide to the electoral process and system.

Moore, John L. *Elections A to Z*. Washington, DC: CQ Press, 1999.

This comprehensive reference tool includes more than 200 entries on all aspects of campaigning and elections, including such topics as debates, consultants, the media, political parties, voter turnout, voting rights, and unique facts and stories.

Renstrom, Peter G., and Chester B. Rogers. *The Electoral Politics Dictionary*. Santa Barbara, CA: ABC-Clio, 1989.

This dictionary includes terms, concepts, cases, and phrases that concern electoral politics. The entries are arranged alphabetically within chapters on political culture and public opinion, political participation, elections, political campaigns, political parties, interest groups, and the mass media.

Young, Michael L. *American Dictionary of Campaigns and Elections*. New York: Hamilton Press, 1987.

This dictionary includes more than 725 entries divided into seven chapters that represent major subject areas. They are: (1) campaign process, (2) media and politics,

(3) polling and public opinion, (4) electoral strategies and tactics, (5) parties and PACs, (6) voting and political behaviors, and (7) money and politics. A complete index of all the entries appears at the end of the volume.

Several excellent reference guides also contain information on the electoral system and political parties of the United States and other countries. All of these tools can be used to find concise information about the American electoral and party system. Because cross-national research is especially prevalent in the areas of election and campaign research, these tools also are very useful for comparative research.

Delury, George, ed. *World Encyclopedia of Political Systems and Parties.* 3d ed. New York: Facts on File, 1999.

Statesman's Yearbook. New York: St. Martin's Press, 1864–.

Worldmark Encyclopedia of the Nations. 8th ed. Detroit, MI: Gale Group, 1998.

Political Parties

The following volumes provide historical information on political parties, conventions, candidates, and elections. In addition to the books listed below, all major political parties and many minor parties have Web sites. Several political party directories are online. Project Vote Smart's section on Political Parties is found at http:www.vote-smart.org/organizations/POLITICAL_PARTIES. Politics1.com's section on political parties is found at http://politics1.com/parties.htm. Yahoo keeps a list of U.S. political parties at http://dir.yahoo.com/Government/U_S__Government/Politics/Parties.

Bass, Harold, F. *Historical Dictionary of United States Political Parties.* Lanham, MD: Scarecrow Press, 2000.

This dictionary contains entries on political parties, party leaders, institutions, and terms associated with parties and elections. The author identifies most of the political parties in American government. Entries exist for all major political party presidential and vice presidential nominees, for noteworthy minor political party nominees, for House Speakers, for the Senate Presidents Pro Tempore, for floor leaders for each party in each chamber, and for all national party chairs of the major parties.

The Democratic and Republican Parties in America: A Historical Bibliography. Santa Barbara, CA: ABC-Clio, 1984.

This bibliography includes more than 1,000 abstracts that summarize journal articles published between 1973 and 1982. It covers such topics as the origin and growth of parties, candidates and campaign platforms, and lobbying. Entries are arranged by chapter and the volume provides a detailed multi-term subject index.

Kurian, George T. *The Encyclopedia of the Republican Party: The Encyclopedia of the Democratic Party.* Armonk, NY: Sharpe Reference, 1997.

This four-volume set provides a history of both parties, profiles of issues, biographies of presidents and vice presidents, losing presidential candidates, speakers of the House, platforms, and brief descriptions of elections. The appendixes include information on the charters and by-laws of each party, leaders and whips of the House, leaders in the Senate, party convention sites and dates, and chairs of the national committees.

Maisel, Sandy L., ed. *Political Parties and Elections in the United States: An Encyclopedia.* New York: Garland, 1991.

This volume includes fifty essay-length articles and more than 1,100 mini-essays that examine events, concepts, personalities, elections, incumbents, platforms, financing, suffrage, and other topics. The longer essays all include bibliographic references, and the work is completely indexed and cross-indexed. The volume also includes a extensive data on individuals, parties, and elections.

Rockwood, D. Stephen, Cecelia Brown, Kenneth Eshleman, and Deborah Shaffer. *American Third Parties since the Civil War.* New York: Garland, 1985.

This bibliography contains more than 1,200 annotated citations organized into chapters by party. Each chapter includes an introductory summary of the party's history. The bibliography primarily includes citations to books and journal articles. It includes an author and title index.

Election Data

Election returns can be found at various Web sites, including news services. Online database services also can be used for finding primary and election data information on campaign funding and analysis of campaigns as they take place. The *National Journal* and *CQ Weekly* each publish the results of congressional and presidential elections in a special issue a week or two following each election. For a week-by-week analysis of a campaign and election, these two journals—as well as the *New York Times* and the *Washington Post*—are indispensable. The *New York Times* and the *Washington Post*, and most other major newspapers, publish unofficial election results the day after an election. Local newspapers also can be very useful sources of information on election returns, including analysis of voting within a state and its major cities. Individual compilations of congressional election statistics also exist for almost every state. These compendiums usually are published by state historical societies, legislative research bureaus, and university institutes.

To find statistical summaries of election statistics, consult general almanacs. The *World Almanac and Book of Facts* (New York: Newspaper Enterprise Association, 1868–) and the *Information Please Almanac* (Boston: Houghton Mifflin, 1947–) are useful ready reference sources that are published annually. While each almanac uses a different format, they all contain essentially the same information. These almanacs often vary from year to year in regard to the data given. Usually almanacs published following an election year will include somewhat more detailed statistics, such as election results by county. The three series published by Congressional Quarterly, *Vital Statistics on American Politics, Vital Statistics on Congress, Vital Statistics on the Presidency,* also provide election statistics.

The National Election Studies (NES) prepared by the Center for Political Studies at the University of Michigan produce data on voting, public opinion and political participation. The best source of information about NES is the program's Web site, located at http://umich.edu/~nes. The site includes information about data sets, study resources, a NES bibliography, reports and papers, and the *Guide to Public Opinion and Electoral Behavior,* which provides summary data from 1952 to the present. A CD-ROM produced by NES and the Inter-University Consortium for Political and Social Research (ICPSR) can be used to find election data information for the period 1948 to 1997. The CD-ROM contains forty-five data collections that cover all presidential and midterm elections from 1948 to 1996, all NES pilot studies from 1979 to 1997, all NES panel and special studies; the 1948 to 1996 Cumulative Data File, and the *NES Guide to Public Opinion and Electoral Behavior.* The NES CD-ROM can be purchased from the ICPSR at the University of Michigan or on the NES Web site and also is available for use at ICPSR member institutions.

The following guides are excellent sources for election returns:

America Votes: A Handbook of Contemporary American Election Statistics. Washington, DC: Elections Research Center, Congressional Quarterly, 1956–.

This biennial work includes data for presidential, congressional, and gubernatorial returns since 1928. It also includes data for primary elections. The handbook reports information on the total vote (Republican and Democratic), pluralities, and percentages by county and congressional district. Sections on each state include: a map of the state depicting counties and congressional districts; a geographical breakdown by county for presidential and senatorial, and gubernatorial returns; and tables of the congressional returns by district.

Austin, Eric W. *Political Facts of the United States since 1789.* New York: Columbia University Press, 1986.

This general statistical compendium has a section on elections. It provides the popular votes for president, senators, and representatives. It also contains data on apportionment and campaign spending.

Burnham, Walter Dean. *Presidential Ballots: 1836–1892*. Baltimore: Johns Hopkins Press, 1955.

This work compiles state and county voting returns for the presidential elections between 1836 and 1892. A backward extension of the series compiled by Edgar E. Robinson, Burnham's book parallels Robinson's series in structure, using the county as the smallest unit. Tables give county, state, regional, and national election returns, broken down into Democratic, Republican, and other categories.

Congressional Quarterly. *Congressional Elections: 1946–1996*. Washington, DC: Congressional Quarterly, 1997.

This volume provides election data for House and Senate races, including popular vote, primary returns, and reapportionment and redistricting data. The work also provides information about the issues and politics of each election.

Congressional Quarterly. *Guide to U.S. Elections*. 3d ed. Washington, DC: Congressional Quarterly, 1994.

This work is the most definitive source of statistical data on U.S. elections from the nineteenth to the twentieth century. Included are the general voting results for elections for the presidency, both houses of congress, and governors. Primary election results also are provided for most presidential, senatorial, and gubernatorial races in the twentieth century. This volume is an excellent reference guide for all aspects of elections, including extensive background material on the history of parties, the Electoral College, demographic data, and redistricting. A topical bibliography accompanies each major section of the work. The format makes this reference work especially useful. Information can be located three ways: (1) a detailed table of contents provides an overall view of the scope and coverage of the work; (2) candidate indexes cover presidential, gubernatorial, Senate, and House candidates; and (3) a general index covers all subjects discussed in the work.

Congressional Quarterly. *Presidential Elections: 1789–1996*. Washington, DC: Congressional Quarterly, 1997.

This book traces the electoral process from presidential primaries through general elections, using tables that contain the votes received by each primary candidate through the 1996 elections. Party nominating conventions and lists of nominated candidates since 1831 are included. The book provides a discussion of voting trends and turnout, along with tables of state-by-state vote totals and percentages for major candidates. The book also covers the Electoral College, including maps and tables displaying Electoral College results since 1789. The appendixes include presidential and vice presidential biographies, texts of constitutional provisions and statutes that relate to presidential elections, and a bibliography.

Dubin, Michael J. *United States Congressional Elections, 1788–1997: The Official Results of the Elections of the 1st through 105th Congresses.* Jefferson, NC: McFarland, 1998.

This volume presents the official returns for all congressional elections arranged in chronological order by Congress and by state. The book also includes data for run-off elections and special elections, and information about incomplete returns.

The Election Data Book: A Statistical of Voting in America. Lanham, MD: Bernan Press, 1993.

This volume presents historical and current statistics on voting results for congressional, senatorial, presidential, and gubernatorial elections. The book includes more than 150 maps and charts and presents statistics on population, race, voting age, registration, turnout, and primaries by state, county, and congressional district.

Israel, Fred L. *Student's Atlas of American Presidential Elections 1789–1996.* Washington, DC: Congressional Quarterly, 1998.

This concise volume tells the story of each presidential election by providing a description of each election along with color maps and tables of the electoral and popular vote by state. The *Student's Atlas* is an easy-to-use reference for each presidential election.

McGillivray, Alice V., and Richard M. Scammon, comps. *America at the Polls, 1920–1956: Harding to Eisenhower: A Handbook of Presidential Election Statistics.* Washington, DC: Congressional Quarterly, 1994.

McGillivray, Alice V., and Richard M. Scammon, Rhodes Cook, comps. *America at the Polls, 1960–1996: Kennedy to Clinton: A Handbook of Presidential Election Statistics.* Washington, DC: Congressional Quarterly, 1998.

The two volumes listed above, which can be purchased separately or together as a set, cover presidential election results from Harding through Clinton. Statistics from 1920 through 1996 are organized by state, down to the county level. The set also provides a summary of popular and Electoral College votes, and tables of the national presidential vote broken down by state by to show pluralities and percentages. The books also include census population by county for each decade, presidential preference primary votes by state and candidate, and full-page maps outlining each county.

Miller, Warren E., Arthur H. Miller, and Edward J. Schneider. *American National Election Studies: Data Sourcebook, 1952–1986.* Cambridge: Harvard University Press, 1989.

The data compendium is the printed version of data archives available at the ICPSR. The surveys were conducted by the Survey Research Center and Center for Political Studies. Each study contains information from interviews with voters for elections from 1952 to 1986. This volume covers areas that include expectations about outcome of election, party identification, interest in politics, issue positions, perception of interest groups, assessment of major problems facing the country, financial and class identity, source of political information, measures of political efficacy, personal data, and post-election voter behavior.

Petersen, Svend. *A Statistical History of American Presidential Elections.* New York: Ungar, 1963.

This volume contains complete statistics for all presidential elections up to 1960 and includes 133 statistical compilations and tables that indicate votes and percentages. The tables are organized according to election, states, and the eleven historical parties examined. The book provides an analysis for each election for which a switch of less than 1 percent of the major-party vote would have changed the outcome. It also presents many miscellaneous tables of specific interest (for example, the number of times parties carried states, high votes for winners and losers by state, the closest Democratic versus Republican races in each state, tables for candidates who ran several times, identification of other votes, and many more). The work is especially useful for finding information concerning minor parties and candidates.

Robinson, Edgar Eugene. *The Presidential Vote, 1896–1932.* Stanford: Stanford University Press, 1934.

————. *The Presidential Vote 1936: Supplementing the Presidential Vote, 1896–1932.* Stanford: Stanford University Press, 1940.

————. *They Voted for Roosevelt: The Presidential Vote, 1932–1944.* Stanford: Stanford University Press, 1947.

The three volume series listed above contains the first publication of election returns by states and counties for the thirteen presidential elections between 1896 and 1944. The works are arranged to facilitate study of all counties for any election or any county for all elections. Tables indicate the distribution of the presidential vote by sections of the country, states, and counties and the distribution of party control by section, state, and county. Vote categories include Democratic, Republican, and Other—a category that is explained in some detail in the appendixes. Maps and other specific tables illustrate additional dimensions of the election results. The narrative essays provide useful analysis and interpretation of the data. In the Roosevelt volume a short introductory essay examines the meaning of Roosevelt's electoral base vis-à-vis his style of government. These three volumes by Robinson and the work by Burham (below) will be of particular interest to researchers seeking election returns by county.

Runyon, John H., Jennifer Verdini, and Sally S. Runyon, eds. *Source Book of American Presidential Campaign and Election Statistics, 1948–1968.* New York: Frederick Unger, 1971.

This comprehensive source of presidential campaign statistics is divided into the following subject areas: presidential preference primaries, national party conventions, presidential campaign staff, campaign itineraries, the cost of presidential campaigns, presidential campaign media exposure, public opinion polls, voting participation in presidential elections, and minor party voting. Each section includes references to data sources. Well designed, the book allows easy access to data and includes a selected bibliography on presidential campaigns and elections. The sections on campaign media exposure demonstrate how creativity can be used in compiling and constructing special types of presidential election statistics. The variety of statistics is useful to students or researchers who have new ideas about how to correlate and combine statistical categories.

Statistical Abstract of the United States. Washington, DC: U.S. Bureau of the Census, 1878–.

This annual document is the basic statistical abstract for social, economic, and political affairs in the United States. First published in 1878, its coverage on elections has changed considerably over the years. Recent volumes include information on votes cast for presidential, congressional, and gubernatorial elections, voter registration and participation, voting-age population, and campaign expenditures. The series includes a wealth of additional background information, such as statistics on education, employment, income, housing, communications, and other topics useful in conjunction with the study of elections. A free online version of the *Statistical Abstract of the United States* for the years 1995 to 1999 is available in PDF format. It can be downloaded from CenStore at http://www.census.gov/mp/www/censtore.html. For retrospective coverage of colonial times, volumes of the *Statistical Abstracts* should be used in conjunction with the *Historical Statistics of the United States, Colonial Times to 1970*, Bicentennial Edition (Washington, DC: U.S. Bureau of the Census, 1975).

Thomas, G. Scott. *The Pursuit of the White House: A Handbook of Presidential Election Statistics and History.* New York: Greenwood Press, 1987.

This volume provides a complete statistical and descriptive guide to the presidential elections between 1789 and 1984, including tables that contain data for all major-party primaries, conventions, and elections. The book also includes profiles of the candidates, parties, and states that shaped the outcome of each election.

U.S. Congress. House. Clerk of the House of Representatives. *Statistics of the Presidential and Congressional Elections.* Washington, DC: U.S. Government Printing Office, 1920–.

This official account of election returns for congressional and presidential elections began with the November 2, 1920, election. The series does not include any geographical breakdown of election returns. It has no real reference value, but is of interest as the official government record. A Web site for the Clerk that includes Electoral College results since the first Congress can be found at http://clerkweb.house.gov.

Students of elections often compare election statistics with similar data of other countries. While this kind of comparison seems natural, it must be conducted carefully and with an awareness of the limitations involved in such a study. Several important distinctions must be kept in mind when making cross-national analyses. You must pay special attention to the differences in the political systems, including party structure, nominating procedures, and forms of elections. In addition to the print sources listed below, several Web sites contain information and data about elections around the world. They are: Election Notes, at http://www.klipsan.com/elecnews.htm, Lijphart Elections Archive, at http://dodgson.ucsd.edu/lij, and Elections Around the World, at http://www.agora.stm.it/elections/indexfrm.htm.

Mackie, Thomas T., and Richard Rose. *The International Almanac of Electoral History.* 3d ed. New York: Facts on File, 1991.

This work provides election results from twenty-four countries, all of which are classified as industrial societies that conduct regular competitive elections. For each country the election results begin with the first competitive national election and include evolution of the electoral system and franchise laws, a list of political parties both in English and the national language, and election returns. The volume reports election returns using a standard format of four tables: total number of votes for each party, percentage of votes for each party, number of seats each party won and percentage of seats each party won. Election returns are provided for each party that secured at least one percent of the vote. The chapter on the United States is an exception: because of the primacy of the presidential elections, the book provides election returns only for those elections. The total vote, percentage of votes, number of electoral votes, and percentage of electoral votes are given for each political party. The value of this book is that it provides a standard format for comparative analysis.

Rokkan, Stein, and Jean Meyriat, eds. *International Guide to Election Statistics.* The Hague: Mouton, 1969.

The first international guide to election statistics, this volume covers fifteen multiparty regimes of Western Europe. It does not include the United States. Like *The International Almanac of Electoral History,* this guide follows a standard list of contents for each country. Each country's chapter begins with a chronology of the electoral system, including franchise qualifications, electoral procedures, and registration procedures. Then the chapters provide descriptions of data sources for each period. The book gives exact bibliographic citations to official and other statistical publications. Descriptions include the organization of the data, specifications of territorial units, contents of major tabulations, and language or languages of the tables. Each chapter also presents a review of period analyses of the data. These reviews are a representative selection of analyses conducted by national statistical agencies, academic research organizations, parties, or individual scholars. The analyses cover such areas as turnout variations, variations in party strength, and recruitment of candidates or electors. Most chapters then include a summary table presenting the national results of elections or referenda. The summary table includes the number of registered voters, number of votes cast, and votes for each party in percent of votes cast or percent of total electorate. This book is more difficult to use than the handbook by Mackie and Rose, but it is especially useful for identifying obscure and little-known election analyses.

Several other handbooks contain comparative information and data on electoral behavior. While they do not include election results, the following handbooks do contain valuable data on election participation and behavior:

Butler, David, Howard R. Penniman, and Austin Ranney. *Democracy at the Polls: A Comparative Study of Competitive National Elections.* Washington, DC: American Enterprise Institute, 1981.

Rose, Richard. *Electoral Behavior: A Comparative Handbook.* New York: Free Press, 1974.

Rose, Richard. *Electoral Participation: A Comparative Analysis.* Beverly Hills: Sage Publications, 1980.

Rose, Richard, ed. *International Encyclopedia of Elections.* Washington, DC: CQ Press, 2000.

Several bibliographies include citations to articles and books about elections on a comparative basis. The following are among the most useful of these bibliographies:

Bloomfield, Valerie. *Commonwealth Elections, 1945–1970.* Westport, CT: Greenwood Press, 1977.

Gorvin, Ian, ed. *Elections since 1945: A Worldwide Reference Compendium.* Chicago: St. James Press, 1989.

Inter-Parliamentary Union. *World-Wide Bibliography on Parliaments.* Geneva: International Center for Parliamentary Documentation, 1978–.

Urwin, Derek W., ed. *Elections in Western Nations, 1945–1968.* Glasgow: Survey Research Centre, University of Strathclyde, 1970.

District Data

When studying elections it is crucial to know something about the voters themselves. Factors such as age, sex, race, education, and income can be used in explanations of why the electorate voted a certain way. This kind of information generally is available only from public opinion surveys.

Congressional Districts in the 1990s (Washington, DC: Congressional Quarterly, 1993) is a political atlas of all the new congressional districts. This volume includes 1990 census data, state and district profiles, and election results since 1986, recalculated to match the new districts. Congressional Quarterly has also published *Congressional Districts in the 1970s* (1973) and

Congressional Districts in the 1980s (1983). A CD-ROM product, the *Census of Population and Housing 1990—Public Law 94-171 Data,* provides the census data gathered for redistricting purposes. The CD-ROM disks can be searched by state, county, census tract, voting district, block group, and block. Maps and data of congressional districts also are irregularly published in the *Congressional District Atlas* (Washington, DC: Bureau of the Census, 1964–). If you are seeking general data about a district, two almanacs—*Almanac of American Politics* and *Politics in America*—can be used as ready reference guides. Both almanacs provide short profiles of districts, including their social and economic structure, political history, and constituent concerns. They are available in print and online. The following volumes provide population data for both the districts and counties, district and county maps, and information about the creation of the counties:

U.S. Bureau of the Census. *Congressional District Data Book: A Statistical Abstract Supplement.* Washington, DC: U.S. Government Printing Office, 1963–.

The *Congressional District Data Book* presents a wide range of data from census and recent election statistics for congressional districts. It includes socioeconomic data, such as population, sex, residency, race, age, households and families, marital status, industry, occupation, migration, and housing. Maps for each state show counties and congressional districts. Appendixes give data on apportionment, redistricting, and district populations. Because the data are based on the decennial census, new editions and supplements of the *Data Book* are irregularly issued. The *Congressional District Data Book* also is available from the Census Bureau in machine-readable form and is in the archival holdings of the Inter-University Consortium for Political and Social Research.

Martis, Kenneth C. *The Historical Atlas of the United States Congressional Districts, 1789–1983.* New York: Free Press, 1983.

This atlas illustrates all congressional districts for the first ninety-seven Congresses. It identifies all representatives and locates their districts on maps. Also a complete legal history of redistricting for every state is included. Thus, the atlas provides an easy way to illustrate voting data and map voting patterns. By mapping the geographical patterns of any roll call vote, you can quickly analyze regional and sectional politics. The atlas also can be used to map the geographical distribution of committee memberships, party membership, and the margin of electoral victory; consequently, it can be used for studying congressional elections and illustrating geographical roll call voting patterns.

Martis, Kenneth C., and Gregory A. Elmes. *The Historical Atlas of State Power in Congress, 1790–1990.* Washington, DC: Congressional Quarterly, 1993.

This atlas provides a visual guide to the history of population shifts and reapportionment that have resulted in the rise and fall of power among the states. Separate chapters for each decade from 1970 through 1990 present snapshots of American demographics and state power throughout a 200-year political history. Color maps and tables clearly illustrate the changes that resulted from each decennial census. The accompanying text provides a historical context for the 1990 census.

Parsons, Stanley B. *United States Congressional Districts, 1883–1913.* New York: Greenwood Press, 1990.

Parsons, Stanley B., William W. Beach, and Michael J. Dubin. *United States Congressional Districts, 1843–1883.* New York: Greenwood Press, 1986.

Parsons, Stanley B., William W. Beach, and Dan Herman. *United States Congressional Districts, 1788–1841.* Westport, CT: Greenwood Press, 1978.

The three volumes listed above provide population data for districts and counties, district and county maps, and information about the creation of the counties. Also given are the names and their party affiliation of representatives for each district by Congress.

Voting and Registration Data

Data on reported voting and registration by various demographic and socioeconomic characteristics are collected in November of congressional and presidential election years in the Current Population Survey. Projections of voting age population by race, age, Hispanic origin, and gender also are produced every other year. Information about available reports can be found at the Census Bureau's Web site under Voting and Registration. Files can be viewed online at http://www.census.gov/population/www.socdemo/voting. html. Data from the Current Population Survey on voting and registration since 1964 also are available on CD-ROM, diskette, and magnetic tape.

The U.S. Census Bureau first published these data as two series within their *Current Population Reports.* The *Population Estimates, P–25 Series* included regular reports on the estimates and projections of population of voting age. The *Population Characteristics, P–20 Series* provided information about the demographic characteristics of the voting population and the degree of participation in general elections by those eligible to vote. Both series also are in the archival holdings of the Inter-University Consortium for Political and Social Research. These older reports, and other reports published by the Census Bureau, are indexed in STATISTICAL UNIVERSE, the *Bureau of the Census Catalog of Publications, 1790–1972* (Washington, DC: U.S. Government Printing Office, 1974), and the *Census Catalog and Guide* (Washington, DC: U.S. Government Printing Office, 1973–). The *Bureau of the Census Catalog* is available online from CenStore at http://www.census.gov/mp/www/censtore. html. Such reports also appear in *American Statistical Index: A Comprehensive*

Index to the Statistical Publications of the U.S. Government (Washington, DC: Congressional Information Service, 1974–).

Party Strength Data

Voting returns by themselves do not convey the entire story of an election. Students of elections can learn considerably more about elections by developing their own statistical measures. Today, political scientists are employing statistical data in highly sophisticated ways. By using data in different configurations, researchers can bring to light new perspectives on elections. The following works are the major studies that have sought to examine concepts of political party strength, competitiveness, and voting behavior:

Cox, Edward F. *The Representative Vote in the Twentieth Century*. Bloomington: Institute of Public Administration, Department of Political Science, Indiana University, 1981.

This volume extends and complements Cox's two previous works. It provides data for all regular and special congressional elections from 1900 to 1972. What makes this statistical compendium special is that it provides complete data for all candidates and parties for elections to the U.S. House of Representatives. Congressional Quarterly's *Guide to U.S. Elections* provides only the data for candidates with percentages in excess of 5 percent. Consequently, this volume is an important statistical compendium for anyone researching minor parties and party performance. It also can be used as a companion to the other data sources on election returns.

Cox, Edward F. *State and National Voting in Federal Elections, 1910–1970*. Hamden, CT: Archon Books, 1972.

This work uses the national elective format as the organization for its data. It organizes tables by nation and state, including the total vote and percentages of all votes. Voting information covers presidential and congressional elections. Data on the election of representatives are compiled on a statewide aggregate basis. Election data for representatives are not broken down by congressional district, which is a serious drawback. The aggregate elective format provides a useful method for comparing the vote of the three national elective positions. This format makes measuring the voting strength of each party for president, senators, and representatives in each election a simple matter.

Cox, Edward F. *Voting in Postwar Federal Elections: A Statistical Analysis of Party Strengths since 1945*. Rev. ed. Dayton, OH: Wright State University, 1968.

As an interpretation of the significance of American voting in federal elections from 1946 to 1966, the book presents measures of party performance, strength, competitiveness, and individual candidate performance. The volume provides geographical analyses by district and state. The author delineates major trends and future directions for party competition. The book includes two chapters on methodological issues related to the statistical analyses employed in the study. The analyses of the eleven federal elections examined are presented in 251 tables. One failing is the lack of an index.

Cummings, Milton C. *Congressmen and the Electorate: Elections for the U.S. House and President, 1920–1964.* New York: Free Press, 1966.

This work provides an extensive analysis of the interrelationships between the votes for members of Congress and the votes for president in presidential election years. The central thrust of the book is the examination of the degree of similarities and differences between presidential and congressional support as polled by the major parties. The book also covers ticket splitting, party strength, the role of minor parties, and the effects of the electoral system on presidential and congressional elections. The work includes fifty-one statistical tables relating to the topics discussed.

David, Paul T. *Party Strength in the United States, 1872–1970.* Charlottesville: University Press of Virginia, 1972.

This book provides index numbers for party strength covering a period from 1872 to 1970. The study contains the percentages of the vote won by Democratic, Republican, and other parties and candidates in presidential, gubernatorial, and congressional elections. The text provides the statistical and technical background to the formulation of the index numbers.

Additional data covering the later elections can be found in the following journal articles:

"Party Strength in the United States: Changes in 1972." *Journal of Politics* 36 (August 1974): 785–796.
"Party Strength in the United States: Some Corrections." *Journal of Politics* 37 (May 1975): 641–642.
"Party Strength in the United States: Changes in 1976." *Journal of Politics* 40 (August 1978): 770–780.

Janda, Kenneth. *Political Parties: A Cross-National Survey.* New York: Free Press, 1980.

This volume provides a systematic and comprehensive empirical study of political parties throughout the world. It includes surveys of 153 parties in fifty-eight countries from 1950 to 1978. The book presents a conceptual framework of political parties using twelve basic concepts. Topics covered include institutionalization, government status, social attraction, concentration and reflection, issue orientation, goal orientation, autonomy, degree of organization, centralization of power, coherence, involvement, electoral data, and validation of the framework. The volume also examines the findings for each country, including data and analysis, party history, and electoral trends. This volume is useful for studying American political parties and for comparing parties cross-nationally. In addition to providing data on party strength, it is an unmatched compendium of data on party characteristics. The data also are available as a file from the ICPSR.

Part II

Selected Bibliography on Elections

3

Nomination and Selection
of Presidents

General

Abramowitz, Alan I., and Walter J. Stone. *Nomination Politics: Party Activists and Presidential Choice.* New York: Praeger, 1984.

The authors employ survey research within a rational choice framework to examine presidential candidate choice by party activists. They focus on twenty-two state presidential conventions in eleven states that use the caucus convention method of candidate selection as opposed to the presidential preference method. Abramowitz and Stone conclude that successful presidential candidates may be less loyal to the party organization, given the increased emphasis placed on presidential primaries at the expense of local and state party organizations.

Barber, James D., ed. *Choosing the President.* Englewood Cliffs, NJ: Prentice-Hall, 1974.

This edited volume evaluates the manner in which the presidency is accountable to the electorate in the wake of the resignation of President Richard M. Nixon. Articles included discuss the relationship between human nature and the office of president, the nominating process and proposed reforms, campaign strategy, the linkage of accountability between the president and the electorate between elections, the role of president as persuader, and postwar electoral trends.

Buell, Emmett H., Jr., and Lee Sigelman, eds. *Nominating the President.* Knoxville: University of Tennessee Press, 1991.

This edited volume addresses what is seen to be a deficiency in the literature concerning the presidential electoral race—analysis of the nomination process. The essays included cover a wide range of subject matter and approach their topics using a variety of methodological and insightful approaches. The authors focus on the 1988 nomination campaign and consider the events of that year as context and attempt to derive patterns that might be applicable to future presidential nomination campaigns. Topics covered in this work include the strategic environment of 1988, the Iowa caucuses, Super Tuesday, financing, outside challengers, media coverage, and the national party conventions.

Ceaser, James W. *Presidential Selection: Theory and Development.* Princeton: Princeton University Press, 1979.

The author examines the development of presidential selection from the founding of the republic. He contends that reformers and scholars have ignored many of the major purposes of the selection system as it was formerly understood. He discusses the theories of selection offered by Thomas Jefferson, Martin Van Buren, and Woodrow Wilson. From these theories Ceaser identifies a set of criteria for a sound selection system that he uses to analyze and evaluate the recent changes in the selection process. Ceaser finds that weak parties and candidate-centered campaigns characterize the present system and lead to the problems of image politics and demagogic leadership appeals. He therefore argues for a selection system in which political parties would be strengthened to serve as a restraining force on popular authority, public opinion, and individual aspirations for executive power.

————. *Reforming the Reforms: A Critical Analysis of the Presidential Selection Process.* Cambridge, MA: Ballinger, 1982.

In this volume Ceaser examines the presidential selection process and the numerous reforms proposed to alter it. Ceaser sketches the evolution of the nominating system from 1789 through 1968 and discusses the era of reform of the late 1960s through the late 1970s. He evaluates the postreform era nominating process and discusses options for changing it. Ceaser argues that parties are strong, contrary to the perception of party decline, and examines four causes of party strength that relate to the nominating process. Finally, he discusses three key issues in choosing the best nominating system: preference, feasibility, and strategy.

Crotty, William J., and John S. Jackson III. *Presidential Primaries and Nominations.* Washington, DC: CQ Press, 1985.

The authors focus on the presidential selection process from the announcement of the candidacy through the national nominating conventions. They examine the way the selection process has evolved in recent decades and evaluate those changes in the context of American political history. The authors examine the history of the nomination process, recent reforms, and the influence of media on the process. They cover issues related to nomination procedures, such as voter participation and representativeness, convention delegates, candidate strategy, campaign finance, and the nominating convention.

Gray, Lee L. *How We Choose a President: The Election Year.* New York: St. Martin's, 1980.

The author divides the presidential campaigning process into five categorical events: the search for candidates, the nomination of candidates, the campaign, election day, and the inauguration. She discusses the evolution of presidential campaigns from 1789 through 1976 and assesses how these parameters might further be transformed or adhered to in future presidential races. The author also provides a glossary of key terms, a table of the electoral votes for all presidential elections through 1976, and selections from the Constitution.

Heard, Alexander. *Made in America: Improving the Nomination and Election of Presidents.* New York: HarperCollins, 1991.

The author examines how Americans choose their president and the consequences that flow from this process. He addresses voters' frustrations with the present means of choosing presidents and defines important functions of the electoral process. Heard discusses his concern about the quality and transformation of political information. He addresses voting, individual participation other than voting, elections, and setting the public agenda. The author examines the current method of executive selection and discusses possible reforms for the system.

Heard, Alexander, and Michael Nelson, eds. *Presidential Selection.* Durham, NC: Duke University Press, 1987.

The articles in this edited volume concern traditional issues regarding the presidential selection process, such as campaign finance, nominations, the media, and electoral participation. The authors also address three additional themes outside the typical boundaries: the international implications and effects of selecting a president; how this process directly affects policy in a variety of issue areas; and the influence of the Constitution on presidential selection.

Jackson, John S., III, and William J. Crotty. *The Politics of Presidential Selection.* New York: HarperCollins, 1996.

The authors give an overview of how we select our presidents and why the system works as well as it does. They examine how presidents are chosen; who succeeds and why; who participates in decision making; how the institutions of selection have evolved; the role of money in the process; the relationship of presidents to congressional, state, and local elections; the conduct and effects of general election campaigns; and the consequences of the outcomes. The authors employ bounded rationality within a rational actor model to explain choice of campaign strategies and how candidates behave once in office. The authors also cover the meaning of the 1994 midterm election and the implications of the Republican Party's Contract with America on the 1996 campaign.

Judah, Charles B., and George W. Smith. *The Unchosen.* New York: Coward-McCann, 1962.

The authors examine nine men who unsuccessfully sought their party's nomination for the presidency. The authors' discussion of the candidates' failures sheds light on the dynamics of the national party convention and specifically on how the convention narrows the field of candidates to one person who can unite the party's warring factions into a single fighting unit. The profiles of the nine unsuccessful candidates explore the genesis and nature of their presidential obsession and factors that may have ultimately contributed to their failure to attain the nomination. The following candidates are examined: Seward (Republicans, 1860); Bristow (Republicans, 1876); Sherman (Republicans, 1880, 1884, 1888); Clark (Democrats, 1912); Lowden (Republicans, 1920); McAdoo (Democrats, 1924); Taft (Republicans, 1952); Kefauver (Democrats, 1956); and Johnson (Democrats, 1960). An epilogue considers the 1964 Republican choice between Barry Goldwater and Nelson Rockefeller.

Keech, William R., and Donald R. Matthews. *The Party's Choice.* Washington, DC: Brookings Institution, 1976.

In this analysis of the presidential nominating process the authors examine the events leading up to the nomination of the major parties' candidates in the ten presidential elections from 1936 to 1972. They find that the crucial period for most presidential aspirants is the three years between one election and the opening of formal campaigning for the next. The search for a consensus candidate often produces a leader whom the press, polls, and party leaders recognize as the unofficial nominee before the first primaries, and such candidates usually survive with their advantages intact. This work examines the mechanics of the nominating process and describes how they affect the chances of contenders inside and outside the party in power. The authors believe that the system of nominating presidential candidates should be changed so as to lengthen the list of promising contestants in the long period of informal campaigning. They further argue that the primaries should serve to narrow the choice to a few candidates whom convention delegates could back as presidential possibilities.

Keeter, Scott, and Clifford Zukin. *Uniformed Choice: The Failure of the New Presidential Nominating System.* New York: Praeger, 1983.

The authors examine how America chooses presidential leadership. Operating from the premise that citizen self-government is important to maintaining a democratic polity, Keeter and Zukin find the presidential nominating system inadequate to support or sustain a democratic community. They maintain that the new system of nominating presidential candidates forces citizens to make uninformed decisions in their selection of possible executive leaders. The authors contend that structures and environment shape political behavior and that the current incentive structure and information exchange through the media are inadequate for educated decision making.

Kirkpatrick, Jeane J., and Michael J. Malbin. *The Presidential Nominating Process: Can It Be Improved?* Washington, DC: American Enterprise Institute for Public Policy Research, 1980.

This monograph contains the transcript from a panel discussion by the authors on how to improve the presidential nomination process. Starting from the observation that there was widespread dissatisfaction with the presidential nominating process as it operated in 1980, they deal with three main issues: the criteria for a good presidential nominating system, the deficiencies of the present system, and how the present system might be reformed. The authors discuss a range of reform proposals: national one-day presidential primaries, complete abolition of presidential primaries, and selection of candidates by conventions composed exclusively of party officers and elected public officials.

League of Women Voters of the United States. *Choosing the President: A Citizen's Guide to the 2000 Election.* Washington, DC: Lyons Press, 1999.

This book goes beneath the political surface to examine how America elects a president. It analyzes the political parties, the selection of convention delegates, primaries, caucuses, and the inner workings of party conventions. The book also takes a thorough look at campaign techniques, strategies and costs, voter behavior, and the actual election process.

Lengle, James I., and Byron E. Shafer, eds. *Presidential Politics: Readings on Nominations and Elections.* New York: St. Martin's, 1983.

This edited collection of readings on the politics of presidential selection begins with an overview of recent reforms. It then follows the politics of presidential selection in roughly chronological fashion, running from the day after one presidential election to the day of the next. Along the way, the authors examine the nomination campaigns, the institutional environment, strategies and tactics, campaign organization and finance, delegate selection, primaries, conventions, the general election, and types of election outcomes. When moving beyond this concrete and chronological approach the authors focus on three fundamental elements: the social base, the institutional structure, and the actions of relevant elites. The readings range from academic classics to journalistic reporting.

Matthews, Donald R., ed. *Perspectives on Presidential Selection.* Washington, DC: Brookings Institution, 1973.

This edited volume examines the process of selecting the U.S. president. After an introduction to comparative approaches to studying this question, the volume delves into the issue of executive selection by comparing the British and French systems with the American one. Some essays include comparisons of the selection of party executives in Britain and the United States, the president and the prime minister, convention systems of Canada and the United States, and the processes for choosing the president of France and the United States. Other essays deal with aspects of the conventions, the electoral college, and alternative methods of electing the president. Most of the chapters in this volume use extended case illustrations, such as the 1968 presidential nomination or an examination of delegate turnover between 1944 and 1968.

Mayer, William G., ed. *In Pursuit of the White House 2000: How We Choose Our Presidential Nominees.* Chatham, NJ: Chatham House, 1999.

This edited volume contains a series of articles that explain various elements of the increasingly important presidential nominating process. While each contribution is specific in its issue area, the authors also attempt to tease out some generally applicable observations and patterns that have emerged since the rule changes on campaign finance and partisan nominating procedures of the late 1960s and early 1970s. Topics covered include forecasting nominations, activists, the New Hampshire primary, the new presidential elite, the role of televised debates, the effect of a divisive nomination race, caucuses, Super Tuesday, the media, campaign finance, the Christian right, third party candidates, and nomination reform.

Novak, Michael. *Choosing Presidents: Symbols of Political Leadership.* 2d ed. New Brunswick, NJ: Transaction, 1992.

The author discusses the elements of symbolic power, moralism and morality, the civil religions of America, and the symbols of the presidential campaign. The introduction traces the shifting and often paradoxical ideological orientations of the Democratic and Republican parties over the past two decades and offers an insightful view of Ronald Reagan's success in grasping the power of symbols in presidential politics. Next, concentrating on the pivotal 1972 campaign, Novak shows how voters seek and choose a candidate with whom they can identify. The author tests the predictive power of the earlier chapters in analyzing the elections and presidencies of Jimmy Carter and George Bush.

Pomper, Gerald M. *Nominating the President: The Politics of Convention Choice, with a New Postscript on 1964.* New York: Norton, 1966.

The author examines the way parties nominate candidates for the office of chief executive. He emphasizes the merits, rather than the deficits, of the presidential nominating system. Pomper notes changes in the system and examines their effects on the political process. He outlines the history of presidential nominations and the formal mechanics involved in making national party decisions. He investigates the process of party action on platforms, internal government, and presidential and vice presidential designations. He investigates patterns and trends in party nominations, which raise questions about the future of the nominating process. He examines several proposed reforms and offers suggestions for improving the system.

Ranney, Austin. *Participation in American Presidential Nominations: 1976.* Washington, DC: American Enterprise Institute for Public Policy Research, 1977.

The author reviews the different ideas held by academics and politicians about who should participate in choosing the major parties' presidential candidates.

Distinguishing three basic views, he finds that in recent years the views of the issue/candidate enthusiasts or even those of the ordinary voters have overborne the views of the party regulars. Analyzing the 1976 primaries, Ranney finds that the overall turnout was about half as large as the turnout in the ensuing general election. Wide interstate variation occurred in the primary turnout, however. The main factors associated with low turnouts were restrictive registration laws, crossover primary laws, and low campaign spending. The author concludes with some predictions about what the turnout would be in a national presidential primary.

Reiter, Howard L. *Selecting the President: The Nominating Process in Transition.* Philadelphia: University of Pennsylvania Press, 1985.

The author examines four causal theories that have been used to examine the presidential nomination process, tests them for accuracy, and determines which changes are the results of which reforms. Reiter isolates a series of causal relationships that support his thesis that the strength of party organization has declined since the 1950s as party control has shifted from a local to a national level.

Rose, Gary L., ed. *Controversial Issues in Presidential Selection.* 2d ed. Albany: State University of New York Press, 1994.

This book examines ten major and controversial issues directly affecting the presidential selection process. Each issue is addressed in a point-counterpoint format. The introduction argues that the modern process of presidential selection has evolved to a point of crisis. The conclusion endorses a proposal that could serve as a first step toward improving the process. In between, the nominating phase, the convention phase and the general election phase are analyzed in detail. The book also examines the media, advertising, public financing, debates, the electoral college, onsite voter registration, degree of representativeness of the process, selection of vice presidential candidates and whether a third major party is needed.

Sanford, Terry. *A Danger of Democracy: The Presidential Nominating Process.* Boulder, CO: Westview Press, 1981.

In this volume, the author offers a study of the history of party nominations. Sanford suggests some inadequacies in the nominating process and recommends adherence to three new principles: (1) the electorate should choose convention delegates who are uninstructed or at least not irrevocably bound; (2) the delegates should be elected in time for them to meet with the candidates, in time for the candidates to electioneer with the delegates, and in time to allow the constituents ample opportunity to communicate with the delegates; and (3) a participatory electorate must inform and guide the process but not distort it.

Thompson, Kenneth W., ed. *The Presidential Nominating Process: Broadening and Narrowing the Debate.* Lanham, MD: University Press of America, 1983.

This edited collection of lectures addresses reforming the presidential nominating process. Some of the contributors call for debate on constitutional reform. Others question whether changes in the current arrangements are necessary or possible. The volume opens with a broad overview of the sectors of government in which change might be considered. Other issues covered include the role of elected officials and party leaders in the nominating process, the political psychology of the process, the effects of presidential primaries on news reporting, and the effect of the media on election politics.

————, ed. *The Presidential Nominating Process: Constitutional, Economic and Political Issues.* Lanham, MD: University Press of America, 1984.

This edited volume focuses on the financial, political, and constitutional issues surrounding the presidential nominating process. One essay focuses on the effects of party and convention rule reform in the nominating process. Another essay examines the intersection of power, money, and the presidential nomination. The book also provides an evaluation of proposed electoral reform in the area of nominations.

Witcover, Jules. *No Way to Pick a President.* New York: Farrar, Straus, and Giroux, 1999.

The author provides a lively account of what is wrong with the way our presidents are chosen. Witcover discusses how campaign professionals are corrupting American politics, how television distorts the electoral process, and how politicians have condoned those developments. He concludes with ideas of how to improve presidential politics and revive public interest in American politics.

Primaries

Bartels, Larry M. *Presidential Primaries and the Dynamics of Public Choice.* Princeton: Princeton University Press, 1988.

The author examines the role of momentum in presidential primaries, using advanced statistical analysis. He analyzes individual voters' attitudes and aggregates that data to study primary campaigns over time. Three appendixes examine media content on presidential primaries, develop the author's formal models, and present the statistical results of his study.

Blackman, Paul H. *Presidential Primaries and the 1976 Election.* Washington, DC: Heritage Foundation, 1975.

The author examines the presidential primary system in an effort to inform the 1976 presidential campaign. He offers a brief historical overview of the development of presidential primaries, followed by an examination of the rationale for primaries and its critique. Blackman examines party and state reforms of the presidential selection process, and federal proposals for reforms.

Davis, James W. *Presidential Primaries: Road to the White House.* 2d ed. Westport, CT: Greenwood Press, 1980.

The author details the shifting trends in the politics of nominating the president. This edition provides a comprehensive update of the presidential nominating process in light of the rapid proliferation of primaries, precedent-shattering congressional legislation on primary and general election campaign finance, and Democratic Party reforms spawned by the 1968 convention. Davis includes a special chapter on polls and primaries. He gives detailed information on state primary laws, especially those statutes approved since the 1976 election. Appendixes detail voting data for primaries from 1912 to 1976 and primary financial receipts and expenditures for 1976.

Ernst, Harry W. *The Primary That Made a President: West Virginia, 1960.* New York: McGraw-Hill, 1962.

The author sees John F. Kennedy's 1960 West Virginia primary victory over Hubert H. Humphrey as the critical event that gave Kennedy the boost he needed to capture the Democratic Party nomination and later the presidency. Ernst offers a detailed case study of that contest, examining examines the strategies and tactics used by both sides, including haggling over a potential televised debate, the role of organized labor, the politics of coal, the role of money and campaign financing, and issues of race and religion.

Geer, John G. *Nominating Presidents: An Evaluation of Voters and Primaries.* Westport, CT: Greenwood, 1989.

The author evaluates presidential nominating techniques and proposes an empirically grounded and nonpartisan reform program. Geer seeks to develop a set of criteria and standards by which to evaluate the qualifications of individuals involved in the nominating process to ensure democratic representativeness. The author also provides an overview of the body of information concerning the role of the voter in presidential primaries.

Hadley, Arthur T. *The Invisible Primary.* Englewood Cliffs, NJ: Prentice-Hall, 1976.

The author examines the period between the election of one president and the start of the first state primary to determine the next presidential candidates. He deals with the people and politics of presidential selection from 1973 through December 1975. Hadley calls this period the invisible primary, claiming that the eventual candidate actually is selected during this period. Hadley traveled with the candidates as they emerged, documenting their rise and fall. He examines candidates (and noncandidates) including Edward Kennedy, Henry Jackson, Gerald Ford, Ronald Reagan, Mo Udall, Walter Mondale, Charles Percy, Elliot Richardson, Lloyd M. Bentsen, and Jimmy Carter. The author concludes that the invisible primary is the key to candidate selection and that the state primaries, caucuses, and party conventions have become largely media events with predictable outcomes.

Lengle, James I. *Representation and Presidential Primaries: The Democratic Party in the Post-Reform Era.* Westport, CT: Greenwood Publishing, 1981.

The author analyzes data from California presidential primaries during 1968 and 1972. He shows that nominating presidential candidates in primaries distorts the outcome compared to a process in which all party members voted. Lengle contends that Democrats who participate in their party's primaries are better educated, more ideological, and wealthier than Democrats who do not vote in primary elections.

Maisel, L. Sandy. *From Obscurity to Oblivion: Running in the Congressional Primary.* Rev. ed. Knoxville: University of Tennessee Press, 1986.

The author recounts his experience as an unsuccessful candidate for his party's nomination to Congress in 1978. He offers anecdotal evidence supplemented by data gathered from questionnaires mailed to other primary candidates across the country and from thirty-nine personal interviews. Maisel provides a thorough treatment of the battle for party nomination. He discusses problems faced by candidates, including lack of funds, poor organization, and having to make decisions based on inadequate information. Maisel concludes with some thoughts about the primary process and a selected bibliography of existing literature on the subject.

Norrander, Barbara K. *Super Tuesday: Regional Politics and Presidential Primaries.* Lexington: University Press of Kentucky, 1992.

The author examines the changing presidential nomination system and the move to Super Tuesday in 1988. She reviews the patterns of presidential nominations of the 1980s and examines how this system developed. Norrander discusses the structure of the 1988 campaign and the campaign strategies used in Iowa, New Hampshire, and on Super Tuesday. She examines participation in presidential primaries, vote choice, and winning the nomination, and concludes with an evaluation of Super Tuesday.

Orren, Gary R., and Nelson W. Polsby, eds. *Media and Momentum: The New Hampshire Primary and Nomination Politics.* Chatham, NJ: Chatham House, 1987.

The editors have collected a series of articles that discuss the pivotal role New Hampshire plays in the presidential nominating process. They maintain that New Hampshire's importance stems from a series of changes in party rules for nominating candidates, federal regulations on fund raising and campaign spending, and an increased role of the media in selecting presidential candidates. The articles cover the history of the nominating process in New Hampshire, the disproportionality of its influence on presidential nominations, newspaper coverage of the primary, the electoral message sent following the primary outcomes, and a statistical analysis of New Hampshire's primary system.

Ranney, Austin. *The Federalization of Presidential Primaries.* Washington, DC: American Enterprise Institute for Public Policy Research, 1978.

The author examines proposals for increasing federal control of presidential primaries. These proposals range in degree from federal limitation of the dates on which state primaries may be held to a national direct primary conducted without regard to state lines or laws. Ranney shows that Congress has a constitutional power to legislate any of these changes. He assesses the probable benefits and costs of each proposal and concludes that the greater the degree of federalization imposed, the greater will be the damage to what remains of national political parties. No probable benefit, he argues, would be worth such a cost.

Sabato, Larry J. *The Democratic Party Primary in Virginia: Tantamount to Election No Longer.* Charlottesville: University Press of Virginia, 1978.

The author examines how the fortunes of the Democratic Party in Virginia have changed over the years. For decades winning the Democratic primary election in Virginia was tantamount to election in November. Now, however, the Democratic primary's position has been greatly diminished. The author follows this decline in fortunes and discusses reasons why this may have occurred. He also reviews and analyzes the origin of the primary system. Finally, the author discusses the future of the Virginia primary system, paying considerable attention to a comparative evaluation of several methods of nomination.

Squire, Peverill, ed. *The Iowa Caucuses and the Presidential Nominating Process.* Boulder, CO: Westview Press, 1989.

This edited volume explains the Iowa caucuses in detail as a singular political phenomenon and in terms of their significance to the larger electoral process. Issues addressed include the representativeness of the Iowa caucus, its significance as the first electoral caucus, and how media coverage of the caucus affects other presidential primaries.

Stein, Leon, ed. *The Caucus System in American Politics.* New York: Arno, 1974.

This collection of papers examines the caucus system and its place in electoral politics. The first two papers, written in 1883 and 1885, examine the origin, purpose, and utility of the caucus system. The final paper, written in 1902, is an essay on the rise and fall of the congressional caucus as a machine for nominating candidates for the presidency. Each article traces the beginnings of the system from the birth of the new nation and uses historical examples to illustrate how caucuses were both efficient and inefficient in helping to select the chief executive.

Conventions

Byrne, Gary C., and Paul Marx. *Great American Convention: A Political History of Presidential Elections.* Palo Alto, CA: Pacific Books, 1976.

The authors attempt to explain the selection of presidents as a two-step process: the nominating convention and the electorate's decision on election day. Arguing that the first step tends to effect the outcome of the second, they develop a typology and formula for ranking party conventions between 1864 and 1968 as strong or weak. They continue by examining the relationship between convention style and electoral outcomes. Byrne and Marx examine eleven presidential elections to support their general hypothesis that nominating conventions are a defining step in the presidential selection process.

David, Paul T., and James W. Ceaser. *Proportional Representation in Presidential Nominating Politics.* Charlottesville: University Press of Virginia, 1984.

The authors examine the consequences of the 1976 Democratic Party delegate selection rules requiring the use of a proportional division of the delegates in many states. They analyze the selection process as a whole, describe the various selection systems in use, and trace the origin, growth, and potential future consequences of the new principle of proportional representation. David and Ceaser look at six independently written state reports representing a cross-section of the various selection procedures in use in 1976. They examine Connecticut, Illinois, Massachusetts, Oklahoma, Texas, and Virginia.

David, Paul T., Ralph M. Goldman, and Richard D. Baia. *The Politics of National Party Conventions.* Rev. ed. New York: Random House, 1984.

The authors offer an account of national party conventions, beginning with their first appearance during Andrew Jackson's initial term in office. The authors examine the following aspects of our political and social system as they affect or are affected by national party conventions: the media, public opinion polls, voter preference, party leadership, candidates, apportionment, voting structure, primaries, delegates, state delegations, and voting strategies. They point out that the fitness of the convention system has been a matter of some dispute historically. They also suggest some reforms. However, the authors' main finding is that the contributions of the convention system to our form of government have proven indispensable.

Davis, James W. *National Conventions in an Age of Party Reform.* Westport, CT: Greenwood, 1983.

The author evaluates the effectiveness and viability of national party conventions during an age in which technology, populism, entertainment, and party reform have transformed the nature and purpose of the nominating conventions. Davis evaluates previously used and suggested nominating procedures throughout American political history and concludes that national partisan conventions are the superior form to date.

Eaton, Herbert. *Presidential Timber: A History of Nominating Conventions, 1868–1960.* New York: Free Press, 1964.

The author offers an account of how and why thirty-two men have, between 1868 and 1960, received their parties' presidential nominations. He focuses on specific events leading up to nomination in the national convention. Eaton analyzes how issues and political events affect the nominations. He devotes each chapter to the two (or in the case of 1912, three) major parties' conventions for a given presidential election year. Eaton uses party documents, correspondence, and anecdotal evidence to illustrate the mechanisms for choosing the nominees.

Mailer, Norman. *Some Honorable Men: Political Conventions, 1960–1972.* New York: Little, Brown, 1976.

This book is a collection of essays written about the political conventions of 1960, 1964, 1968, and 1972. Mailer examines the mood of the events rather than simply the facts of each story. Each essay was written around the time of that particular convention and so provides a short-term rather than long-term look back. In the preface the author suggests that, in the light provided by distance, one notices the events not noted as much as the events noted, especially given the book's post-Watergate publication date.

Martin, Ralph G. *Ballots and Bandwagons.* Chicago: Rand McNally, 1964.

The author discusses the politics of national conventions. He examines the events behind the ballots. In particular, Martin focuses on the behind-the-scenes wheeling and dealing, the bandwagoning, and intraparty campaigning that goes on at conventions. He analyzes five conventions: the Republican National Conventions of 1900, 1912, and 1920 and the Democratic National Conventions of 1932 and 1956.

Moos, Malcolm, and Stephen Hess. *Hats in the Ring.* New York: Random House, 1960.

The authors offer an account of political conventions from 1832 to 1960. They examine the backstage manipulations in the near-mythical smoke-filled rooms, the intraparty campaigning and deal making necessary to put forth a candidate, and the onstage shows of unity necessary at the end of each convention to propel the party into the general election campaign. They examine different paths to a party nomination, the national committee, delegates, convention committees, the party platforms, running mates, and the nomination process. An appendix lists all major-party presidential candidates from 1856 to 1956.

Parris, Judith H. *The Convention Problem: Issues in Reform of Presidential Nominating Procedure.* Washington, DC: Brookings Institution, 1972.

The author examines the political implications of convention rules and reform proposals issued after the 1968 Democratic National Convention. She discusses the purposes of convention reforms, proposed convention reforms, the apportionment and selection of convention delegates, the organization of convention debate, and party platform drafting. Parris examines the role of the media in the convention process, as television is the primary source of information about conventions. The author recommends fairness in media coverage.

Schier, Steven E. *The Rules and the Game: Democratic National Convention Delegate Selection in Iowa and Wisconsin.* Washington, DC: University Press of America, 1980.

The author demonstrates the significant effect of broad reforms of national party delegate selection on both the conduct and outcomes of delegate selection in post-1968 Democratic nomination races in Iowa and Wisconsin. Schier uses comparative case studies to examine relationships within each state over time, assessing demographic participation, candidate competition variables, and delegate selection outcomes. Schier assembles data in chapter-long descriptive case studies and draws conclusions from each case. Survey data were rarely available, but the author's use of county aggregates augments the descriptive purposes of the case studies.

Sullivan, Denis G., Jeffrey L. Pressman, and F. Christopher Arterton. *Explorations in Convention Decision-Making: The Democratic Party in the 1970s.* San Francisco: Freeman, 1974.

The authors offer research conducted at the 1972 Democratic National Convention and the 1974 Democratic Charter Conference. Drawing on firsthand observations and interviews with delegates, they have developed models of intraparty conflicts and how they are resolved, convention decision making, and the process of legitimation. The authors relate their findings to current concerns about party reform and to the more general problem of the survival of political parties in a changing environment.

Sullivan, Denis G., Jeffrey L. Pressman, Benjamin I. Page, and John J. Lyons. *The Politics of Representation: The Democratic Convention 1972.* New York: St. Martin's, 1974.

The authors examine some of the central problems that came to the fore at the 1972 Democratic convention in Miami. The main questions driving this examination are: Who is entitled to participate in the nomination process, and how do shifting patterns of participation affect the representation of interests both within and without the party? The research is based on firsthand observations of caucuses, state delegation meetings, and convention floor proceedings, and structured interviews in Miami with a random sample of 234 delegates, and the results of a preconvention CBS poll of all delegates. The effects of the McGovern-Fraser Reform Commission rule changes on patterns of representation at the convention are examined in depth. The relative success of the new modes of convention participation also is examined, as are issue voting in the making of a platform and the significance of the "new political style"—the style of the purist as opposed to the traditional politician.

Tillett, Paul, ed. *Inside Politics: The National Conventions, 1960.* Dobbs Ferry, NY: Oceana, 1962.

This edited volume examines the 1960 national party conventions and interprets the significance of each party's decisions and nominations. Each chapter is written by a political scientist who spent time during the convention as a member of a particular committee or delegation. The first part of the book summarizes the Democratic and Republican preconvention campaigns and developments at the conventions. The second part shows how the front-running candidates dominated both conventions. The third part develops the conflicts between national platform requirements for the presidential nominees and the pressures from party wings, sections, or states for planks more suited to the political needs of their more limited constituencies. The fourth part discusses the behavior of individual delegates and the relationships between state delegation leaders and the delegates. The final part examines state delegation organization and communication.

4

Campaigns

General

Agranoff, Robert, comp. *The New Style in Election Campaigns.* 2d ed. Boston: Holbrook Press, 1976.

    This compilation of essays and articles focuses on the shift the author perceives from a party-based political campaigning style to one based on individual candidates. Agranoff maintains that electors are fundamentally questioning the role and function of political parties. The author's introduction precedes a series of topical sections on professional campaign management, information systems, campaign media (focusing upon television), and the reforms and ethical considerations that arise from this new era of politics.

Anderson, Walt. *Campaigns: Cases in Political Conflict.* Pacific Palisades, CA: Goodyear, 1970.

    The author examines fourteen electoral campaigns in terms of the candidates, the strategies used during the campaigns, and the particular events that shaped the outcomes of these elections. Themes highlighted throughout the book include the role of African Americans in electoral politics, the presidential primaries, radicalism and reactionaryism, progressivism and reform, the agrarian revolt, political trends of the 1960s, and the mass media. Anderson also has constructed the book to account for geographical differences in campaigns, issues, and strategies.

Bowler, Shaun, and David M. Farrell, eds. *Electoral Strategies and Political Marketing.* New York: St. Martin's, 1992.

    This volume presents a comparative study of contemporary election campaigning in nine countries: Austria, Britain, Denmark, Finland, France, Germany, the

Netherlands, New Zealand, and the United States. Each chapter begins with an outline of the particular national context in which the election occurred. The chapters examine party control of elections, campaign themes, and images. The chapter on the United States examines the 1980 congressional campaign and focuses on the candidate-centered nature of American campaigns.

Butler, David, and Austin Ranney, eds. *Electioneering: A Comparative Study of Continuity and Change.* New York: Oxford University Press, 1992.

This work is a comparative study of electioneering in the United States, Latin America, the United Kingdom, Australia, New Zealand, India, France, Germany, Italy, Scandinavia, and Japan. Each chapter describes how electioneering has changed in these geographical areas over the last few generations. The book examines the extent of "Americanization" of politics and elections in other countries and explores how new techniques of American electioneering have interacted with different political cultures.

Congressional Quarterly. *Congressional Quarterly's Guide to the 1976 Elections.* Washington, DC: Congressional Quarterly, 1977.

This book provides comprehensive and in-depth information about the 1976 elections. The main divisions of the book focus on the nominating conventions, congressional and gubernatorial elections, campaign financing, electoral college votes, and popular primary and general election returns for the presidency. Appendixes present comprehensive information on voting returns for 1976 and more general information on presidential elections from 1860 to 1976.

——. *The People Speak: American Elections in Focus.* Washington, DC: Congressional Quarterly, 1990.

This volume examines in detail the elections from 1985 through 1988, including the 1988 presidential election. The first section deals with political parties in the 1988 contests, examining delegate selection, the primaries, national conventions, convention texts, key convention ballots, and the party nominees. The second section focuses on the presidential election. Official results for the 1984 and 1988 elections follow a history and chronology of presidential elections. A third section examines congressional and gubernatorial elections of 1986 and 1988 and off-year and special elections from 1985 to 1989. The section begins with a history of politics and issues from 1945 to 1989, followed by descriptions and results of the regular and special elections. A final section includes primary returns from the 1986 to the 1988 Senate and gubernatorial races.

Davies, Philip J. *US Elections Today.* 2d ed. New York: Manchester University Press, 1999.

The author examines congressional and presidential elections as a way of understanding the constitutional and historical principles of American government. Davies discusses political campaigns occurring in the last 200 years. He covers the use of technology in campaigns, political parties, electoral regulations, and campaign finance. Tables present information about the main presidential candidates from 1932 to 1996, election results from 1980 to 1998, and electoral votes by state.

Dinkin, Robert J. *Campaigning in America: A History of Election Practices.* Westport, CT: Greenwood, 1989.

The author offers a comprehensive historical examination of campaign activities. The introductory chapters account for watershed events in the history of electioneering, including the rise and fall of political parties. The later chapters attempt to track shifts in campaign styles during the twentieth century. While not concerned with detailed accounts of each campaign, the author attempts to trace the evolution of campaigning techniques over time. Dinkin concludes that while electioneering may not directly affect outcomes, it does illuminate patterns of political culture and behavior.

Felknor, Bruce L. *Dirty Politics.* New York: W. W. Norton, 1966.

The author discusses dirty campaigning and political chicanery in America. He begins with the first election in 1789, a time when politics was the province of an elite and news traveled slowly. He closes with the 1960s, a time when every citizen could vote and news had begun to travel quickly. Felknor focuses on the use of dirty campaign tactics by and against the president, Congress, political organizations, unions, and political parties. He examines intrigue, espionage, deception, the buying or stealing of votes, the manipulation of candidate records, and the use of guilt by association and whipping-boy tactics.

————. *Political Mischief: Smear, Sabotage, and Reform in U.S. Elections.* Westport, CT: Praeger, 1992.

The author examines two forms of political mischief in elections. The first form of mischief is the attempt to subvert rational discourse by deception or by hiding or altering information needed by voters to make choices. The second form of mischief is the attempt to deny voters access to the electoral process, either by discouraging or preventing voting or making an accurate count difficult.

Friedenberg, Robert V. *Communication Consultants in Political Campaigns: Ballot Box Warriors.* New York: Praeger, 1997.

The author provides an overview of political consulting in America. He examines the role of polling consultants, speech and debate consultants, newspaper and radio consultants, and television consultants. Friedenberg concludes with a discussion of the future of political consulting.

Hershey, Marjorie R. *The Making of Campaign Strategy.* Lexington, MA: D.C. Heath, 1974.

The author shows how high-ranking campaign operatives formulate campaign strategies. She finds that the more tolerant the campaigner is the more open will be the campaign style. Also, candidates differ from managers in nearly every area of decision making. The chances of winning also affect attitudes and behavior. Hershey also finds that most campaigners believe that winning the election is more important than educating the voters. Few candidates believe in the importance of party identification as a motivator. Managers are less personally involved in the campaign and its outcome than candidates, and incumbents put forth less campaign effort than challengers. Candidates have more face-to-face contact with voters than do campaign managers. Most campaigners disapproved of name-calling and other forms of unethical campaigning.

Johnson-Cartee, Karen S., and Gary A. Copeland. *Inside Political Campaigns: Theory and Practice.* Westport, CT: Praeger, 1997.

The authors present the theories that political communications specialists use to make strategic and tactical decisions in political campaigns. This provides an understanding of what motivates political consultants to choose a particular strategy by explaining how various strategies work with the voting public. While the book is research-driven, its academic findings are enhanced by the authors' personal political consulting experiences.

King, Anthony S. *Running Scared: Why America's Politicians Campaign Too Much and Govern Too Little.* New York: Free Press, 1997.

The author examines why elected politicians are obsessed with their electoral futures and why these preoccupations have deleterious consequences for the political system. King argues that American politicians devote more of their time to electioneering than do politicians in other countries and contends that this affects their conduct in office, as they are more concerned about the electoral considerations of policies.

Luntz, Frank I. *Candidates, Consultants, and Campaigns: The Style and Substance of American Electioneering.* New York: Basil Blackwell, 1988.

The author examines political consultants' influence on and relationships with candidates and their parties. Luntz uses in-depth personal interviews and questionnaires to gather relevant information on thirty-seven campaign practitioners. Topics covered include candidate marketing, mass mailings, political action committees, and modern technology. The author concludes by assessing how these political trends affect the democratic electoral process. Appendixes provide the results of the consultant questionnaire and a list of those interviewed.

Menefee-Libey, David. *The Triumph of Campaign-Centered Politics.* New York: Chatham House, 2000.

The author discusses the transformation of American national campaigns and electoral politics and how the political parties have responded. He discusses the role of national party organizations in an environment shaped by new party rules, ballot access, political action committees, and campaign professionals. Menefee-Libey provides a new perspective on critical elections and party decline in recent elections.

Napolitan, Joseph. *The Election Game and How to Win It.* Garden City, NY: Doubleday, 1972.

The author covers political communications techniques and how political consultants use them. Napolitan discusses electronic campaigning, polls, and the role of political consultants. He also discusses much of the new politics by using examples from his campaign experiences in the 1968 presidential election, the 1966 Pennsylvania gubernatorial primary, and the 1970 Alaska Senate election.

Nelson, Michael, ed. *The Elections of 1988.* Washington, DC: CQ Press, 1988.

The essays in this volume focus on the 1988 election and its impact on future politics. Along the way the authors examine the history of presidential politics from 1960 to 1988; the nominating process; the election; the press; issues and themes of the campaign; Congress; the presidency; and constitutional aspects of the election. Several essays address split-level realignment—Republican dominance of the presidency and Democratic dominance of Congress. Other essays address whether the 1988 election fulfilled even minimally the requirements of democratic government.

———, ed. *The Elections of 1992.* Washington, DC: CQ Press, 1993.

The editor has collected a set of essays that analyze the 1992 presidential and congressional elections as unique events and as events within an historical context. The essays cover a broad array of issues, including the historical and political settings of the elections, the procedures used to nominate the candidates, the general campaigns and elections, the role of the media in the elections, the campaigns' issues, and the implications of the presidential and congressional outcomes. The last chapter summarizes and synthesizes the articles.

———, ed. *The Elections of 1996.* Washington, DC: CQ Press, 1996.

The essays in this edited volume analyze the 1996 presidential and congressional elections as unique events and as events within an historical context. The essays cover a broad array of issues, including the perils of a second-term presidency, the nominations of the candidates, the general election campaigns and results, the role of the media in the elections, the campaigns' issues and themes, and the implications of the presidential and congressional outcomes.

Nimmo, Dan. *The Political Persuaders: The Technique of Modern Election Campaigns.* Englewood Cliffs, NJ: Transaction Publishers, 1999.

The author attempts to summarize and evaluate the literature on political campaigns and their effects on voters. Nimmo also describes and assesses how advanced technological methods of campaigning will affect future elections. The author uses a variety of sources to examine the modern campaign process, including case studies from local, state, and national levels; state and national surveys of public opinion that focus on the impact of the media; and personal interviews with party and campaign activists. In the new introduction Nimmo discusses political management and consulting in the past thirty years.

Pomper, Gerald M., et al. *The Election of 1976: Reports and Interpretations.* Chatham, NJ: Chatham House, 1976.

The essays in this edited volume evaluate and assess the elections of 1976. The topics include the nominating process, the presidential campaign, the presidential election, congressional elections, state and local elections, the outlook for the Carter administration, and an interpretation of the meaning of the elections of 1976. The book concludes with a copy of Jimmy Carter's inaugural address.

————. *The Election of 1980: Reports and Interpretations.* Chatham, NJ: Chatham House, 1981.

The essays in this edited volume evaluate and assess the presidential and congressional elections of 1980. The topics include the nominating process, the presidential campaign, the presidential election, public opinion, congressional elections, and an interpretation of the outcome of the elections. One essay also evaluates the implications of the Ronald Reagan victory.

————. *The Election of 1984: Reports and Interpretations.* Chatham, NJ: Chatham House, 1985.

This edited volume presents an in-depth analysis of the 1984 presidential and congressional elections. It covers the nomination process, campaign issues, public opinion, the implications of Ronald Reagan's second term, and Reagan's inaugural address. The authors maintain that a subtextual reading of the sound bites, speeches, and debates reveals a competition not only for seats of political power but also for America's soul.

————. *The Election of 1996: Reports and Interpretations.* Chatham, NJ: Chatham House, 1996.

The essays in this edited volume evaluate and assess the presidential and congressional elections of 1996. The topics include presidential nominations, candidate strategies, the media campaign, public opinion, financing the election, the presidential election, congressional elections, and an interpretation of the outcome of the elections. An introductory chapter examines the confluence of luck, skill, and adaptability in the success of Bill Clinton's campaign. Appendixes provide the text of Clinton's second inaugural address and a list of members of the second Clinton administration.

Ranney, Austin, ed. *The American Elections of 1980.* Washington, DC: American Enterprise Institute for Public Policy Research, 1981.

The authors in this edited volume analyze the 1980 congressional and presidential elections. Topics covered include primary campaigns, issues, public opinion, conventions, party platforms, media, general election campaigns, and election results. Some of the findings include the heavy party influence in Ronald Reagan's campaign, the importance of special interests and congressional staff in writing party platforms, the public's shifting opinion of Jimmy Carter's ideology, and seniority rather than liberalism as an explanation of the results in the Senate elections.

————, ed. *The American Elections of 1984.* Washington, DC: American Enterprise Institute for Public Policy Research, 1985.

The authors in this edited volume analyze the 1984 presidential and congressional elections. Topics covered include campaigns, conventions, party platforms, media, and election results. The authors of the articles also examine the significance of Ronald Reagan's campaign for a second term and the possibility that the United States is experiencing a fundamental shift in partisan politics similar to the realignments of the mid-1800s and early 1900s.

Sabato, Larry J. *The Rise of Political Consultants.* Cambridge, MA: Ballinger, 1982.

The author examines the role of the political consultant in modern campaigns. He looks at both the consultants' profession and their much-acclaimed techniques. Sabato dissects the new campaign technology and consultants' attitudes about it for the three main consulting specialties: political polling, paid media, and direct mail. Sabato examines the love-hate relationship between consultants and political parties, and the effects of recent campaign finance laws and the growth of political action committees on the consultants and the parties. He also addresses questions of ethics and democracy. He concludes by analyzing the ills apparent in the new age of political consultants and prescribes remedies for some of the most severe ailments. Appendixes list and give brief profiles of some major political consultants.

Salmore, Stephen A., and Barbara G. Salmore. *Candidates, Parties, and Campaigns: Electoral Politics in America.* 2d ed. Washington, DC: CQ Press, 1989.

The authors examine the declining role of parties in political campaigns and the simultaneous rise of candidate-centered strategies. They attempt to address how and why these changes have occurred and offer a list of characteristics of successful and unsuccessful campaigns for political office. The authors provide a political history of candidates and campaigns, address the current state of political campaigning in terms of its candidate-centered and media-driven forms, and discuss emerging strategies and the prospects for a return to campaigns in which the party is emphasized.

Sandoz, Ellis, and Cecil V. Crabb Jr., eds. *A Tide of Discontent: The 1980 Elections and Their Meaning.* Washington, DC: CQ Press, 1981.

This edited volume assesses the events, outcomes, and implications of the 1980 presidential and congressional elections. In their attempt to evaluate the 1980 elections as being either a watershed or an accident, the editors have assembled a series of essays that concern themselves with a variety of topics. The topics include an historical overview of elections that situate the 1980 election; the presidential race; the increased Republican membership in the House; the Republican takeover of the Senate; the role of interest groups, media, and parties in the elections; and the economic and foreign issues that dominated the electoral agenda.

Scher, Richard K. *The Modern Political Campaign: Mudslinging, Bombast, and the Vitality of American Politics.* Armonk, NY: M. E. Sharpe, 1997.

The author puts the modern political campaign into its political context. He discusses how old-style and modern campaigns differ. Scher discusses the role of money, the media, and issues in modern campaigns.

Selnow, Gary W. *High-Tech Campaigns: Computer Technology in Political Communication.* Westport, CT: Praeger, 1994.

The author examines the influence of technological development on the process of political campaigning. In part one he discusses the technologies available and how they are employed through public opinion polls. Databases are the primary focus. In part two he discusses the effects of campaign technology on the voter, the press, and the system of governance.

Thurber, James A., and Candice J. Nelson, eds. *Campaigns and Elections American Style.* Boulder, CO: Westview Press, 1995.

This edited volume contains eighteen articles on campaigns and elections. The central thesis of the book is that election campaigns influence voter behavior. The chapters examine campaign strategy, campaign financing and spending, media advertising, the press, polling, and campaign ethics.

Trent, Judith S., and Robert V. Friedenberg. *Political Campaign Communication: Principles and Practices.* 3d ed. Westport, CT: Praeger, 1995.

The authors view political campaigns as a communicative process and examine how the principles of language and communication are essential to electoral campaigns. They examine the theoretical implications of the campaign as communication and examine the principles of communication in terms of function, style, distribution, and televised advertising. They delineate and evaluate the practical applications of campaign communications, including public speaking, ceremonial and institutionalized speech, debates, interpersonal forms, and advertising.

Advertising

Ansolabehere, Stephen, and Shanto Iyengar. *Going Negative: How Political Ads Shrink and Polarize the Electorate.* New York: Free Press, 1995.

The authors discuss the use of attack advertisements in political campaigning. They discuss six campaigns, including the 1992 Senate primary and general elections and the presidential campaign in California. Information includes data the authors gathered in more than 3,500 interviews. They examine the effects of advertising on voter choice and citizen's involvement in campaigns. Ansolabehere and Iyengar propose electoral reforms aimed at curtailing negative advertising.

Biocca, Frank, ed. *Television and Political Advertising. Vol. 1, Psychological Processes; Vol. 2, Signs, Codes, and Images.* Hillsdale, NJ: L. Erlbaum Associates, 1991.

These edited volumes attempt to derive a better understanding of how televised political advertisements organize and disseminate political information and how that information is evaluated and filtered. Volume 1 addresses the cognitive processes and psychological effects political ads have on the viewer, such as the processing of information, the effects of positive and negative campaign advertising, and the contextualization of information by viewers. Volume 2 examines in depth the form and content of televised political advertisements, such as language, image, signs, codes, rhetoric, and symbolic speech.

Diamond, Edwin, and Stephen Bates. *The Spot: The Rise of Political Advertising on Television.* Cambridge, MA: MIT Press, 1984.

The authors argue that the political television advertisement depends so heavily on high technology and big dollars that it may be turning campaigns and elections into a spectator sport that voters watch but in which they do not participate. Diamond and Bates show how media strategy fits within the wider campaign, using a case study from the 1984 primary campaign of John Glenn and discussing the fall campaigns of 1984 and 1988. They discuss television's role in presidential elections from 1952 to 1988. They analyze the major persuasive techniques and visual styles of the political television advertisement, based on examples found in the News Study Group Archive at New York University. Diamond and Bates bring together the political narrative and the media techniques. They explain how political television advertisements work, assess the effects of television campaigns, and evaluate some proposals for reform.

Jamieson, Kathleen H. *Dirty Politics: Deception, Distraction, and Democracy.* New York: Oxford University Press, 1992.

The author examines how traditional genres of campaign discourse are being reduced to visually evocative ads, with the boundaries between news and ads blurring in the process. She first examines the uses of attack in political campaigning, past and present. She then focuses on the relationship between news and ads and addresses news coverage in general. Jamieson discusses the norms of discourse that should govern not just campaign ads and news but also speeches, debates, interviews, and press conferences. The author argues the case for fair, accurate, contextual, comparative, engaged campaign discourse by candidates ready to take responsibility for the arguments they make and to either defend or repudiate claims made by others on their behalf. She argues for news coverage that engages the candidates on matters of public concern, while holding them accountable for their pasts and their promises.

————. *Packaging the Presidency: A History and Criticism of Presidential Campaign Advertising.* 3d ed. New York: Oxford University Press, 1996.

The author offers an interpretation of presidential campaign advertisements in various formats, including print, radio, and television. She compares advertising rhetoric for consistency, accuracy, and effectiveness within and between campaigns. Jamieson also examines how changing campaign financing laws and other campaign regulations affect presidential campaigns. By providing an inclusive historical analysis of presidential elections between 1952 and 1992, the author illuminates how political advertising has evolved.

Johnson-Cartee, Karen S., and Gary A. Copeland. *Manipulation of the American Voter: Political Campaign Commercials.* Westport, CT: Praeger, 1997.

The authors examine the theoretical and practical reasons for successful political advertising. They analyze political commercials and present the motives behind advertising strategies and tactics used in politics. Johnson-Cartee and Copeland show how political campaign commercials manipulate voters.

————. *Negative Political Advertising: Coming of Age.* Hillsdale, NJ: L. Erlbaum Associates, 1991.

Operating from the premise that politics is based on a system of dichotomous symbols, the authors examine the negative side of that division as manifest in political advertisements to explain the phenomenon of negative campaigning. They use and critique an array of disciplinary approaches to the issue, formulate a framework by which one can analyze negative political advertising, and consider the ethical and legal ramifications of this form of advertisement. The authors conclude with an overall assessment of negative political advertising and its societal impact.

Kaid, Lynda L., Dan Nimmo, and Keith R. Sanders, eds. *New Perspectives on Political Advertising.* Carbondale: Southern Illinois University Press, 1986.

This edited volume focuses on the evolution and importance of political advertising as a form of political communication. The articles in this collected work examine the history, forms, styles, settings, uses, and effects of political advertising. The authors' central concerns are the effects of political advertising on public opinion and what, if anything, should be done to restrict the content of political advertising. The volume concludes with comparative studies of political advertising in Britain and Australia.

Kamber, Victor. *Poison Politics: Are Negative Campaigns Destroying Democracy?* New York: Insight Books, 1997.

Written by a campaign consultant, this book aims to provide an analysis about what is fair and foul in campaign debate and strategy. The author focuses on the ethics of negative campaign strategy and examines the role of political consultants in negative campaigning.

Kern, Montague. *30-Second Politics: Political Advertising in the Eighties.* New York: Praeger, 1989.

The author maintains that since 1972 political advertising has developed into a vehicle for negative campaigning and the dissemination of information other than issue-related facts. In addition, the purpose of the political ad has changed to provide entertainment, present a message, and elicit reactions of various sorts. The author traces the use, content, and form of political advertising since 1972 and focuses primarily on the political ads used during the 1984 congressional and presidential campaigns.

Levine, Myron A. *Presidential Campaigns and Elections: Issues and Images in the Media Age.* 2d ed. Itasca, IL: F. E. Peacock, 1995.

The author offers an in-depth look at contemporary presidential elections, with a focus on political advertising, inasmuch as the advertising contains the messages that are presented to the voter. He examines the stages of the presidential selection process, campaign finance reform, issue voting, retrospective voting, and the role of the media. Levine analyzes elections from 1960 to 1992 as case studies. He reviews contemporary election trends through 1992, including the evidence on voter realignment and dealignment. He concludes with a discussion on which strategies Republicans and Democrats should follow in their pursuit of the White House.

Nesbit, Dorothy D. *Videostyle in Senate Campaigns.* Knoxville: University of Tennessee Press, 1988.

The author focuses on how candidates and their media consultants think voters arrive at their decisions. She studies the use of television advertising in three 1982 Senate races, examines the process by which candidates' self-presentation strategies are developed, and discusses their implications for the democratic system. Nesbit contrasts her concept of *videostyle* (in other words, the candidate's composite television image) to that of Richard Fenno's *home style*. She also analyzes how a given videostyle may vary with the circumstances or stages of a particular campaign.

Patterson, Thomas E., and Robert D. McClure. *The Unseeing Eye: The Myth of Television Power in National Politics.* New York: Putnam, 1976.

The authors examine television's role in building a candidate's public image, educating the electorate about critical issues and events, and influencing how people vote. They find that political commercials have almost no power to overcome a voter's preexisting view of a candidate and his or her party. However, Patterson and McClure find that while television ads are a significant source of issue information for voters, television campaign news coverage is no more influential than newspaper coverage in affecting the voters' views of the candidates. In a survey of every evening news program on the three major networks during the 1972 general election, the authors find little information about the candidates' issue positions or qualifications but a great deal of information about superficial aspects of the presidential election.

Spero, Robert. *The Duping of the American Voter: Dishonesty and Deception in Presidential TV Advertising.* New York: Lippincott, 1980.

The author investigates the way presidents have been elected since the appearance of the political television commercial. He shows how presidential candidates, with the aid of political advertising, lay down smokescreens to mask their true intentions on assuming office. Spero discusses the deception and distortions employed in the dueling campaign ads of the 1976 contest between Gerald Ford and Jimmy Carter. He discusses the origins of the political ad in the 1952 Dwight D. Eisenhower campaign and follows the historical development of political advertising on television through the 1960, 1964, 1968, 1972, and 1976 campaigns. The author concludes with a discussion of whether televised political advertisements should be banned, and how the voter can get around the information gaps in television ads.

West, Darrell M. *Air Wars: Television Advertising in Election Campaigns, 1952–1996*. 2d ed. Washington, DC: CQ Books, 1997.

The author evaluates the evolution of political advertising in electoral campaigns from 1952 to 1996. Issues addressed include the development of political advertisements; the messages, media, and controversy of election ads; the impact of televised political advertising on the electorate in terms of political learning, agenda-setting, and evaluative standards; and the implications of advertising for democratic politics. In this second edition, West also incorporates changes in technology, the use of the Internet, free televised advertising, and the increased emphasis on visual imagery in more recent political ads.

Presidential

Abels, Jules. *The Degeneration of Our Presidential Elections: A History and Analysis of an American Institution in Trouble*. New York: Macmillan, 1968.

The author examines how elections have become sparring matches between candidates rather than substance-filled debates over issues. He examines the rhetoric, strategies, candidates, and issues of the campaigns of 1948, 1952, 1956, 1960, and 1964. Abels traces a history of earlier campaigns from 1789 through World War II to show the gradual decline of debate, issue-laden polices, and even civility in electoral politics. The author discusses the repercussions that this erosion might have for the future of American politics.

Adams, William C., ed. *Television Coverage of the 1980 Campaign*. Norwood, NJ: Ablex, 1982.

The studies in this edited volume examine how the television networks presented the 1980 presidential campaign. In the first chapter the editor surveys some of the central issues on campaign coverage and reviews the 1980 change in popular media coverage. The next eight chapters consider in detail how the networks treated the 1980 campaign. A comparative study of CBS and UPI coverage reveals stark differences in the networks' approaches. The authors examine coverage of the primaries, the party conventions, the debates, and election night. They analyze the treatment of energy issues and the use of public opinion polls. They discuss the implications of a typical campaign story. The editor's concluding chapter proposes seven factors—themes, agenda, treatment, endorsements, advertisements, persona, and entertainment—with which to estimate the impact of television content.

Aldrich, John H. *Before the Convention: Strategies and Choices in Presidential Nomination Campaigns.* Chicago: University of Chicago Press, 1980.

The author uses the 1976 presidential campaign to study the process of campaigning for a party's presidential nomination. His work rests on three premises: institutions shape behavior, candidates are rational actors, and nomination campaigns are dynamic political events. Aldrich examines candidate motivations; the rules, regulations, and procedures of the nominating process; and the individual citizen as a political actor. He also maintains that preconvention campaigns are time-related phenomena and that politicians respond rationally to events by selecting regions in which to campaign and shifting their policy platforms.

Barber, James D., ed. *Race for the Presidency: The Media and the Nominating Process.* Englewood Cliffs, NJ: Prentice-Hall, 1978.

This edited volume examines the interplay among candidates, their backers, the press, and television that spells victory or defeat for every presidential hopeful. The book examines Jimmy Carter's victory over incumbent Gerald Ford. The authors focus on strategies used by campaign managers to shape press coverage, the role of New Hampshire in the primary season and nomination process, the perceptual environment in which the candidates compete, and how the campaign weeds out political contenders. The authors examine how the media plays a major role in whittling down the number of possible candidates, and how it is an important factor in shaping the public choice.

Barker, Lucius J., and Ronald W. Walters, eds. *Jesse Jackson's 1984 Presidential Campaign: Challenge and Change in American Politics.* Urbana: University of Illinois Press, 1989.

This edited volume offers an in-depth examination and assessment of the presidential campaign mounted by Jesse Jackson under the auspices of the Rainbow Coalition in 1984. The book is divided chronologically into five parts that evaluate the context in which Jackson and the coalition emerged and were able to mobilize support, the response of white America given the general political culture of the United States, the typical Jackson supporter, the effects of Jackson's campaign and platform on the Democratic National Convention, and the effect of Jackson's candidacy on a national and local level.

Barrus, Roger M., and John H. Eastby, eds. *America through the Looking Glass: A Constitutionalist Critique of the 1992 Election.* Lanham, MD: Rowman and Littlefield, 1994.

The editors of this volume maintain that the use of new campaign methods made the 1992 presidential election a watershed event in American politics. The book's contributors praise the town-meeting format, televised infomercials, and other nontraditional modes of campaigning for their effectiveness and utility. The articles evaluate the use of these methods, their ramifications for the electorate's expectations, and the implications they present for future presidential elections. The book is primarily concerned with three larger themes of the 1992 presidential campaign: campaign methods, institutions of government, and political issues.

Blumenthal, Sidney. *The Permanent Campaign.* Rev. ed. New York: Simon and Schuster, 1982.

The author focuses on the rising influence of political consultants in national politics and elections since the age of television. Demonstrating that consultants constantly reinvent candidates' images, marketing the politicians as if they were commodities through television commercials and mass mailings, the author makes the case that the line between politics and government has been blurred. The book is divided into case studies of major political consultants for Lyndon Johnson, Ted Kennedy, Jimmy Carter, Ronald Reagan, and others.

Boller, Paul F., Jr. *Presidential Campaigns.* Rev. ed. New York: Oxford University Press, 1996.

The author offers the history of presidential elections from George Washington to Bill Clinton. Brief essays describe every presidential election from 1789 to 1992.

Brams, Steven J. *The Presidential Election Game.* New Haven: Yale University Press, 1978.

The author uses modern decision theory and game theory to analyze presidential campaigns and elections. Brams develops models to analyze the three major phases of the presidential election game: state primaries, national party conventions, and the general election. He develops three models around themes of coalition politics. Brams then uses Richard Nixon's 1974 confrontation with the Supreme Court as a case study of how an election mandate can be upset. Finally, the author proposes the adoption of approval voting based on these mathematical models.

Broder, David S., Lou Cannon, Haynes Johnson, Martin Schram, and Richard Harwood. *The Pursuit of the Presidency, 1980.* New York: Berkley Books, 1980.

The authors, journalists for the *Washington Post,* examine the 1980 presidential election race. They report on the context of the election, including the general feelings among the electorate, the role of industry, and the place the media held in the election. They examine the primaries, with particular emphasis on Democratic contenders Jimmy Carter and Edward Kennedy. They also examine the role and actions of the parties during the campaign. They discuss each major-party candidate: Jimmy Carter, Ronald Reagan, and John Anderson. The authors chronicle the stretch run from Labor Day to election day 1980. The appendixes offer electoral vote counts and state-by-state popular vote totals for all presidential elections between 1960 and 1980, a demographic table, the partisan distribution of the House and Senate following the 1980 election, a transcript of the presidential debates, and candidate speeches.

Buchanan, Bruce. *Electing a President: The Markle Commission Research on Campaign '88.* Austin: University of Texas Press, 1991.

The author examines the intricate relationships among the electorate, the candidates, and the media to improve our understanding of what a presidential campaign entails. Using focus groups, content analysis, and public opinion polls, Buchanan discusses problems with the 1988 presidential campaign, the electorate's learning processes, and how the media's treatment of campaign events may have affected voters' preferences. He concludes with a set of three policy recommendations made by the Markle Commission: polling hours should be increased to twenty, public projections and announcements should be restrained until after polls close, and the voter registration process should be simplified.

Carlson, Jody. *George C. Wallace and the Politics of Powerlessness: The Wallace Campaigns for the Presidency, 1964–1976.* New Brunswick, NJ: Transaction Books, 1981.

The author explores the political appeal of George Wallace, a candidate for the presidency in 1964, 1968, and 1972. She employs content analysis of official documents, speeches, and other Wallace campaign materials and data analysis of demographic and attitudinal data on Wallace supporters to explore the nature of Wallace's politics. She supplements these with historical accounts to draw a picture of the presidential races in which Wallace played a major role. Carlson concludes that Wallace's politics were the politics of powerlessness.

Carney, Francis M., and H. F. Way Jr., eds. *Politics 1960.* New York: Wadsworth, 1960.

This edited volume presents the major economic, social, and international issues confronting the nation and the voters in the 1960 presidential election. A collection of writings of leading statesmen and political analysts, the book is divided into two major sections. The first section analyzes the political processes operating in a presidential election year. These articles focus on political parties, the electorate, pressure groups, the presidency, and the processes of persuasion. The second section deals with the major issues of the day. Those issues include budget and welfare legislation, labor and business and their relationship with politics and the public, civil rights, foreign policy in general, and the balance of terror specifically.

Ceaser, James W., and Andrew E. Busch. *Losing to Win: The 1996 Elections and American Politics.* New York: Rowman and Littlefield, 1996.

The authors offer an analysis of the unique characteristics and events of the 1996 election. They examine Bill Clinton's administrative record, the Republican nomination process and candidate selection, the Robert Dole campaign, the congressional elections, and the implications for American politics that stem from the outcome of the 1996 presidential race, focusing primarily on a new era of coalition partnership. An appendix lists the presidential vote by state.

————. *Upside Down and Inside Out: The 1992 Elections and American Politics.* Lanham, MD: Rowman and Littlefield, 1993.

The authors offer an analysis of the unique characteristics and events of the 1992 election. They examine the Republican and Democratic presidential nomination processes and candidate selections, the entry of independent candidate Ross Perot, the congressional elections, and the implications for American politics stemming from the outcome of the 1992 presidential race.

Chagall, David. *The New Kingmakers.* New York: Harcourt Brace Jovanovich, 1981.

The author examines campaign consultants as political kingmakers between the presidencies of John Kennedy and Ronald Reagan. He recounts the career of Joe Napolitan, the most important consultant and strategist behind the 1960 Kennedy campaign. Chagall examines critical political moments and the men and women who made them happen, including successfully run campaigns by Jimmy Carter in 1976 and Ronald Reagan in 1980, and near losses by Richard Nixon, and a loss by Edward Kennedy. He focuses specifically on campaign strategy and tactics by the consultants. He discusses Hal Evry, Gerald Rafshoon, and other key consultants, as well as the use of issues such as race, the economy, and ideology. The author illustrates the central role that campaign consultants have played in electoral politics from 1960 to 1980.

Colton, Elizabeth O. *The Jackson Phenomenon: The Man, the Power, the Message.* New York: Doubleday, 1989.

As press secretary for Jesse Jackson's 1988 bid for the Democratic nomination for president, the author provides an insightful and in-depth account of the evolution of the Jackson campaign. Items covered in this book include the organization of the Rainbow Coalition, the events and campaigns in more than eleven caucuses and primaries, preconvention negotiations, and the 1988 Democratic National Convention.

Congressional Quarterly. *Selecting the President: From 1789 to 1996.* Washington, DC: Congressional Quarterly, 1997.

This basic work examines all the major aspects of the presidential selection process, including campaign strategy fundraising, primaries and caucuses, national party conventions, the general election, and the electoral college. The work contains detailed historical summaries of each presidential election from George Washington to Bill Clinton's second election in 1996.

Cravit, Lawrence. *The Forty-Year Parallel in Presidential Elections.* New York: Vantage Press, 1980.

The author examines historical parallels in presidential elections from the first, in 1789, to the 1976 election. Working from an earlier finding that history is most likely to repeat itself after a period of forty years, Cravit outlines the numerous parallels between these elections. During each forty-year period, ten presidential elections take place. Each chapter divides the elections so that each can be compared with one that took place forty years earlier or forty years later.

Crotty, William J., and Jerome M. Mileur, eds. *America's Choice: The Election of 1996.* Guilford, CT: Duskin-McGraw Hill, 1997.

This edited volume includes chapters on the 1996 presidential election, campaigning, and campaign finance. The volume also covers topics such as media coverage, public opinion, women voters and the gender gap, African American voters, and ethnic voters.

Cummings, Milton C., Jr., ed. *The National Election of 1964.* Washington, DC: Brookings Institution, 1966.

This edited volume presents several interpretive and analytical essays that probe selected aspects of the 1964 election campaign. The book considers the dynamics and consequences of the national conventions, the presidential campaign, media performance, campaign finance, and House and Senate nominations and elections. It examines the strategic considerations in detail. The final chapter tries to interpret the presidential victory in the context of the election and the political environment. It examines long-term and short-term consequences.

Denton, Robert E., Jr., ed. *The 1992 Presidential Campaign: A Communication Perspective.* Westport, CT: Praeger, 1994.

This edited work includes ten chapters focusing on the 1992 election. They cover the campaign, nominating conventions, presidential debates, political advertising, the issues, voter rationality, town hall meetings, the role of C-SPAN, and the role of television news. All the essays discuss the relationship between politics and communication.

————, ed. *The 1996 Presidential Campaign: A Communication Perspective.* Westport, CT: Praeger, 1998.

This edited volume on the 1996 presidential campaign includes chapters on topics such as the use of television, videostyle and campaign advertising, use of rhetoric, editorial cartooning, the campaign online, and the rhetorical constraints of first ladies and vice presidents. All the articles showcase communication studies as a discipline.

Devlin, L. Patrick, ed. *Political Persuasion in Presidential Campaigns.* New Brunswick, NJ: Transaction Books, 1987.

This work focuses on how politicians run for the presidency and how the media cover a presidential campaign. All the articles focus primarily on the 1984 campaign. The eighteen chapters cover polling, campaign financing, press conferences, television and radio advertising, news coverage at all levels, political action committees and campaign strategies, and commercials.

Divine, Robert A. *Foreign Policy and U.S. Presidential Elections, 1940–1948.* New York: New Viewpoints, 1974.

The author examines the role that foreign policy has played in presidential elections from 1940 to 1948. He discusses how the issues of war and peace were used by the candidates in their quest for votes.

———. *Foreign Policy and U.S. Presidential Elections, 1952–1960.* New York: New Viewpoints, 1974.

The author examines the central role that foreign policy has played in presidential elections from 1952 to 1960. He discusses how the candidates used the issues of war and peace in their quest for votes.

Drew, Elizabeth. *American Journal: The Events of 1976.* New York: Random House, 1977.

Assigned by the *New York Times* to keep a journal of the events of the 1976 presidential campaign, the author recorded both factual accounts and her own impressions of the campaign. Drew traveled and talked with candidates and their staffs, pundits, and others close to the action of the campaign season. Beginning on January 2, 1976, and running through election day in November, the book places the campaigns in the context of the larger questions being confronted by the nation that year.

———. *Campaign Journal: The Political Events of 1983–1984.* New York: Macmillan, 1984.

The author, a staff writer for the *New Yorker*, presents a journal of the 1984 presidential campaign and its surrounding events. It is a contemporary account, with periodic entries, of what was happening and why. Combining on-the-scene reporting, interviews with the candidates, their advisers, and other insiders, and her own experiences, the author provides a picture of what was taking place as it happened. The account begins in 1983, with an overview of the previous term and the beginning of the campaigning and jockeying for position, and ends with the election returns in November 1984.

———. *Portrait of an Election: The 1980 Presidential Campaign.* New York: Simon and Schuster, 1981.

The author analyzes the candidates running for president in the 1980 election. The appendix contains strategy memoranda written during the campaign by pollsters Richard Wirthlin and Patrick Caddell.

Ewing, Cortex A. *Presidential Elections from Abraham Lincoln to Franklin D. Roosevelt.* Norman: University of Oklahoma Press, 1940.

This book is a history of election results, focusing on sectionalism, the role of minor parties, and the role of the electoral college. The volume provides an overview and analysis of the presidential elections from 1864 to 1928.

Faber, Harold, ed. *The Road to the White House: The Story of the 1964 Election by the Staff of the New York Times.* New York: McGraw-Hill, 1965.

This book offers an account of the 1964 presidential election by *New York Times* staff writers. The authors chronicle the Republican and Democratic primaries; Barry Goldwater's victory at the Republican convention; the selection of vice presidential candidates and how they affected the campaigns, strategies, and tactics on each side; and the general election campaign. They recount strategies and tactics used in the campaign; the rise and decline of the conservative movement in the Republican Party; the role of foreign affairs, race, and rights in shaping the campaign; and how the Johnson win affected the composition of the House and Senate and gubernatorial races.

Fenno, Richard F., Jr. *The Presidential Odyssey of John Glenn.* Washington, DC: CQ Press, 1990.

The author provides a detailed analytical narrative of a six-year period of John Glenn's political career as a senator campaigning for the office of president. Fenno intends to provide political scientists, journalists, and historians with a stronger sense of patterns that may exist or emerge for other, similarly grounded presidential candidates. The author also examines the interplay between personal character and public perception, the differences between nominating and electoral campaigns, the evolution of campaign strategies, the influence of the media, and campaign organization.

Fishel, Jeff. *Presidents and Promises: From Campaign Pledge to Presidential Performance.* Washington, DC: CQ Press, 1985.

The author examines the congruency between presidential campaign promises and a president's actual activity. Fishel focuses primarily on domestic issues and presidentially advanced legislation and executive orders from 1960 through Reagan's first term. Employing data obtained from interviews, content analysis of campaign speeches, public papers, platforms, and presidential libraries, the author constructs detailed case studies of the campaigns and presidencies during this time period.

Forest, John. *Warriors of the Political Arena: The Presidential Elections of 1984.* New York: Vantage Press, 1986.

The author provides a history and analysis of the 1984 presidential campaign. He details the antagonism between the two major constituencies of the Democratic Party and the long and bitter Democratic primary that brought the problem to a head. Forest also illustrates changes in major constituencies within the party, including the breakthroughs for women and the dissatisfaction and polarization of African Americans. He also details the national conservative trend, the strong resurgence of the Republican Party, and the dilemmas that these events presented to the Democrats.

Germond, Jack W. *Blue Smoke and Mirrors: How Reagan Won and Why Carter Lost the Election of 1980.* New York: Viking, 1981.

The author examines the 1980 presidential campaign. He shows how professional manipulation was less effective than in past elections and that mistrust in government and dramatic unforeseen events combined to give Ronald Reagan the victory over Jimmy Carter. Among the events and issues Germond covers are the role of the media, Ted Kennedy's challenge to Carter, the Republican primary and caucus battles, the role of professional campaign strategists, the national mood, the Anderson campaign, the hostage crisis in Iran, the debates, and the possibility of an October Surprise.

Germond, Jack W., and Jules Witcover. *Wake Us When It's Over: Presidential Politics of 1984.* New York: Macmillan, 1985.

The authors, both journalists, examine the 1984 presidential election. They briefly follow the careers of the two principals, Ronald Reagan and Walter Mondale, from their early beginnings to their participation in the contest for the presidency. They primarily chronicle the caucus and primary battles, the conventions, debates, campaign inside dealings, tactics and strategies, and political maneuvering that defined the 1984 election. Germond and Witcover examine the role of the campaign handlers, the media, campaign financing, and voter disenchantment with the system and the candidates.

Gibbons, Arnold. *Race, Politics and the White Media: The Jesse Jackson Campaigns.* Lanham, MD: University Press of America, 1993.

The author reviews Jesse Jackson's presidential campaigns in 1984 and 1988. His account of these campaigns reveals the class, race, and gender fault lines in American society. Gibbons also acknowledges the critical role of the national media. He focuses on Jackson's remarkable success in reaching a national constituency without major access to or support from the mass media, particularly television.

Goldman, Peter, and Tony Fuller. *The Quest for the Presidency 1984.* Toronto: Bantam Books, 1985.

The authors, two journalists, chronicle of the events of the 1984 presidential campaign, showing the process and the participants. They focus on President Ronald Reagan's campaign to retain his office and examine the contenders for the Democratic Party's nomination, focusing particularly on Walter Mondale, Gary Hart, and Jesse Jackson, and whether Edward Kennedy would run. Goldman and Fuller examine the primaries and convention dynamics. The authors chronicle the fall campaign, including strategies, tactics, candidate blunders, the debates, and the election's result. The appendix compiles campaign documents from both sides of the 1984 race. Some of these papers appear in their entirety, while others are excerpted.

Goldstein, Michael L. *Congressional Quarterly's Guide to the 1988 Elections.* Washington, DC: Congressional Quarterly, 1988.

The author provides a comprehensive and in-depth look at the 1988 elections. He presents a brief overview on the electoral process in historical context. Goldstein focuses on the changing political context, national party conventions, the campaign trail, and future controversies. He includes brief profiles of the 1988 presidential and vice presidential hopefuls.

Greenberg, Stanley B. *Middle Class Dreams: The Politics and Power of the New American Majority.* Summit, PA: Times Books/Random House, 1995.

The author examines the historic forces that surrounded Bill Clinton's rise to the presidency and the long-term changes they reflected. These forces have set the stage, roles, and tests that have defined his presidency and tested the Republican leaders in Congress. Greenberg's core argument focuses on the breakdown of party traditions and the social contract. The author sets the historical stage in an effort to understand what was really at issue in the 1992 presidential election and whether it constituted an historic break that could change the course of American politics. Greenberg immersed himself in a single suburban county, Macomb County, Michigan, and in the book he uses this setting to show how national political forces play out in the lives and politics of middle America.

Greenfield, Jeff. *The Real Campaign: How the Media Missed the Story of the 1980 Campaign.* New York: Summit Books, 1982.

The author attempts to analyze the 1980 presidential race by examining the public records covering the campaign and assessing the influence the daily media had on the outcome of the election. The author uses news reports, broadcasts, and print media in conjunction with interviews and discussions with many of the people involved with reporting on the campaign.

Grimes, Ann. *Running Mates: The Making of a First Lady.* New York: William Morrow, 1990.

The author focuses on the role that the candidates' wives played in the 1988 presidential campaign. She illustrates how the candidates' wives must present themselves to the media, perform like candidates, and play numerous roles, including wife, mother, cheerleader, and possibly the "ill-defined, unpaid job" of being First Lady. She discusses Barbara Bush and Kitty Dukakis, Hattie Babbitt, Beryl M. Bentsen, Elizabeth Dole, Tipper Gore, Jane Gephardt, Jackie Jackson, Marilyn Quayle, and Jeanne Simon. Grimes illustrates how each of these women played major roles in the 1988 presidential campaign and discusses how the campaign season affected them.

Herzke, Allen D. *Echoes of Discontent: Jesse Jackson, Pat Robertson, and the Resurgence of Populism.* Washington, DC: CQ Press, 1993.

The author argues that Jesse Jackson and Pat Robertson were able to legitimately challenge the partisan mainstream by appealing to individuals on the economic, social, and cultural periphery of American society during the 1992 presidential nominations. The author employs ethnographic, interpretive, and historical approaches to explain how these candidates were able to tap the discontent of the populace, how the partisan mainstream approached and dealt with their rhetoric and demands, and what the increasingly populist nature of national politics holds for future political contests.

Herzog, Arthur. *McCarthy for President.* New York: Viking Press, 1969.

The author offers a firsthand account of the 1968 presidential run by Democrat Eugene McCarthy. He examines the candidate, traces the origins of the senator's decision to run, and details the strategies and tactics of the campaign. Along the way Herzog documents McCarthy's confrontations with President Lyndon Johnson, Robert Kennedy, and Hubert H. Humphrey, among others. He discusses the travails of the campaign trail, beginning with the first primary in New Hampshire, the bitter battle in Wisconsin through the Midwest, and the fight for California. Finally, the author details the dynamics of the 1968 Democratic National Convention in Chicago.

Hess, Stephen. *The Presidential Campaign: The Leadership Selection Process after Watergate: Essay.* 3d ed. Washington, DC: Brookings Institution, 1988.

The author shows the shifting roles of presidential campaigns. He argues that the system places great demands on persons seeking the office. Hess lists important presidential qualities: trustworthiness, high intelligence, broad interests, the ability to communicate with the public, being able to mobilize the nation, possessing long-range vision, and being a talented executive. He shows that the campaign serves many functions: leadership selection plus policy formulation, national self-examination, a check on executive action, and entertainment. Hess discusses the importance of media in the selection process and places money in its political context. There are limits to what money can do in a quest for the presidency and underfinancing is more typical than overfinancing in campaigns. Hess proposes legal and procedural reforms.

Huckfeldt, Robert, and John Sprague. *Citizens, Politics, and Social Communication: Information and Influence in an Election Campaign.* New York: Cambridge University Press, 1995.

The authors investigate the political implications of interdependent citizens within the context of the 1984 presidential campaign as it was experienced in the metropolitan area of South Bend, Indiana. National politics is experienced locally through a series of filters unique to a particular setting. This study is concerned with understanding that setting and its consequences for the exercise of democratic citizenship. The authors examine the dynamic implications of social communication among citizens, the exercise of citizen purpose in locating sources of information, the constraints on individual choice that arise as a function of contexts and environments, and the institutional and organizational effects that operate on the flow of information within particular settings.

Johnson, David E., and Johnny R. Johnson. *A Funny Thing Happened on the Way to the White House.* New York: Beaufort Books, 1983.

The authors examine the history of political mudslinging in presidential campaigns. They provide insight into the tradition of presidential rhetoric and its evolution from 1828 through the modern, televised era. The authors focus on the more colorful statements, slogans, and political cartoons of each race.

Kessel, John H. *The Goldwater Coalition: Republican Strategies in 1964.* Indianapolis: Bobbs-Merrill, 1968.

The author sets forth a theory that will aid in understanding political parties. Using a detailed analysis of nomination and electoral politics of 1964, the author argues that voters' attitudes are subject to modification by the behavior of coalitions in their various institutional settings. The flow of new information modifies voter attitudes. Normally voters cognize new information in accordance with previous attitudes, but occasionally highly visible behavior by a particular coalition provides information on an important subject about which there is heretofore inadequate knowledge. The author argues that this is what happened in the early 1950s, and again in 1964.

———. *Presidential Campaign Politics.* 4th ed. Pacific Grove, CA: Brooks/Cole, 1992.

The author focuses on the multifaceted and complex nature of presidential campaigns by analyzing both the campaign process and voting. He provides an in-depth but broad examination of nomination politics, electoral politics, campaign strategies, and citizen response. The fourth edition of this work benefits greatly by the inclusion of data collected in a massive 1988 study of presidential parties that allows for the detection of partisan shifts through the 1970s and 1980s. An appendix provides details concerning the indexes and measures used to manipulate the data used in the study.

Kingdon, John W. *Candidates for Office; Beliefs and Strategies.* New York: Random House, 1968.

The author investigates candidates for office using personal interviews, politicians' images of constituencies, beliefs about the behavior of voters, and views on coalition building. He examines a variety of sources of information about their election districts, their reliability, and their reasons for adopting various campaign strategies. Kingdon also discusses the broader implications of his findings for understanding representation in a democratic system.

Krukones, Michael G. *Promises and Performance: Presidential Campaigns as Policy Predictors.* Lanham, MD: University Press of America, 1984.

The author challenges the negative public attitude toward political campaigns by examining the degree to which presidential candidates adhered to campaign pledges once in office. Krukones collects the promises of successful candidates from Woodrow Wilson to Jimmy Carter from sources of campaign information available to the electorate, such as newspapers, newsmagazines, and television reports. He then examines each administration to determine whether the presidents executed the campaign pledges. The author finds that successful candidates keep approximately three-fourths of issue-positions taken in their campaigns. He concludes that campaigns fulfill a highly useful informative function for the public and are good indicators of presidents' future policy performance.

Lamb, Karl A., and Paul A. L. Smith. *Campaign Decision-Making: The Presidential Election of 1964.* Belmont, CA: Wadsworth, 1968.

The authors examine the 1964 presidential campaign and election in terms of a rational decision-making process. Using direct observation, informal discussions, and interviews with campaign leaders, the authors evaluate the evolutionary process of decision making in the Barry Goldwater and Lyndon Johnson campaigns. They tease out the differences in the two candidates' decision-making styles: Goldwater's more comprehensive organizational style and Johnson's incrementalism.

Loevy, Robert D. *The Flawed Path to the Presidency, 1992: Unfairness and Inequality in the Presidential Selection Process.* New York: State University of New York, 1995.

The author interprets the 1992 presidential campaign state-by-state and event-by-event from the perspective of the average voter. The author offers numerous reforms to give the average voter a larger voice in the process while reducing and minimizing systemic and structural inequalities that value some citizens over others. These reforms include a model calendar for state caucuses and primaries, preprimary party conventions, and the abolishment of the electoral college.

Lorant, Stefan. *The Glorious Burden: The History of the Presidency and Presidential Elections from George Washington to James Earl Carter, Jr.* Lenox, MA: Author's Edition, 1976.

The author offers a history of the presidents and presidential elections from 1789 to 1976. Each presidential term is given a chapter, beginning at the start of the new administration and running until the election of the next president. Each chapter opens with portraits of the leading candidates for president and vice president. Along with detailed historical text about the administrations, the volume also includes political cartoons of the day, pictures, and descriptions of the presidents. An appendix details the election vote from 1789 to 1976.

Mann, Thomas E., and Norman J. Ornstein. *The American Elections of 1982.* Washington, DC: American Enterprise Institute for Public Policy Research, 1983.

This edited volume examines national and state elections during the midterm of the first Reagan administration. The first chapter provides a detailed historical analysis of the political events and campaigns leading to the 1982 elections. Subsequent chapters evaluate the effects on the election of reapportionment and redistricting, examine the roles of political action committees and the national political parties; study the implications of state legislative and gubernatorial outcomes for national politics; and examine outcome interpretations by politicians, the press, and the public. Several appendixes contain selected statistical data on state and national legislative electoral outcomes.

McCubbins, Mathew D., ed. *Under the Watchful Eye: Managing Presidential Campaigns in the Television Era.* Washington, DC: CQ Press, 1992.

This edited volume examines the changes that have occurred in presidential campaigns in the past three decades. The essays reexamine the claims that television and party decline have altered presidential campaigns, the evidence that presidential campaigns have been transformed, and the effects of these changes on American democracy. The book begins with a review of the literature on the evolution of presidential campaigns. Next is a discussion of the rise of candidate-centered campaigns and the role of momentum, followed by essays on the use of television advertising by presidential candidates; the sensationalized, frenzied nature of modern political reporting; and the ability of the voters to extract the intended messages from the political imagery they receive.

McGinnis, Joe. *The Selling of the President, 1968.* New York: Trident, 1969.

The author focuses on the 1968 campaign, showing how Richard Nixon's campaign team managed his image through the press, television, and in person. The author offers a behind-the-scenes view of how the image makers operate.

Melder, Keith. *Hail to the Candidate: Presidential Campaigns from Banners to Broadcasts.* Washington, DC: Smithsonian Institution Press, 1992.

The author examines the changes in political expression and campaign materials. He begins with an overview of the diverse languages and imagery of campaign techniques and devices, showing how different approaches have been used to appeal to voters. Melder traces the development of campaign images and public participation from the election of 1789 to the campaigns of the twentieth century. He includes chapters on the gradual inclusion of women in mainstream politics and the images that appealed to them, the effect of television on campaigning, the decline of political parties and the rise of consultants, and the effects of new technologies. Melder offers reproductions and photographs of political Americana from the collection of the National Museum of American History of the Smithsonian Institution.

Mendelsohn, Harold A., and Garrett J. O'Keefe Jr. *The People Choose a President: Influences on Voter Decision Making.* New York: Praeger, 1976.

Using a panel research design covering the four months before the November 1972 presidential election, the authors delineate those variables influencing voter decision making, including the impact of campaign communications media on voter choice. They discuss the influences of sociological, psychological, and political dispositions on voter decision making. Voter profiles include questions dealing with demographic characteristics, stability of voter intentions, issue importance, and candidate image. Mendelsohn and O'Keefe examine campaigns' influences on voter decision making, focusing on the role of the mass media and the influence of televised political commercials. The authors find demographic characteristics provide weak predictability in determining overall voter choice. They conclude that selective exposure to campaign news and advertising media by the electorate no longer applies, that national campaign events by themselves produce little change in voter decisions, that exposure does not equate with effect, and that approximately 20 percent of the electorate surveyed indicated that their vote in 1972 had been influenced by the media.

Miller, Arthur H., and Bruce E. Gronbeck, eds. *Presidential Campaigns and American Self Images.* Boulder, CO: Westview Press, 1994.

The editors of this volume maintain that a political campaign is not merely a process by which the electorate selects its president, but is a large process of social construction that provides a window onto the political culture of the United States. Miller and Gronbeck present three primary centers of activity through which political images are shaped: candidate-generated activities, mass print and broadcast media, and the images constructed by the voter as citizen. The concluding section of the book develops the links between these spheres of activity that further define the relationships between American self-images and presidential campaigning.

Miller, Warren E., and Teresa E. Levitin. *Leadership and Change: Presidential Elections from 1952 to 1976.* Cambridge, MA: Winthrop, 1976.

For the authors, the unrest associated with the 1960s marks the beginning of a new politics that they maintain deviates significantly from the traditional partisan political behavior that preceded it. Using survey data for the period between 1952 and 1976, the authors construct an argument that considers the period between 1970 and 1972 as pivotal in the institutionalization of this transformed style of citizen politics. Miller and Levitin review recent political history, analyze advocates' and opponents' positions on new politics, and offer hypotheses for the transformation of American electoral politics in the early 1970s. The authors also identify those hypotheses that are determinate for the 1972 presidential election. They conclude by examining the effects of the new politics on the 1976 election and speculate on its long-term implications for American politics.

Morreale, Joanne. *The Presidential Campaign Film: A Critical History.* Westport, CT: Praeger, 1993.

The author examines the unexplored genre of the presidential campaign film, which has developed with visual broadcast media. She argues that the subordination of the word to image in a post-literate context has fundamentally transformed the way political campaigns and electoral politics are conducted. Using content analysis of campaign films, Morreale focuses on archetypal, personal, and party images; and film structure; narration, testimony, and rhetoric; stock footage; music; and special effects.

Morris, Lorenzo, ed. *The Social and Political Implications of the 1984 Jesse Jackson Presidential Campaign.* New York: Praeger, 1990.

The chapters in this edited volume originally were part of a conference on the significance and implications of Jesse Jackson's 1984 presidential campaign. Initially the volume examines the social and political context of the campaign. Next it looks to social and economic policy in party politics, including race and the party system. The book provides an explication of, critique of, and alternative to the Jackson campaign's economic policy. The book then turns to the campaign's influence on racial issues, including articulation of interests, control of issue framing, and use of symbols by the Jackson campaign. The next section deals with foreign policy, history, and issues. Finally, the book discusses political mobilization, charisma, and coalition building in the campaign.

Nelson, Michael, ed. *The Elections of 1984.* Washington, DC: CQ Press, 1985.

This collection of essays focuses on the 1984 elections. The editor includes articles about realignment, the nomination process, candidates' strategies, media coverage, the role of foreign policy and the economy in the election, and the outcomes for Congress and the presidency. The volume concludes with two essays about the elections' long-term consequences.

Newman, Bruce I. *The Marketing of the President: Political Marketing as Campaign Strategy.* Thousand Oaks, CA: Sage, 1994.

The author argues that a strategically market-oriented approach to presidential campaigns is viable because of the collapse of communism in East-Central Europe; increasing access to information via television, radio, satellite, and the Internet; and a growing cynicism about the parties and candidates that compete for power in the United States. Using Bill Clinton's 1992 campaign as an example of how marketing and presidential politics have become linked, the author offers a model that illustrates the role of marketing techniques in modern politics. After examining the rise of marketing as a campaign technique and demonstrating in detail how it has been used, Newman concludes by exploring the ramifications of this trend for future presidential elections.

Ogden, Daniel M., and Arthur L. Peterson. *Electing the President.* Rev. ed. San Francisco, CA: Chandler, 1968.

The authors describe the process of choosing the chief executive officer. They report the experiences of the two major parties in the 1960 election and examine the expectations for the 1964 campaign. Ogden and Peterson include discussions of history and of constitutional and legal determinants in the detail needed to support the book's practical emphasis. The authors' main foci include nominations, platforms, campaign organization, state and local support, special interest groups, candidate image, meeting the public, and financing campaigns. Both authors write with the combined knowledge of a practicing political worker and a scholar in political science. They have expert and intimate familiarity with the 1960 campaign, having been faculty fellows assigned to national committees of the two major parties.

Page, Benjamin I. *Choices and Echoes in Presidential Elections: Rational Man and Electoral Democracy.* Chicago: University of Chicago Press, 1978.

The author investigates the behavior of political parties and candidates in response to voter demands, expectations, and perceptions. Relying on campaign speeches, advertisements, platforms, and other public materials from 1932 to 1976, he systematically analyzes the links between presidential candidate rhetoric and the electorate. Page employs an economic rational argument to construct spatial models of public opinion and candidate positioning. This approach emphasizes the dynamic component of candidate rhetoric and positioning in response to voter demands and other candidate issue stances. Other issues addressed include ambiguity in political rhetoric and party platforms, incumbent records, candidates' personal character and presentation, and candidates' ability to manipulate or lead the electorate.

Phillips, Kevin P. *The Politics of Rich and Poor: Wealth and the American Electorate in the Reagan Aftermath.* New York: HarperPerennial, 1991.

The author examines the new political economics of the post-Reagan era and how electoral politics had a role in shaping that new reality. Phillips documents the intensifying inequality and pain of the poor, the unprecedented growth of upper bracket wealth, the surprisingly related growth of federal debt, global economic realignment, the new rush of foreign investment in real estate, and the millionaire culture of the 1980s. He shows how the 1988 election signaled an end to that era and a swing back to a distaste for survival-of-the-fittest economics, new talk of a "kinder, gentler nation," belief in a more activist role for government, and a demand for more attention to the weaker portions of society.

Pika, Joseph A., and Richard A. Watson. *The Presidential Contest.* 5th ed. Washington, DC: CQ Press, 1996.

The authors examine all aspects of the race for the presidency. Using a chronological, step-by-step analysis and a common framework, they illuminate similarities and differences between the nomination and election phases of the campaign. The authors elucidate the rules, discuss the kinds of people chosen as candidates, and analyze the voters. They also examine the strengths and weaknesses of the presidential selection process and suggest reforms.

Pious, Richard M., ed. *Presidents, Elections, and Democracy.* New York: Academy of Political Science, 1992.

The essays in this book, reprinted from *Political Science Quarterly,* provide the background essential to understanding the functioning of the modern presidency and presidential elections. Issues examined include restoring balance to presidential power, the new politics of deficits, prerogative power, the procedural presidency, the myth of presidential mandate, and the 1988 elections as the continuation of the post–New Deal system. Also included are discussions of political reforms that might make a difference in the prospects for American democracy.

Polsby, Nelson W. *Citizen's Choice: Humphrey or Nixon.* Washington, DC: Public Affairs Press, 1968.

The author offers a consideration of the main candidates, issues, and strategies of the 1968 presidential race. Polsby compares the records and respective styles of Hubert Humphrey and Richard Nixon. He examines the dilemmas that these candidates faced because each had held the office of vice president. Polsby focuses on the campaign for the nomination, the conventions, and the Republican southern strategy. He attempts to counter three voter questions that might decrease voter turnout. Polsby argues against the notion of president as hero. He argues that, despite failed policies and considerable unrest, the system did rather well in choosing the nominees and providing a forum for dissent. The author explores the problems of opting out and not voting, arguing that the long-run costs outweigh the short-term benefits.

Polsby, Nelson W., and Aaron B. Wildavsky. *Presidential Elections: Strategies of American Electoral Politics.* 9th ed. Chatham, NJ: Chatham House, 1996.

The authors try to explain the strategic choices of differently situated actors by seeking to understand how incentives and prohibitions, habits, customs, regulations, and opportunities organize their world. To that end Polsby and Wildavsky examine voter attitudes, interest groups, and parties and analyze the environment within presidential campaigns. They discuss strategies in primaries, conventions, and campaigns. The authors examine how mass communications have affected the nominating process and the importance of issues and parties to victory in elections.

Pomper, Gerald M., et al., eds. *The Election of 1988: Reports and Interpretations.* Chatham, NJ: Chatham House, 1989.

This edited volume brings together seven essays by prominent political scientists that analyze the results of the 1988 federal elections. Ross Baker contributes a chapter in which he explains the outcomes of the congressional elections. Baker describes them as evidence of continuity and safety for the incumbent party (for example, the Democrats) and details the advantages of incumbency. He discusses what it took to win or lose a seat in 1988 and concludes with a preview of the new Congress and the George Bush agenda. Other essays look at the presidential race, the campaign and the media, and public opinion trends.

————, eds. *The Election of 1992: Reports and Interpretations.* Chatham, NJ: Chatham House, 1993.

The fifth in a series on presidential elections, this volume of essays explores the unique characteristics of the 1992 elections. The authors maintain that some traditional preconceptions about presidential elections were challenged by the 1992 election, including the incumbency effect, the outcomes of nomination campaigns, and the attention to issues and candidates paid by the electorate. Essays deal with the George Bush legacy, the nomination process, campaign tactics and strategies, public opinion, and the congressional elections. They also evaluate the implications of the outcome of the 1992 presidential election and include President Bill Clinton's inaugural address.

Pool, Ithiel de Sola, Robert P. Abelson, and Samuel L. Popkin. *Candidates, Issues, and Strategies: A Computer Simulation of the 1960 and 1964 Presidential Elections.* 2d ed. Cambridge, MA: MIT Press, 1965.

The authors conduct a mathematical and behavioral simulation of the 1960 and 1964 presidential elections. The project uses symbolized voters and behavioral theories about how persons interact to formulate a series of equations. The authors offer a breadth and depth of analytical modeling that concerns itself with real-world issues and by which the authors hope future electoral outcomes can be predicted.

Rabinowitz, George B. *Spatial Models of Electoral Choice: An Empirical Analysis.* Chapel Hill: Institute for Research in Social Science, University of North Carolina, 1973.

The author attempts to take advantage of spatial representations of electorates in an empirical political context. He focuses on the 1968 presidential campaign. Rabinowitz delineates how information gleaned from thermometer questions on surveys can be used to form a political space in which both mass and elite can be located. The author finds the extent to which a space of limited dimensionality can represent the rich diversity of politics striking and somewhat unexpected.

Reed, Adolph L., Jr. *The Jesse Jackson Phenomenon: The Crisis of Purpose in Afro-American Politics.* New Haven: Yale University Press, 1986.

The author's central thesis is that the 1984 Jesse Jackson phenomenon is emblematic of the inadequacy of conventional patterns of discourse concerning African American political activity, which originated in a pre–civil rights context of racial protest. Reed uses the Jackson phenomenon as a window onto the larger dynamics that have structured post–civil rights era African American political activity, including the development of competing criteria for legitimation of claims to African American political leadership, the sharpening of lines of socioeconomic stratification within the African American population, and the growth of centrifugal pressures within the external attacks on national policy consensus represented by the Democratic coalition. The author also examines electoral mobilization, leadership ratification, the role of the church in African American politics, tensions with labor, relations between African Americans and Jews within the Democratic Party coalition, and the role of the media.

Renshon, Stanley A., ed. *The Clinton Presidency: Campaigning, Governing, and the Psychology of Leadership.* Boulder, CO: Westview Press, 1995.

This edited volume examines the relationship between public and candidate psychology in presidential elections and governing processes. The articles focus on the psychology of political leadership in the 1992 presidential contest between George Bush, Bill Clinton, and Ross Perot; the immediate postelection period; and the first year of the Clinton presidency. The stated purpose of the volume is to evaluate the Clinton campaign and administration and examine the intersection between campaign rhetoric and in-office performance. Drawing on a variety of disciplinary strengths, such as political science, psychology, and psychiatry, the articles discuss the campaign lessons of 1992, public psychology and leadership style, presidential leadership, public perception of President Clinton, and the psychology of public policy.

Roseboom, Eugene H., and Alfred E. Eckes. *A History of Presidential Elections, From George Washington to Jimmy Carter.* New York: Macmillan, 1979.

The authors offer a history of the quadrennial contest for the presidency from the first election in 1789 to the 1976 election of Jimmy Carter. They explain the political trends in the social and economic settings of the different periods, with particular attention to periods of change. Roseboom and Eckes present facts about conventions, campaigns, and elections, assess the effectiveness of the presidents and other important political leaders, and discuss the more significant congressional electoral and political struggles.

Rosenbloom, David L. *The Election Men: Professional Campaign Managers and American Democracy.* New York: Quadrangle Books, 1973.

The authors present professional campaign managers as a menace because they care only about winning elections, enriching themselves, being close to the powerful, and satisfying their egos instead of being concerned about the issues, party government, representation, and solving the world's problems. The sole concern of the new manager is the election at hand. The new manager uses commercial advertising, radio, television, direct mail, and telephone banks as demographic and survey research in campaigns. Rosenbloom says the parties are the losers when professional managers take charge.

Russell, Francis. *The President Makers: From Mark Hanna to Joseph P. Kennedy.* Boston: Little, Brown, 1976.

The author examines eight men who helped their respective candidates achieve the office of the presidency. Each was a campaign manager, political boss, strategist, or behind-the-scenes ally. The success of their respective candidates can be largely attributed to these men. They are (with their presidential protégés in parentheses): Mark Hanna (William McKinley), Thomas Collier Platt (Theodore Roosevelt), Theodore Roosevelt (William H. Taft), George Harvey (Woodrow Wilson), Harry Daughterty (Warren Harding), Frank Stearns (Calvin Coolidge), Louis Howe (Franklin D. Roosevelt), and Joseph P. Kennedy (John F. Kennedy). Each chapter is devoted to one of these men and how he influenced the election of his respective candidate.

Sabato, Larry J., ed. *Toward the Millennium: The Elections of 1996.* Boston: Allyn and Bacon, 1997.

This edited volume of eleven chapters focuses on the 1996 presidential election. The essays are by prominent scholars and journalists, who explain how Bill Clinton won the election and analyze the critical elements of the election. The book looks at the campaign process and the role of the media and political money. It also covers the nomination process and conventions.

Schantz, Harvey L., ed. *American Presidential Elections: Process, Policy, and Political Change.* Albany: State University of New York Press, 1996.

The authors of the essays in this volume analyze presidential elections and examine how presidential elections affect the political system and society. They chart vote patterns for the 1992 election and contrast the election's outcome with those of the 1984 and 1988 elections. They also analyze state-level presidential election results. The authors examine the effectiveness of political parties in the democratic process and test the link between elections and major policy change. They examine divided government and probe the impact of a postindustrial society on parties and elections. They also examine sectional voting patterns in presidential elections from 1824 to 1992.

Schramm, Peter W., and Dennis J. Mahoney, eds. *The 1984 Election and the Future of American Politics.* Durham, NC: Carolina Academic Press, 1987.

The editors intend this volume to be a coherent and comprehensive account of the events and procedures of the 1984 election. Each of the fourteen chapters describes and analyzes a particular important element of the 1984 electoral process. The editors' focus is on the issues dividing the candidates and the parties. The chapters cover such issues as foreign policy, economics, ethnicity, entitlements, and the media. Chapters also address platforms, campaign strategy, campaign finance, and incumbency.

Semetko, Holli A., et al. *The Formation of Campaign Agendas: A Comparative Analysis of Party and Media Roles in Recent American and British Elections.* Hillsdale, NJ: L. Erlbaum Associates, 1991.

The authors compare and analyze the roles of party and media in recent American and British elections. They discuss how campaign agendas are formed and the agenda-setting role of television journalists. They look at the 1984 American presidential election and the 1983 British general election.

Simon, Roger. *Road Show.* New York: Farrar, Strauss, and Giroux, 1988.

The author offers an account of the 1988 presidential campaign. The account begins with George Bush's announcement, follows the Democratic and Republican primaries and conventions, describes the viciousness of the general election campaign, and ends with the Bush victory on election day. Simon pays particular attention to the tone of the rhetoric, the interaction between candidates and the media, and the general negative atmosphere surrounding the race.

Stacks, John F. *Watershed: The Campaign for the Presidency, 1980.* New York: Times Books, 1982.

The author examines the 1980 presidential campaign. He focuses on the political patterns that did or did not hold to form in 1980, the men who subjected themselves to the process of choosing a president, and the nature of the process. Stacks examines the Ted Kennedy challenge to Jimmy Carter for the Democratic nomination, the Republican battle for the nomination, the conventions, the John Anderson independent campaign, the debates, the general election campaign, and the election results.

Stephenson, D. Grier, Jr. *Campaigns and the Court: The U.S. Supreme Court in Presidential Elections.* New York: Columbia University Press, 1999.

The author discusses the relationship between the Supreme Court and presidential campaigns. He examines the role that the Court has played in presidential elections. Stephenson looks at the Court's involvement in partisan politics and the evolution of constitutional law as it relates to campaigns and elections.

Stout, Richard T. *People.* New York: Harper and Row, 1970.

The author examines Eugene McCarthy's 1968 campaign for the Democratic presidential nomination. Stout examines McCarthy's campaign in detail, focusing on the ordinary people who volunteered and helped him effect change despite his defeat. Stout recounts the events surrounding the Vietnam War and the administration's policies that led to the development of the grassroots movement that McCarthy spearheaded. The author also details the events of the Democratic National Convention in Chicago, which was effectively the end of the McCarthy campaign.

Taylor, Paul. *See How They Run: Electing the President in an Age of Mediaocracy.* New York: Alfred A. Knopf, 1990.

The author, a journalist, critiques the current electoral system by showing how the politicians, press, and voters bring out the least in each other. He fleshes out his argument by chronicling the actions of each actor during the 1988 presidential election campaign. Taylor gives a general overview of the campaign and its various dysfunctions. He describes the interaction between candidates and reporters. Taylor examines the political handlers, the press, and the voters. He argues that each of these actors responds to built-in incentives and therefore is trapped in a vicious circle. He offers a proposal for modest structural change in modern media campaigns that might help these actors break the cycle.

Tenpas, Kathryn D. *Presidents as Candidates: Inside the White House for the Presidential Campaign.* New York: Garland Publishing, 1997.

The author examines eight reelection efforts, from Dwight D. Eisenhower through Bill Clinton. She presents a typology of three standard types of reelection campaigns: the victorious, defeated, and takeover. She examines each president's campaign committee, the national party organization, and the campaign inside the White House. She concludes with a discussion of the implications of a White House-centered reelection campaign.

Thompson, Kenneth W., ed. *Lessons from Defeated Presidential Candidates.* Lanham, MD: University Press of America, 1994.

This edited volume addresses the literature on defeated presidential candidates. The campaigns examined are: Charles Evans Hughes, in 1916; John W. Davis, in 1924; Calvin Coolidge, in 1928; Herbert Hoover, in 1932; Wendell Willkie, in 1940; Thomas Dewey, in 1944 and 1948, Adlai Stevenson, in 1952 and 1956; Hubert H. Humphrey, in 1968; and Walter Mondale, in 1984. The two unusual cases are Coolidge—who decided not to run for reelection in 1928—and Hoover, who had already won an election in 1928 but lost reelection in 1932. The other candidates all ran and lost each time out. Each chapter of this book focuses on one particular failed candidacy and examines it in depth, looking for lessons that can be drawn from each campaign.

Troy, Gil. *See How They Ran: The Changing Role of the Presidential Candidate.* Rev. ed. Cambridge, MA: Harvard University Press, 1996.

The author examines every presidential election campaign from 1840 to 1992 to explore why candidates campaign as they do. Troy reveals what our presidential campaign tells us about democracy itself. He reveals that campaigns always have reflected tensions within the electorate. There never has been a golden age of campaigning. Rather, voters have complained about the presidential campaign, and their choice of candidates, for the last two centuries. However, while the complaints have not changed much, the targets have shifted. Candidates, not parties, receive most of the blame in more recent times, while the opposite was true previously.

Tugwell, Rexford G. *How They Became President: Thirty-Five Ways to the White House.* New York: Simon and Schuster, 1965.

The author examines how each president attained his office. He places emphasis on background, qualifications, political careers, and personal characteristics. Tugwell chronicles each president's ascent to the office and examines the similarities and differences among the presidents. The author considers partisanship, ethics, past careers, leadership, and the selection process itself.

Wattenberg, Martin P. *The Rise of Candidate-Centered Politics: Presidential Elections of the 1980s.* Cambridge, MA: Harvard University Press, 1991.

The author evaluates the decline of partisan-centered electoral politics and the rise of candidate-centered politics in the 1980s. Placing the candidate-oriented presidential campaigns in historical context, Wattenberg argues that this shift in emphasis has reshaped electoral processes and might continue to produce governments divided along partisan lines in the legislative and executive branches. By examining theories of voting, psychological variables, and dealignment, Wattenberg finds that candidates have become less popular and that a widening gap is developing between voters' policy preferences and their evaluation of presidential performance.

Wayne, Stephen J. *The Road to the White House 2000: The Politics of Presidential Elections.* New York: St. Martin's, 1999.

The author examines how the institutions created to elect the president are constructed and operate. In part one Wayne focuses on the electoral arena in which candidates vie for the office of president: the electoral system, campaign finance, and the political environment. In parts two and three he examines delegate selection, nominating conventions, campaign organization, strategy and tactics, and media politics. In part four, the author evaluates the implications these institutions and practices have for democratic politics and the election of the president. He also examines the forecasting of elections and electoral reform.

Wead, Doug, and Bill Wead. *Reagan in Pursuit of the Presidency: 1980.* Plainfield, NJ: Logos International, 1980.

The authors chronicle Ronald Reagan's campaign for his party's nomination for president. in 1980. They begin with Reagan's decision to run, follow the campaign to New Hampshire and beyond, and conclude with Reagan's primary season victory and nearly assured nomination. They examine campaign strategy, Reagan's opponents, and his views on the issues. Appendixes include an interview with Reagan; Reagan's official announcement of his candidacy; and the candidate's views on abortion, the SALT treaty, and the state of the economy.

Weil, Gordon L. *The Long Shot: George McGovern Runs for President.* New York: Norton, 1973.

The author examines George McGovern's 1972 presidential campaign. Weil, a former aide to the senator's campaign, depicts the major events of the campaign, focusing particularly on strategy mistakes and uncontrollable events. In particular, Weil discusses the Nixon campaign's tactics to beat McGovern, the Thomas Eagleton affair, and failures in the McGovern campaign organization. The author also examines the roots of the candidacy in the conflict in Vietnam, the beginnings of the campaign, the primaries that eventually led to the Democratic nomination, the general election campaign, and the election results.

West, Darrell M. *Making Campaigns Count: Leadership and Coalition-Building in 1980.* Westport, CT: Greenwood, 1984.

The author focuses on candidates and their campaign advisors to examine the relationship between coalition formation and partisan leadership during the 1980 presidential campaign. He examines candidate strategies; the coalitions that candidates attempted to construct; the rhetoric, symbolism, and geographic focus of candidates; the candidates' learning processes during the campaign; and the implications these items held for leadership and coalition building. The research is framed within a dynamic framework in which campaign technology, mass media, the nominating process, and the nature of the political parties have changed.

White, F. Clifton, and William J. Gill. *Why Reagan Won: A Narrative History of the Conservative Movement, 1964–1981.* Chicago: Regnery Gateway, 1981.

The author argues that the conservative movement that Ronald Reagan led to victory is not merely political but, rather, represents a deep philosophical, intellectual, and spiritual upheaval. White argues that Reagan's victory can be traced back and attributed to the unsuccessful 1964 campaign of Barry Goldwater and the political movement it sparked. He traces the development of that movement, and in the process traces the career of Ronald Reagan. The book ends with Reagan's 1980 victory and a look ahead to the future of politics and the conservative movement.

White, Theodore H. *America in Search of Itself: The Making of the President, 1956–1980*. New York: Harper and Row, 1982.

The author examines politics, and in particular presidential politics, from the 1950s to 1980. White's main thesis is that the 1980 election marked the end of the post–World War II era. He begins by examining the campaigns of Dwight Eisenhower in the 1950s, then looks to the transformation of politics from 1960 to 1979. He examines the role of the media, social programs, activism, inflation, change in the U.S. role abroad, and the presidency of Jimmy Carter. White devotes the third section of the book to the 1980 election. He examines Carter and the Democrats, Ronald Reagan and the Republicans, the primaries, conventions, general election campaign, and election results.

———. *The Making of the President, 1960*. New York: Atheneum, 1961.

The author discusses the politics of the 1960 presidential election. White traveled with the candidates from the fall of 1959 to election day 1960 and here recounts the history of this campaign from his perspective. The first part of the book follows the campaign before the primaries, the dynamics of the primaries, and party conventions. It covers the seven major candidates and their respective jockeying for position. The second part of the book examines the issues and strategies of the John F. Kennedy and Richard Nixon campaigns, the television debates, and the final judgment of the people on which of the two nominees was the best choice for president.

———. *The Making of the President, 1964*. New York: Atheneum, 1965.

The author discusses the politics of the 1964 presidential election. He follows the procession from the crest of the late John F. Kennedy's vision to the alternate visions offered by Lyndon Johnson and Barry Goldwater, to the final judgment of the people on which of the two party nominees was the best choice for president. White covers the quarrels between leaders, the rivalries of the groups, riots in the streets, and the bitterness of clashes over race. He examines the repercussions of the Kennedy assassination, the dynamics of the primaries and party conventions, and the issues and strategies of the two major campaigns.

———. *The Making of the President, 1968*. New York: Atheneum, 1969.

The author offers an historical account of the politics of the 1968 presidential election year. He follows the rise of the Republican Party from the ashes of the 1964 Barry Goldwater campaign, the mass politics that forced the president to back out of the race, the ascent of Richard Nixon, the rise and demise of Robert Kennedy, primary and convention battles, the campaign endgame, and the final judgment of the people on which of the two party nominees was the best choice for president. White covers the quarrels between leaders, the rivalries of groups, the riots in the streets of Chicago, and the bitterness of clashes on the issues. He examines campaign dynamics and tactics in depth.

————. *The Making of the President, 1972.* New York: Atheneum, 1973.

The author offers an historical account of the politics of the 1972 presidential election year. He follows the changes in the Democratic Party from the seeming chaos of the primaries to the eventual rise of George McGovern. White details the advantages inherent in Richard Nixon's incumbency. He examines campaign dynamics and tactics in depth on both sides. He discusses problems of the McGovern campaign, including the Thomas Eagleton affair, and Nixon's problems posed by the war in Vietnam, the press, and Watergate. White examines the campaign endgame and the final judgment of the people on which of the two party nominees was the best choice for president.

Wildavsky, Aaron B. *Presidential Elections: Strategies and Structures in American Politics.* 9th ed. New York: Scribner's, 1996.

The author gives a comprehensive overview of presidential elections by examining voters, parties, special interest groups, the rules and resources of elections, the electoral college, and the media. Wildavsky covers all aspects of the nomination process and campaigning. He concludes with a look at reforms of parties, conventions, the nomination process, and the electoral process in general.

Witcover, Jules. *85 Days: The Last Campaign of Robert Kennedy.* New York: G. P. Putnam's Sons, 1969.

The author chronicles Robert Kennedy's 1968 presidential campaign. Witcover explains why Kennedy chose to hasten what appeared to be the inevitable decision to run and how he implemented that decision in a time of great political upheaval. He covers the trials and tribulations of the campaign trail, the state-by-state battle for the nomination, the triumphs of the campaign, and its tragic ending with the assassination of Robert Kennedy.

————. *Marathon: The Pursuit of the Presidency, 1972–1976.* New York: Viking, 1977.

The author follows the quest for the presidency in the years leading up to the 1976 election. Witcover examines where America found itself before and through the presidential election, the individuals who ran, the changes they wrought, and their failures. The author shows what the campaign did to the candidates, their families and friends, their campaign workers, the press, the political parties, and the country itself. Along the way Witcover documents the jockeying for position within the two parties, the hunt for delegates in the primary season, the party conventions, the general election campaign, and the outcome on election day.

Zernicke, Paul H. *Pitching the Presidency: How Presidents Depict the Office.* Westport, CT: Praeger, 1994.

The author examines the rise of presidential rhetoric and the ramifications it has for the public's perception of the role of the president. Zernicke analyzes the modern presidency's reliance on rhetoric during three phases of the presidential term: during the campaign, while holding office, and after leaving the seat of governance. He examines and compares Lyndon Johnson's, Richard Nixon's, and Jimmy Carter's use of rhetoric in these three stages of their presidencies. The author concludes by positing that a cyclical pattern in the use of presidential rhetoric causes the electorate to shift their assessment of the office between power and accountability. Finally, he examines the presidencies of Ronald Reagan through Bill Clinton in light of this pattern.

Presidential Debates

Anderson, John B. *A Proper Institution: Guaranteeing Televised Presidential Debates.* Winchester, MA: Unwin Hyman, 1988.

The author maintains that the American political system needs to redevelop and reinforce its levels of representative accountability to the electorate. Anderson offers a systematic program for overhauling the way presidential debates are carried out to make candidates' statements and issue positions legitimate.

Bishop, George F., Robert G. Meadow, and Marilyn Jackson-Beeck, eds. *Presidential Debates: Media, Electoral, and Policy Perspectives.* New York: Praeger, 1978.

This volume collects various perspectives and research on the 1976 presidential debates. The authors discuss the selling of the debates, the effects of communications context, the behavioral and cognitive consequences of the debates, and the analysis of the debate contest. The work includes the transcripts of the 1976 presidential and vice presidential debates.

Bitzer, Lloyd, and Theodore Rueter. *Carter vs. Ford: The Counterfeit Debates of 1976.* Madison: University of Wisconsin Press, 1980.

The authors examine the debates between incumbent Gerald Ford and challenger Jimmy Carter during the 1976 presidential race. They discuss what was wrong with the Ford-Carter debates and how future debates can be improved. Bitzer and Rueter examine the campaign context, panelists, candidates, the questions asked, skills of verbal combat, argumentation, the defective debate format, and potential designs for future debate formats. They provide accurate and readable transcripts of the three presidential debates and the one vice presidential debate between Bob Dole and Walter Mondale.

Carlin, Diana B., and Mitchell S. McKinney, eds. *The 1992 Presidential Debates in Focus.* Westport, CT: Praeger, 1994.

This edited volume contains fourteen chapters on the 1992 presidential debates, including chapters on how the debates are structured and the impact of the debates. Chapters examine voter reactions to the debates, voter ambivalence, the gender gap, and the effect on students. The book concludes with a chapter on implications for future debates.

Friedenberg, Robert V., ed. *Rhetorical Studies of National Political Debates: 1960–1992.* 2d ed. Westport, CT: Praeger, 1994.

This edited volume on presidential debates brings together the thoughts and ideas of thirteen scholars of political communication and debate. It provides a systematic analysis of the ten series of national political debates held between 1960 and 1992. Each analysis addresses the factors motivating the candidate to debate, the goals of each candidate in debating, the rhetorical strategies used by each candidate, and the impact of the debate. The final chapter examines trends and patterns in the debates since 1960.

Hellweg, Susan A., Michael Pfau, and Steven R. Brydon. *Televised Presidential Debates: Advocacy in Contemporary America.* New York: Praeger, 1992.

The authors examine how television has fundamentally altered the way presidential debates are staged and conducted. Arguing that television is a medium unlike print, radio, or live performance, they maintain that presidential debates have taken on a conversational and interpersonal character. While image and style are important, the authors argue that verbal content also is important. They examine how television has shaped presidential debates in function, structure, message, image, and persuasive effects.

Hinck, Edward A. *Enacting the Presidency: Political Argument, Presidential Debates, and Presidential Character.* Westport, CT: Praeger, 1993.

The author argues that presidential debates yield four primary opportunities: to present a presidential image palpable to the public, to demonstrate Aristotelian political and rhetorical skills, to present an image through discourse, and to renew democratic and communal values. In sum, he claims that presidential candidates are required to perform as if they were president. Using five presidential debates and three vice presidential debates, the author examines the influence of candidate language and rhetoric and their effects on the public image of those candidates.

Jamieson, Kathleen H., and David S. Birdsell. *Presidential Debates: The Challenge of Creating an Informed Electorate.* New York: Oxford University Press, 1988.

Jamieson and Birdsell argue that presidential debates do not use their power to educate voters because of their confrontational style, the brevity of responses given by candidates, and the superficial coverage of a large number of issues. The authors examine voters' potential to learn more about specific public policies and issues if these problems are remedied by examining the origins and history of the presidential debate and its transformation with the onset of broadcast media. The authors also discuss the effects, power, problems, and promise of broadcasted presidential debates.

Kraus, Sidney, ed. *The Great Debates: Background, Perspective, Effects.* Bloomington: Indiana University Press, 1962.

This edited volume includes numerous articles by political scientists, journalists, and commentators on the 1960 presidential debates. They examine the background of the debates, such as the issues, personalities, and backstage conditions. They also examine the effects of the debates. The volume includes the texts of all four debates.

————, ed. *The Great Debates: Carter vs. Ford, 1976.* Bloomington: Indiana University Press, 1979.

This edited volume includes numerous articles by political scientists, journalists, and commentators on the 1976 presidential debates. They examine the background of the debates, such as the issues, personalities, and backstage conditions. They also examine the effects of the debates. The volume includes the texts of all four debates.

————. *Televised Presidential Debates and Public Policy.* 2d ed. Mahwah, NJ: L. Erlbaum Associates, 2000.

The author reviews what has been learned about televised presidential debates, evaluates their electoral impact, and projects possible policy influences. Kraus assesses the effects of televised politics on the electorate, offers a brief examination of four televised presidential debates, and evaluates the coverage, the effects, and the policy of debate in the context of campaigning.

Lanoue, David J., and Peter R. Schrott. *The Joint Press Conference: The History, Impact, and Prospects of American Presidential Debates.* Westport, CT: Greenwood, 1991.

The authors contend that—contrary to the traditional view—presidential debates do shape the electorate's preferences. Their model, based on quantitative data from content analysis and qualitative evaluations of presidential debates, accounts for the direct and indirect paths between voter preference and debate watching. Lanoue and Schrott offer a critical and analytical history of presidential debates, examine the content of presidential debates, and evaluate previous scholarly literature on the effects of debates since 1960.

League of Women Voters Educational Fund. *Presidential Debates: 1988 and Beyond.* Washington, DC: Congressional Quarterly, 1987.

This book is a comprehensive resource book on the status of presidential debates. It examines the various cultural, political, journalistic, and legal issues raised by debates. It contains annotated highlights of debate transcripts, all existing data about each broadcast debate from 1948 to 1984, and selected Gallup Poll results from 1960 to 1987. The book also examines issues and implications of political debates and debate sponsorship.

Lemert, James B., William R. Elliott, James M. Bernstein, William L. Rosenberg, and Karl J. Nestvold. *News Verdicts, the Debates, and Presidential Campaigns.* New York: Praeger, 1991.

The authors examine the influence that media verdicts on presidential and vice presidential debates have on voters' perceptions of the candidates. The book uses more than 2,000 survey interviews conducted after debates and uses a sophisticated time-series model to evaluate the media's influence on voter opinion. The authors conclude that voters tend to think that the candidate they preferred before the debate emerged as the victor.

Martel, Myles. *Political Campaign Debates: Images, Strategies, and Tactics.* New York: Longman, 1983.

The author analyzes the process of political debate in an historical and pragmatic manner that focuses on the strategies employed by participating candidates. Using a variety of sources, including oral histories, Congressional Debate Surveys, multimedia sources from forty-nine debates, and personal accounts from participants in the debate process, the author constructs an in-depth examination of the political debate process. Martel provides a case study of the 1980 presidential debates, the variables considered when deciding whether to participate in debates, candidates' goals and strategies, tactical options available to candidates, the format of political debate, and the media's discussions about the role of debates. He concludes with a set of recommendations for campaign strategists, candidates, and journalists that may improve the character of future political debates.

Ranney, Austin, ed. *The Past and Future of Presidential Debates.* Washington, DC: American Enterprise Institute for Public Policy Research, 1979.

This edited volume analyzes the arguments for and against mandatory nationally televised debates. The contributors discuss several issues, such as disputes over formats, the effect on voters, and legal obstacles. The book focuses on the 1976 presidential debates in particular but provides an historical overview of earlier debates.

Swerdlow, Joel L. *Beyond Debate: A Paper on Televised Presidential Debates.* New York: Twentieth Century Fund, 1984.

The author assembles data and insights from presidential elections from 1960 to 1980 to facilitate considering the consequences of debates and to seek means of improving them. He examines debate format, including single debates versus a series of debates, and the importance of face-to-face confrontations. He analyzes non-majority candidates' participation. Swerdlow examines why candidates commit themselves to debate, why they may resist debates, excuses they use, and what the debate sponsor can do to encourage candidates to debate. The author looks at the possible sponsors of debates, including television networks, other journalists, political parties, a federal debate commission, the Senate or House, and the League of Women Voters.

Twentieth Century Fund. *With the Nation Watching: Report of the Twentieth Century Task Force on Televised Presidential Debates.* Lexington, MA: Lexington Books, 1979.

This task force report deals with the role of television debates in political campaigning, and in particular with their importance in presidential elections. The task force finds two major problems. First, while a revolutionary change in political communication has resulted in television becoming the primary campaign medium, television's great promise to inform and involve the citizenry remains unfulfilled. Second, federal law and regulations on broadcast practices have restricted robust political debate on television during the formal election campaign, which is precisely the time it could be most beneficial. The report focuses on the 1960 and 1976 presidential debates in illustrating these problems, then makes recommendations to alleviate the problems. The report also includes a background paper examining the origins, history, and effects of campaign debates. Allocating responsibility for future debates, financing, candidate participation, and the role of minor party participation in debates are among the items considered in the background paper.

Congressional

Arico, Susan M. *Trends in the 1980 Congressional Elections: A Conference Report*. Washington, DC: Free Congress Research and Education Foundation, 1981.

This volume is the result of a four-day conference held by the Free Congress Foundation. The foundation invited seven campaigners to discuss what techniques succeeded and failed during the 1980 election cycle. The first chapter provides a general description of the seven districts, candidates, and key factors in the campaigns. The remaining two chapters go into more detail on the aid of attracting attention, both in primaries and elections, and the management and internal functions of running a successful campaign.

Clem, Alan L., comp. *The Making of Congressmen: Seven Campaigns of 1974*. North Scituate, MA: Duxbury Press, 1976.

This collaborative work examines congressional campaigns in Massachusetts, Ohio, Georgia, Wisconsin, South Dakota, Texas, and California in 1974. Each essay in this collection covers the mechanical questions of how and why political campaigns are conducted and why congressional electoral arrangements tend not to promote representative accountability. The book includes an introductory theoretical chapter on elections and representation and a concluding chapter that compares the cases.

Coffey, Wayne R. *How We Choose a Congress*. New York: St. Martin's, 1980.

The author describes how a politician pursues a seat in Congress. Coffey follows imaginary candidates for both the Senate and the House from the primaries through the elections. He describes all aspects of campaigning, including financing, staff organization, use of the media, and campaigning techniques in general. The volume also provides an excellent introduction to understanding Congress, as it details the structure and function of both chambers, the committee system, seniority, and the process by which a bill becomes a law.

Ginsberg, Benjamin, and Alan Stone, eds. *Do Elections Matter?* 3d ed. Armonk, NY: M. E. Sharpe, 1996.

The underlying question driving this edited volume is whether elections matter. In the first section, the authors examine the implications of the 1994 congressional elections. In the second section they provide a more general analysis of how elections can affect policy. Ginsberg and Stone focus on more general questions about the conditions under which elections are and are not likely to be important in the political process. In the third section the authors focus on the growing role of ideology in elections. This, in turn, has implications for how much elections matter.

Herrnson, Paul S. *Congressional Elections: Campaigning at Home and in Washington.* 2d ed. Washington, DC: CQ Press, 1998.

The author provides a comprehensive description of congressional elections. He focuses on congressional campaigns but also gives considerable attention to voters, candidates, governance, and campaign reform. Herrnson draws on surveys of and interviews with hundreds of candidates, campaign aides, party officials, political action committee managers, and political consultants. He concludes that the norms and expectations associated with congressional campaigns affect who runs, the kinds of organizations the candidates assemble, how much money they raise, and whether they win or lose. He also observes that candidates adopt different strategies to win votes in their home districts than to gain access to resources in Washington, DC.

Hinckley, Barbara. *Congressional Elections.* Washington, DC: CQ Press, 1981.

The author examines contemporary research on congressional elections. After establishing a framework for analyzing congressional elections, Hinckley looks at how voters receive and process information about the candidates and issues. She then examines the impact of incumbency and the influence of parties on electoral outcomes, the role of issues and candidate attributes, and the similarities and differences between midterm and presidential election years. In a concluding section, the author discusses the policy and research implications of her findings.

Huckshorn, Robert J., and Robert C. Spencer. *The Politics of Defeat: Campaigning for Congress.* Amherst: University of Massachusetts Press, 1971.

The authors offer a study of the losing candidates in a congressional election. They focus on the phenomenon of political defeat and the congressional campaign as a manifestation of a unique universe in politics. Huckshorn and Spencer survey the effects of party, recruitment, campaign techniques, and issues on election outcomes, and provide insights into why men and women seek high public office when chances of victory are remote.

Jacobson, Gary C. *The Politics of Congressional Elections.* 4th ed. New York: HarperCollins, 1997.

The author explores congressional election politics up to and including the 1994 elections. Jacobson discusses the legal and institutional context in which elections take place and examines candidates and campaigns, covering topics such as incumbency, the role of money in campaigns, and campaign strategies and tactics. He also looks at various aspects of congressional voting, including turnout, partisanship, and issues. Jacobson examines congressional elections as aggregate phenomena and discusses the relationship between elections and the politics of Congress. He concludes with an in-depth analysis of the Republican takeover of the House and Senate in 1994, a detailed examination of the new Republican majority's impact on congressional operations and reflections on the likely duration of its tenure.

Kazee, Thomas A., ed. *Who Runs for Congress? Ambition, Context, and Candidate Emergence.* Washington, DC: CQ Press, 1994.

This edited volume presents a series of case studies of candidate emergence in nine districts during the 1991–1992 election cycle. The book begins with a brief overview chapter that examines the emergence of congressional candidates. The chapters that follow examine: the process that led to the creation of a new African American majority district in North Carolina; candidate emergence in a majority Hispanic district in Texas; running for Congress in Virginia under the shadow of Washington, DC; vanishing candidates in a district in Colorado; challenging a strong incumbent in North Carolina's 9th District; old-style politics and invisible challengers in two Iowa districts; noncandidates in Oklahoma's 4th District; and a successful defense of weakened incumbency in a district in Illinois. The concluding chapter evaluates the case studies and discusses running for Congress as a strategic calculation.

Klinkner, Philip A., ed. *Midterm: The Elections of 1994 in Context.* Boulder, CO: Westview Press, 1994.

This edited volume examines the importance, reasons for, and effects of the Republican victory in the 1994 midterm elections. The first chapter places the 1994 election in perspective. Next, the Senate and House victories are examined separately, as qualitatively different phenomena. The election also is viewed as a loss by the Democratic Party. Klinkner examines the role of the Christian Right, campaign finance, the angry white male voter, and the possibility of realignment or dealignment in the South. He also re-explores the weak challenger hypothesis. The author ultimately finds the 1994 midterm election an innovative election as compared to other elections.

Morris, Dwight, and Murielle E. Gamache. *Gold-Plated Politics: The 1992 Congressional Races.* Washington, DC: CQ Press, 1994.

The authors analyze the role money played in the 1992 House and Senate races. Morris and Gamache examined every expenditure reported to the Federal Election Commission by the 933 candidates who sought congressional office in 1992, and they conducted hundreds of personal interviews with campaign staffers, political consultants, and candidates themselves. The result is a comprehensive analysis of campaign spending that reveals where funds come from and how they are spent. Phenomena analyzed along the way include the House freshmen, the Year of the Woman, the angry electorate, the role of political consultants, and campaign finance reform.

Silbey, Joel H., ed. *The United States Congress: The Electoral Connection, 1789–1989.* Brooklyn, NY: Carlson Publishing, 1991.

The articles in this edited volume address the nature and range of Congress's electoral connection. Authors address how popular elections shape Congress's central impulse and drive its behavior different moments. Each article provides a larger context for particular episodes, events, careers, pressures, and actions. Some of the essays recall an earlier world of partisan-determined elections, with occasional party realignments and their consequences. Other essays explore the new incumbency-driven world and its different behavior patterns.

House of Representatives

Brady, David W., John F. Cogan, and Douglas Rivers. *The 1996 House Elections: Reaffirming the Conservative Trend.* Stanford: Hoover Institution Press, 1997.

The authors assess the 1996 House elections. They find no evidence that House Republicans who lost were defeated because of their support for conservative votes. In fact, Republican winners had slightly more conservative voting records than did Republican losers. This pattern holds even when the analysis is confined to Republicans in moderate-to-liberal congressional districts. Likewise, the authors find no evidence that voting for the Contract with America harmed the reelection prospects of Republicans from moderate-to-liberal districts. Finally, they find no statistical evidence that organized labor's campaign had any impact on election outcomes involving Republican freshmen. The authors forecast continued Republican dominance of Congress for the remainder of the twentieth century.

Goldenberg, Edie N., et al. *Campaigning for Congress.* Washington, DC: CQ Press, 1984.

This volume is based on research conducted on eighty-six contested House races in 1978. The authors provide an overview of congressional campaigns, including the role of the mass media. They detail campaign strategies and tactics, including the roles of parties and issues, and examine the raising of money, patterns of campaign expenditures, and the use of money. The authors conclude with an analysis of voter response to campaigns and the electoral success of campaigns.

Sullivan, Gerald, and Michael Kenney. *The Race for the Eighth: The Making of a Congressional Campaign: Joe Kennedy's Successful Pursuit of a Political Legacy.* New York: Harper and Row, 1987.

The authors examine the 1986 primary race for the 8th Congressional District of Massachusetts between James Roosevelt and Joseph P. Kennedy II. An historically and economically important district, the primary proved to be one of the most informed, issue-oriented, and costly, races of the 1986 election year. The authors consider the events from Tip O'Neill's decision to retire and Joseph Kennedy's decision to enter the race through the immediate post-election victory. Appendixes provide information concerning other 8th District primary and election results, 1986 polls, campaign expenditures and contributions, and the demographic composition of the 8th District.

Senate

Abramowitz, Alan I., and Jeffrey A. Segal. *Senate Elections.* Ann Arbor: University of Michigan Press, 1992.

The authors contend that, because Senate elections are more competitive than House elections, the Senate is more responsive to shifts in the political climate. They focus on the 1974 Senate elections but also discuss earlier elections. The authors' model explains Senate election outcomes since World War II. Topics include a discussion of Robert Bork's rejection by the Senate, an analysis of voter behavior in Senate elections, an examination of the nomination process, presentation of three statistical models of Senate election outcomes, a discussion of campaign financing, and a look at four Senate campaigns that illustrate modern Senate elections.

Fenno, Richard F., Jr. *Learning to Legislate: The Senate Education of Arlen Specter.* Washington, DC: CQ Press, 1991.

The author provides a case study of one freshman senator, Republican Arlen Specter of Pennsylvania, and his first-term adjustment to the ways of the Senate. Fenno, who has produced a series of such profiles, maintains that the institution can be better understood by trying to see it through the eyes of its members. The centerpiece of this work is a detailed account of Specter's introduction, nurturing, and attempts to pass three crime-control bills. Fenno also devotes attention to Specter's successful campaigns for election and reelection to the Senate. The author paints a portrait of a modern Senate that is more egalitarian, outward-looking, and individualistic than it once was. He combines firsthand observation with ongoing interviews with Specter and his key staff.

———. *Senators on the Campaign Trail: The Politics of Representation.* Norman: University of Oklahoma Press, 1996.

The author presents a Senate campaign from the perspective of the candidate for the purpose of understanding representation. Fenno traveled with ten senators as they campaigned, focusing on pursuing a career, campaigning for office, and building constituency connections.

Haynes, George H. *The Election of Senators.* New York: Holt, 1906.

This volume is useful for the early history of the election of senators. The author discusses how senators were elected by state legislatures. He also discusses the movement for their popular election. Haynes discusses the arguments for and against popular elections of senators.

Hershey, Marjorie R. *Running for Office: The Political Education of Campaigners.* Chatham, NJ: Chatham House, 1984.

The author uses social learning theory to explain campaign behavior. She studies the experiences of six Senate incumbents targeted for defeat by pro-life groups. Hershey examines the journalistic record and draws on data from a series of interviews with important actors. Her research explores changing conditions in the modern campaign environment, details the strategies of antiabortion groups, and notes how Senate candidates reacted to their shifting surroundings. She concludes with a discussion of the implications of her findings for understanding campaigns in general and suggests ways to improve the quality of learning.

Kahn, Kim F., and Patrick J. Kenney. *The Spectacle of U.S. Senate Campaigns.* Princeton: Princeton University Press, 1999.

The authors discuss the nature of political campaigns and ways of measuring the content and consequences of campaigns. They examine candidates' campaign strategies, the news media's coverage of campaigns, citizen reactions to campaigns, and how voters make decisions in Senate campaigns.

Westlye, Mark C. *Senate Elections and Campaign Intensity.* Baltimore: Johns Hopkins University Press, 1991.

The author contends that Senate election outcomes in the same constituency can best be explained by variation in the amount and quality of information available to voters. Westlye uses content analysis of the journalistic record, state-level and national survey data, and detailed case studies of selected Senate campaigns to develop a measure of intensity that separates hard-fought and low-key Senate campaigns. He finds different patterns of information dissemination, candidate recognition, and subsequent voting behavior. In low-information contests voters tend to opt for the candidate they know. He concludes with an extended discussion of new directions for research in Senate elections, including suggestions for theoretical and methodological advancement, and a call for greater attention to the interaction between voters and candidates by looking beyond the static features of the political landscape.

5

Candidates

General

Asher, Herbert B. *Presidential Elections and American Politics: Voters, Candidates, and Campaigns since 1952.* 5th ed. Pacific Grove, CA: Brooks/Cole, 1992.

The author analyzes presidential elections from the perspectives of the candidate seeking support from the electorate and the citizen choosing among competing candidates. Asher views elections as an interplay between citizens and candidates, with each actor imposing constraints upon the other. In the first part of the book, Asher focuses on factors that influence citizens' voting choices and on conditions that affect candidates' strategic choices. In a section on citizens and elections, he examines the role of party identification and voting, the issue-voting controversy, and trends in voting behavior. Asher includes an election-by-election analysis of voting behavior from 1952 to 1988. In a section on candidates and elections, he focuses on the role of the media, political change and realignment, campaigning for the nomination, and running as the party standard-bearer.

Brown, William B. *The People's Choice: The Presidential Image in the Campaign Biography.* Baton Rouge: Louisiana State University Press, 1960.

The author explores the nature of the symbols that represent the electorate's ideals and beliefs about a presidential candidate. Brown discusses a variety of symbols focusing on the candidates' forebears, youth, military career, apprenticeship for statecraft, and the concept of being everyman.

Fishel, Jeff. *Party and Opposition: Congressional Challengers in American Politics.* New York: McKay, 1973.

The author examines the incentives offered by the major political parties to challengers for political office and the relation of these incentives to the future of the parties and the political system. Fishel profiles the challengers for House seats in 1964. He explores which challengers are most likely to succeed electorally and analyzes how successful challengers—House freshmen elected in 1964—reacted to their experience in the House, how the institution changed and failed to change them, and how they affected the policy outcomes of the legislative process though their first three terms.

Fowler, Linda L. *Candidates, Congress, and the American Democracy.* Ann Arbor: University of Michigan Press, 1993.

The author discusses the importance of candidates to our system of government. She argues that they provide both stability and change and have been an important force throughout American political history. Fowler traces the influence of candidates, focusing on Congress in particular.

Fowler, Linda L., and Robert D. McClure. *Political Ambition: Who Decides to Run for Congress.* New Haven: Yale University Press, 1989.

The authors use a case study of developments in New York's 30th Congressional District to illustrate the electoral consequences of the political reasoning of ambitious elites. Drawing mainly on information gathered in interviews with the principal actors, Fowler and McClure try to explain why some individuals choose to run for Congress while others opt not to. They suggest that the individualistic cast of the party system depends on ambitious individuals presenting themselves as eager rivals for elective office and that the continued health of the electoral system requires a sufficient supply of these men and women. The authors focus on what they call the unseen candidates—qualified individuals who nevertheless choose not to run—and the political and personal calculations that motivate their decisions.

Hacker, Kenneth L., ed. *Candidate Images in Presidential Elections.* Westport, CT: Praeger, 1995.

This edited volume presents major, varied approaches to studying candidate images. The book presents a history of how candidate images have progressed through the years. It proposes a cybernetic framework. The authors cover how candidate images relate to political socialization, communications, television debates, campaigns in general, and the role of interpersonal communication in presidential elections. The authors also explain the effects of political advertising on candidate images. The book also addresses research methodology, including chapters that show how meta-analysis can benefit candidate image researchers, explore the role of semantic differential measurement, and focus on intensive analysis, Rashomonian perspective, and linguistic discourse analysis.

Heale, M. J. *The Presidential Quest: Candidates and Images in American Political Culture, 1787–1852.* New York: Longman, 1982.

The author examines the history of American presidential elections from its beginning in 1787 to the 1850s. He discusses the rise of the party system, an active mass electorate, and national nominating conventions. Heale also examines the origins of image politics and the approach to campaigning taken by presidential candidates.

Krasno, Jonathan S. *Challengers, Competition, and Reelection: Comparing Senate and House Elections.* New Haven: Yale University Press, 1994.

The author argues that Senate elections are more competitive than House elections because Senate challengers are more likely to be experienced politicians. Krasno draws on the National Election Study to dispose of these explanations for senator vulnerability: that the public holds senators responsible for national policy development while it looks to representatives to provide district service; that districts are easier to represent because of their smaller populations; and that voters use different standards for House and Senate performance. The author contends that the reason senators lose more often than representatives do is the quality of their opponents.

Nimmo, Dan, and Robert L. Savage. *Candidates and Their Images: Concepts, Methods, and Findings.* Pacific Palisades, CA: Goodyear, 1976.

The authors employ a variety of research methods and techniques to examine how candidate image affects the electorate's preferences. Nimmo and Savage consider previous theories and studies that have attempted to address the role of candidate image in electoral politics. Maintaining that candidate image is multidimensional and that numerous variables may determine the image radiated by political candidates, the authors examine how styles of campaigning and candidate image affect strategic decision making by campaign leaders. In addition, the authors detail the media's influence on candidate image, the effect victory or defeat has on candidates following an election, and whether or not candidate image significantly affects voting behavior.

Pessen, Edward. *The Log Cabin Myth: The Social Backgrounds of the Presidents.* New Haven: Yale University Press, 1984.

The author examines the social backgrounds of presidents from George Washington to Ronald Reagan. He finds that most presidents were born to families at or near the top of the American social and economic order. Aided by these advantages, they forged successful presidential careers. Over time, the tendency to elect presidents from among the elite further widened the gulf between presidents and the populations they led. The evidence contradicts several enduring and widespread myths about the rise of ordinary Americans to the pinnacle of power.

Pierce, Roy. *Choosing the Chief: Presidential Elections in France and the United States.* Ann Arbor: University of Michigan Press, 1995.

This book is a systematic comparative study of how presidents are chosen in France and the United States. The author shows how the constitutional frameworks, electoral laws, party systems, social structures, and historical developments have produced presidential politics in the two countries. Pierce describes the basic institutional arrangements and reviews the succession of presidential contenders in each country. He examines candidate choice, split-ticket voting, presidential coattails, and midterm elections. He evaluates each country's system in historical perspective. Results are assessed by looking at popular satisfaction and how political results are affected by institutional arrangements. The appendixes include a survey of the French electorate, left-right scoring of French candidates and parties, sources of constituency-level electoral data, presidential electoral results from 1964 to 1992, and a copy of the original questionnaire Pierce used in France to gauge public opinion.

Sheehy, Gail. *Character: America's Search for Leadership*. New York: William Morrow, 1988.

The author examines the character and leadership potential of six presidential candidates in 1988. Sheehy uses evidence from research into the candidates' life histories and their conduct during the campaign to evaluate this elusive variable. The author examines Gary Hart, Michael Dukakis, Albert Gore, Jesse Jackson, George Bush, and Bob Dole. Sheehy also looks at the character of Ronald Reagan, the outgoing president, in an attempt to get beyond the public persona.

Stone, Irving. *They Also Ran: The Story of the Men Who Were Defeated for the Presidency*. Garden City, NY: Doubleday, Doran, 1943.

This volume presents a popular history of the candidates who ran for president and lost. The author discusses nineteen candidates who were defeated in their quest for the presidency in the years between 1824 and 1940.

Gender

Burrell, Barbara C. *A Woman's Place Is in the House: Campaigning for Congress in the Feminist Era*. Ann Arbor: University of Michigan Press, 1994.

The author examines the structural, societal, and systemic factors that have traditionally produced a dearth of women representatives in the House. Burrell investigates trends in political attitudes toward women as candidates and lawmakers, the numbers of women candidates for the House between 1968 and 1992, and their occupational status in comparison to that of men before their decision to run for office. She evaluates the structural constraints (political parties) that limit female participation; campaign experiences, such as contributions and voter response; the trends that have led to increased support of female candidates; and their status as policymakers and congressional candidates.

Carroll, Susan J. *Women as Candidates in American Politics*. 2d ed. Bloomington: Indiana University Press, 1994.

The author focuses on the circumstances facing candidates for public office, including election to congressional, statewide, and state legislative offices. Carroll examines aspects of women as candidates, including their recruitment, electoral outcome, political ambitions, and views on issues that are related to women.

Darcy, Robert E., Susan Welch, and Janet M. Clark. *Women, Elections, and Representation.* 2d ed. Lincoln: University of Nebraska Press, 1994.

The authors examine the phenomenon of female underrepresentation in political institutions. They employ surveys, aggregate data, and election returns to assess the causes of this underrepresentation. They find possible impediments to women's access to representative institutions, including voter prejudice, party leaders and other political elites, gender socialization, and institutional constraints (such as election structures, incumbency, and turnover rates). Darcy, Welch, and Clark's revised edition includes theoretical insights into the plight of women's representation in several advanced industrial democracies.

Fox, Richard L. *Gender Dynamics in Congressional Elections.* Thousand Oaks, CA: Sage, 1997.

The author examines how the presence of women candidates affects the electoral process. He analyzes the 1992 and 1994 congressional races in California, in which nineteen women were candidates for House seats. Fox compares and contrasts the experiences of the male and female candidates and discusses the different challenges that women candidates face.

Mandel, Ruth B. *In the Running: The New Woman Candidate.* New York: Ticknor and Fields, 1981.

The author shows that the campaign of a woman candidate differs from that of a male candidate. She covers more than seventy women running for office at federal, state, and local levels in 1976. By contextualizing the problems women face as political candidates in terms of the women's movement, the author evaluates the prospects for gender equity in public office.

Seltzer, Richard A., Jody Newman, and Melissa V. Leighton. *Sex as a Political Variable: Women as Candidates and Voters in U.S. Elections.* Boulder, CO: Lynne Rienner, 1997.

The authors examine the role of women in the electoral system. They begin by exploding ten myths about women in politics. Seltzer, Newman, and Leighton examine the electorate in terms of how men and women differ on issues and demographics. The authors discuss the gender gap and break down women's voting patterns by demographic group. The women's vote is considered an important percentage of the electorate. The authors find that when women run for office, they are as likely to win elections as are men. Gender is less an impediment to success than is incumbency. The authors also find that while women are slightly more likely than men to vote for women candidates, some percentage of women will vote against women candidates. The authors also engage in a multivariate analysis of women voters to better explain the gender gap. Finally, the authors examine the 1996 election to illustrate that the gender gap is not a chasm, as is often claimed.

Thomas, Sue, and Clyde Wilcox, eds. *Women and Elective Office: Past, Present, and Future.* New York: Oxford University Press, 1998.

This edited volume includes fourteen articles on various aspects of women and elective office. It includes chapters on campaign finance, political advertising, roll call voting behavior of women, and the representation of women's interests in the House. The volume also discusses the role of women in state legislatures.

Witt, Linda, Karen M. Paget, and Glenna Matthews. *Running as a Woman: Gender and Power in American Politics.* New York: Free Press, 1993.

The authors approach the subject of women running for and holding political office from a multidisciplinary standpoint that incorporates journalism, political science, and history. They maintain that the way female office-seekers approach politics has fundamentally shifted since the early 1970s. Witt, Paget, and Matthews contend that women candidates have changed their campaigning style from one that emphasized a woman's ability to do as well in office as a man to one that plays on gender issue differences. The authors interpret the 1990s as the beginning of a new era of gender politics.

Constituencies

Bernstein, Robert A. *Elections, Representation, and Congressional Voting Behavior: The Myth of Constituency Control.* Englewood Cliffs, NJ: Prentice-Hall, 1989.

The author sets out to debunk the rarely challenged myth that constituencies control the behavior of their elected representatives. He examines the logic undergirding this myth and then subjects it to empirical investigation using information drawn from survey data, election results, and congressional voting behavior. Bernstein looks at this question with respect to constituencies, citizens, and members of Congress. He finds that the representative's relationship has been fundamentally misstated to exaggerate and distort the role of constituents. He discusses the implications of his findings and suggests possible changes in the electoral system.

Cain, Bruce E., John A. Ferejohn, and Morris P. Fiorina. *The Personal Vote: Constituency Service and Electoral Independence.* Cambridge, MA: Harvard University Press, 1987.

The authors look at the interactions between constituents and their elected representatives in the United States and Great Britain. They analyze survey data gathered from 1978 to 1980 and aggregate electoral outcome information collected in hundreds of interviews to determine the nature of and motivations for constituency service and to identify changes since earlier studies conducted in the 1950s. The authors also examine constituent responses to member behavior, especially with respect to reelection. They conclude with a discussion of the implications of their findings for legislative behavior, job satisfaction, and political institutions.

Fenno, Richard F., Jr. *The Making of a Senator: Dan Quayle.* Washington, DC: CQ Press, 1989.

Written before Dan Quayle's bid for the office of vice president, this book chronicles Quayle's public and political life as a candidate and senator from Indiana. The book is part of a larger project in which Fenno observed senatorial campaigns from 1978 through 1986. The author's guiding question is to determine the relationship between senatorial activities in Washington and in the senators' home states. The book is organized into the patterns of behavior that Fenno observes among the senators he has studied: campaigning and adjustment, governing, and phases of campaigning. Issues of particular concern are Quayle's interpretation of his election to the Senate, an explanation of his legislative activities, the early adjustment period following his election, and the contextual framework within which Quayle made decisions.

Mayhew, David R. *Congress: The Electoral Connection.* New Haven: Yale University Press, 1974.

The author argues that the principal motivation of a member of Congress is reelection, and this affects his or her behavior and the structure and policy making of Congress. Mayhew groups the reelection activities of legislators into three categories: advertising the member's name to constituents through newsletters, press conferences, visits, and reports to the media; advertising the member by receiving credit for activities favoring constituents; and taking positions on policies and programs.

Incumbents

Fenno, Richard F., Jr. *When Incumbency Fails: The Senate Career of Mark Andrews.* Washington, DC: CQ Press, 1992.

The author analyzes the twenty-three year career of Senator Mark Andrews of North Dakota to examine why the incumbency effect did not hold in Andrew's final bid for reelection. Using his two-pronged theory of senatorial behavior (campaigning and governing both at home and abroad), Fenno attempts to explain Andrews's defeat in terms of generalizable variables: constituency size, previous election margins, challenger quality, national and local issue salience, policy- and candidate-centered variables, and campaigns. He also assesses the vulnerability of the candidates in this narrative account of Andrews's senatorial career.

Leuthold, David A. *Electioneering in a Democracy: Campaigns for Congress.* New York: Wiley, 1968.

The author constructs a comparative study of electoral constituencies with special attention to the problem of acquiring campaign resources. Topics addressed include candidacy, party, issues, support of typically nonpolitical groups, money, and people. The author examines ten districts in 1962 that border San Francisco Bay to study the effects of incumbency and resource competition among congressional candidates. Using a variety of resources, including candidate observation, interviews with members of the campaigns, the literature and advertising of the campaigns, questionnaires, and financial reports, Leuthold finds that incumbency increases the probability of successful congressional bids and concludes that this does not bode well for democratic politics.

Mann, Thomas E. *Unsafe at Any Margin: Interpreting Congressional Elections.* Washington, DC: American Enterprise Institute for Public Policy Research, 1978.

The author refines voting behavior theory in congressional elections in an age of incumbent reelection. Mann uses data from forty congressional districts surveyed by the Democratic Study Group in the 1974 and 1976 elections. Mann focuses on the candidate rather than national tides. He finds candidate preference is more consistently related to the voter's choice than to the voter's party identification.

Merriner, James L., and Thomas P. Senter. *Against Long Odds: Citizens Who Challenge Congressional Incumbents.* Westport, CT: Praeger, 1999.

The authors discuss why incumbents almost always win a return to their seats in the Senate or House. Merriner and Senter present fourteen races that show the advantages that congressional incumbents have in an election, and the struggles that challengers face.

6

Campaign Finance

General

Adamany, David W. *Campaign Finance in America*. North Scituate, MA: Duxbury Press, 1972.

The author examines campaign finance using a combination of resource theory and incentive and exchange theory. Adamany compares campaign finance in Connecticut and Wisconsin, examining the role of money in party politics, the different sources of funds, and spending strategies of the aspirants for office. He redefines issues raised by private political finance and critiques proposals for reform.

Alexander, Herbert E. *Financing Politics: Money, Elections, and Political Reform*. 4th ed. Washington, DC: CQ Press, 1992.

The author traces the history of campaign finance law and examines recent controversial trends: the proliferation of political action committees, the use of soft-money donations from wealthy contributors, and the effects of independent expenditures made on behalf of or against candidates. Alexander includes information pertaining to the 1988 presidential election and the 1988 and 1990 congressional elections.

———. *Money in Politics*. Washington, DC: Public Affairs Press, 1972.

The author provides an overview of money and politics. Alexander identifies sources of campaign funds, the uses of money by candidates and committees, and the advantages and disadvantages that accrue to the political system as a result of the patterns of raising and spending money. He uses data from elections at local, state, and national levels to examine these topics. Alexander examines attempts to regulate the role of money in politics and campaign finance reform. He describes legal regulation in the states, the Federal Corrupt Practices Act of 1925, and the history of reform, and he evaluates the provisions of the Revenue Act of 1971 and the Federal Election Campaign Act of 1972.

Donnelly, David, Janice Fine, and Ellen S. Miller. *Money and Politics: Financing Our Elections Democratically.* Boston: Beacon Press, 1999.

The authors argue that only full public funding of campaigns can ensure democratic elections. The volume includes seven responses to Donnelly, Fine, and Miller from activists, scholars, and politicians. A response from Senator Russell Feingold discusses the status of the McCain-Feingold Act.

Drew, Elizabeth. *Whatever It Takes: The Real Struggle for Political Power in America.* New York: Viking Books, 1997.

The author discusses campaign spending in the 1996 presidential and congressional elections. She examines how parties and interest groups struggle to control the House agenda to win the presidential election. She describes how activists use improper strategies to obtain the necessary political power to win. Drew also offers suggestions about campaign finance reform.

Green, John, ed. *Financing the 1996 Election.* Armonk, NY: M. E. Sharpe, 1999.

The authors in this collection of essays look at campaign spending, financing the 1996 elections, regulation, the role of interest and advocacy groups, the role of individual donors, campaign laws, and campaign finance.

Gunlicks, Arthur B., ed. *Campaign and Party Finance in North America and Western Europe.* Boulder, CO: Westview Press, 1993.

The author examines and compares campaign and party finance practices in North America and Europe, including Great Britain, France, Germany, Austria, and Sweden. Gunlicks examines European campaign and party financing practices and contrasts them with the American emphasis on candidate financing.

Malbin, Michael J., ed. *Money and Politics in the United States: Financing Elections in the 1980s.* Washington, DC: American Enterprise Institute for Public Policy Research, 1984.

This edited volume addresses the effects of extensive changes in campaign finance laws made during the 1970s. Three chapters focus on specific campaigns: the 1980 presidential campaigns, congressional elections of 1980 and 1982, and state campaigns for governor, state legislature, and ballot issues in 1980 and 1982. Another three chapters concentrate on organizational developments in political parties and political action committees. A seventh chapter surveys major court cases of the 1970s and 1980s that could have dramatic consequences in future elections. The final chapter looks ahead to future research and the potential effects of proposals for further changes in the law.

Nugent, Margaret L., and John R. Johannes, eds. *Money, Elections, and Democracy: Reforming Congressional Campaign Finance.* Boulder, CO: Westview Press, 1990.

The editors bring together scholarly research on the ongoing controversy over congressional campaign finance. Opening chapters provide an overview of the main issues. Succeeding chapters address topics such as problems arising from the source of campaign funding, the undesirable consequences of the campaign finance system, and difficulties with reforming the current system. Further topics include the use of independent expenditures, the advantages of incumbency, the relationship of political action committees to the parties, public opinion on campaign finance, and the weakness of the Federal Election Commission. The concluding chapter presents the editors' views regarding congressional campaign finance reform and the preservation of a representative democracy.

Sabato, Larry J. *Paying for Elections: The Campaign Finance Ticket.* New York: Priority Press, 1989.

Operating from the premise that it is necessary to identify real and apparent political corruption, the author targets campaign financing as a real cause of public dissatisfaction with politics. Sabato proposes specific policy recommendations to remedy problems such as those associated with political action committees, a relative decline of partisan politics, fewer truly competitive elections, and increasing campaign costs.

Thayer, George. *Who Shakes the Money Tree? American Campaign Financing Practices from 1789 to the Present.* New York: Simon and Schuster, 1974.

The author examines how money has been raised and spent in political elections from 1789 to the 1970s, with particular emphasis on developments since 1945. He concentrates on presidential, House, Senate, and certain gubernatorial and mayoral races. Thayer's purpose is to show, not only who gives the money, who raises it, and how it is spent, but also to examine why people give, what they give, what they expect to get, what they actually get, the techniques of raising and spending money, the nature of campaign financing law and attitudes toward it, and changing styles in the reaction to campaign financing practices.

Presidential

Alexander, Herbert E. *Financing the 1960 Election.* Princeton: Citizens' Research Foundation, 1962.

The author examines the voting and financing trends of the 1960 presidential election. The book's sections cover preconvention campaigns, financing the conventions, general election campaigns, sources of funds, the influence of business and labor, and the postelection period. Alexander also addresses future issues of party and public policy. Appendixes offer detailed information on presidential campaign expenditures for the 1960 election year.

————. *Financing the 1964 Election.* Princeton: Citizens' Research Foundation, 1966.

The author examines the voting and financing trends of the 1964 presidential election in the second of his series on campaign financing. The book's sections cover preconvention campaigns, financing the conventions, general election campaigns, sources of funds, the influence of business and labor, and the postelection period. Appendixes offer detailed statistical information on the 1964 presidential campaign expenditures.

————. *Financing the 1968 Election.* Lexington, MA: Lexington Books, 1971.

The author examines the voting and financing trends of the 1968 presidential election in the third of his series on campaign financing. He explains the Democratic loss in terms of its inability to match the money raised and spent by the Republicans. The 1968 election was the most expensive presidential campaign up to this point because of increased campaign costs in the areas of travel, polling, computers, and broadcast advertising. Alexander also maintains that the heated prenomination contests in both parties resulted in excessive spending. The book's sections cover prenomination campaigns, financing the conventions, general election campaigns, sources of funds, the influence of external actors, and the postelection period. Appendixes offer detailed statistical information on the 1968 presidential campaign expenditures.

————. *Financing the 1972 Election.* Lexington, MA: Lexington Books, 1976.

The author examines the voting and financing trends of the 1972 presidential election in the fourth of his series on campaign financing. Alexander discusses campaign funds in the 1972 presidential campaign. He provides a history of the Federal Election Campaign Act of 1971 and the effects of Watergate on campaign finance financing of the prenomination campaigns, the general election campaigns, and the conventions. Alexander examines business and labor in politics and the sources of funds for presidential campaigns.

————. *Financing the 1976 Election.* Washington, DC: CQ Press, 1979.

The author examines the voting and financing trends of the 1976 presidential election in the fifth of his series on campaign financing. The book's sections cover the impact of new laws since the last election, the role of the Federal Election Commission, campaign spending in the 1976 election, the prenomination campaigns, financing the conventions, general election campaigns, specialized expenditures, sources of funds, the influence of business and labor in politics, reform, and the postelection period. Two appendixes offer detailed statistical information on the 1976 presidential campaign expenditures and summaries of four major pieces of campaign finance legislation from 1971 to 1976.

————. *Financing the 1980 Election.* Lexington, MA: Lexington Books, 1983.

This book is Alexander's sixth text on campaign finance in presidential elections using data gathered by the Citizens' Research Foundation. While this study focuses on the presidential campaign, some attention is paid to various aspects of congressional elections. Alexander addresses subjects such as campaign finance reforms, funding sources, and campaign and convention expenses. He assesses the aftermath of the 1980 election. The book discusses Congress most directly in the sections of independent expenditures, public financing, campaign finance reform, and spending by party committees.

Alexander, Herbert E., and Monica Bauer. *Financing the 1988 Election.* Boulder, CO: Westview Press, 1991.

This book is Alexander's eighth text on campaign finance using data gathered by the Citizens' Research Foundation. The authors devote one chapter exclusively to issues of campaign finance in House and Senate elections, including a section on token challengers to incumbents in both houses of Congress. Alexander and Bauer also discuss congressional elections in relation to the roles of soft money and independent expenditures in relation to proposed electoral reforms. Their research reveals that more than $2.7 billion was spent during the 1988 election cycle; this represents a 50 percent increase over the previous cycle, topping all previous records.

Alexander, Herbert E., and Anthony Corrado. *Financing the 1992 Election.* Armonk, NY: M. E. Sharpe, 1995.

Alexander's ninth quadrennial book on the financing of presidential-year elections, this volume includes a wealth of data on campaign spending and financing. Alexander and Corrado discuss the prenomination campaigns of all candidates and the financing of the national conventions and general campaigns. They also discuss Senate and House financing, political action committee trends, use of soft money, possible campaign reforms, and postelection trends.

Alexander, Herbert E., and Brian A. Haggerty. *Financing the 1984 Election.* Lexington, MA: Lexington Books, 1987.

Alexander's seventh text on campaign finance focuses primarily on the financing of the 1984 presidential election campaign. Alexander and Haggerty include some discussion of both House and Senate 1984 campaign expenditures. The authors offer data gathered by the Citizens' Research Foundation and the Federal Election Commission. They also examine election law, exploring topics such as legislative efforts at reform in Congress and the workings of the Federal Election Commission.

Bennett, W. Lance. *The Governing Crisis: Media, Money, and Marketing in American Elections.* 2d ed. New York: St. Martin's, 1996.

The author examines how new technologies are changing the nature of democratic government. He examines in depth three themes that help to explain the crisis in governing: media, money, and marketing. Bennet uses the 1988 and 1992 presidential campaigns to discuss the origins and workings of the electoral system. The author also investigates the policy-election-leadership connection, using analyses of the 1994 midterm elections.

Brown, Clifford W., Jr., Lynda W. Powell, and Clyde Wilcox. *Serious Money: Fundraising and Contributing in Presidential Nomination Campaigns.* New York: Cambridge University Press, 1995.

The authors provide a detailed analysis of the relationship between fundraising methods and contributing decisions in presidential campaigns. They use the 1988 and 1992 presidential campaigns as examples and discuss the differences between direct-mail solicitation and personal solicitation. Brown, Powell, and Wilcox analyze candidate resources for fundraising, such as home-state power bases, access to national party networks, and congressional office. They also examine the motives of contributors.

Corrado, Anthony. *Paying for Presidents: Public Financing in National Elections.* New York: Twentieth Century Fund, 1993.

The author explores some of the major developments in public financing to increase our understanding of the effects of the law and highlight some of the major issues. Corrado seeks to provide a foundation for assessing alternatives for further reform and the future direction of campaign finance regulation. He documents considerable weaknesses in the way the process has been operating, yet he remains convinced of the value of the public financing approach. The author examines in detail financing both primary and general election campaigns, especially in light of the 1992 election.

Sorauf, Frank J. *Inside Campaign Finance: Myths and Realities.* New Haven: Yale University Press, 1992.

The author explores the dynamics and consequences of campaign finance and explodes the myths about this widely debated subject. He examines the period from 1907 through Watergate and explores the reforms that resulted from the Nixon era and those of subsequent years. He also focuses on the sources and sums of campaign finance. Sorauf examines the organizational factors driving campaign finance and the reform efforts and discusses campaign finance in the context of the 1992 presidential election.

Congressional

Drew, Elizabeth. *Politics and Money: The New Road to Corruption.* New York: Macmillan, 1983.

The author examines the role of money in politics. She concentrates on the effects on candidates and the political system of raising the requisite sums of money to run an effective campaign. Her research indicates that the real and imagined pressure to raise large amounts of money (and prevent large amounts from being spent by the opposition) has become a full-time preoccupation on Capitol Hill. Before turning her attention to proposed reforms, Drew examines the sources of campaign funding, the influence they can exert on legislators, and their effects on legislative behavior and the legislative process.

Fritz, Sara, and Dwight Morris. *Gold-Plated Politics: Running for Congress in the 1990s.* Washington, DC: CQ Press, 1993.

The authors offer an overview of the current campaign spending system and analyze what this system means to candidates running for Congress in the 1990s. Fritz and Morris focus on where campaign money comes from and where it goes. They discuss campaign costs, political machines, challengers, consultants, television, fundraising, political action committees, and campaign finance reform.

Goidel, Robert K., Donald A. Gross, and Todd G. Shields. *Money Matters: Consequences of Campaign Finance in U.S. House Elections.* New York: Rowman and Littlefield, 1999.

The authors examine the effects of campaign finance reform on partisan control of the House and the effect of campaign finance reform on electoral competition, voter turnout, and voter information. They also discuss excessive spending, candidate viability, and free speech. The authors conclude with ideas for improving the electoral process through reform.

Jacobson, Gary C. *Money in Congressional Elections.* New Haven: Yale University Press, 1980.

The author explains how campaign spending, especially by challengers, influences congressional elections. He analyzes data from postcampaign finance reform election cycles using multiple regression to test competing models that explain electoral outcomes. Jacobson examines campaign contributions from the perspective of the motives and strategies of those giving money and from the perspective of the candidates who receive the funds. A simultaneous equation model that accounts for reciprocal causation suggests that spending by nonincumbents is the critical variable. The author uses this finding to assess the effects of proposed and previously passed reforms, concluding that their net result has been to decrease electoral competitiveness.

Makinson, Larry. *The Price of Admission: Campaign Spending in the 1994 Elections.* Washington, DC: Center for Responsive Politics, 1995.

This book is a guide to the money that drove the congressional elections of 1994. It contains more than 1,500 charts and graphs that illustrate the patterns behind the flow of money from industries and interest groups to members of Congress. The book includes miniprofiles showing the primary sources of campaign money for every member of Congress elected in 1994; information on the spreading patterns of political action committees in the 1994 election, broken down by industry and group; and big-picture patterns that show the role that money played in the congressional elections in the Republican sweep of 1994.

McKeough, Kevin L. *Financing Campaigns for Congress: Contribution Patterns of National-Level Party and Non-Party Committees, 1964.* Princeton: Citizens' Research Foundation, 1970.

The author describes the extent of monies reported by national-level party, labor, and miscellaneous committees as contributed to candidates in the 1964 campaigns for House and Senate seats. He analyzes the considerations that determine recipients and amounts. McKeough finds that since 1964 the national-level funds have become increasingly important elements in the financing of a congressional campaign.

Theilmann, John M., and Allen Wilhite. *Discrimination and Congressional Campaign Contributions.* New York: Praeger, 1991.

The authors examine the influence of money on the election of African American and female candidates to the House in the 1980s, a period when these candidates were exercising greater political clout and when campaign finance regulations were in transition. Theilmann and Wilhite provide a historical overview of the changing political outlook for African Americans and women and explore the impact of money on congressional elections. They combine their historical and narrative approach with a theoretical exploration of campaign decisions grounded in a statistical analysis of contributions by parties, individuals, and political action committees. A concluding chapter offers some informed predictions about the future for African American and female congressional candidates.

Interest Groups

Baker, Ross K. *The New Fat Cats: Members of Congress as Political Benefactors.* New York: Priority Press Publications, 1989.

The author examines the phenomenon of leadership political action committees (PACs), which are organized by members of Congress to aid present or potential colleagues. Increasingly, legislators with surplus campaign funds and little opposition use these PACs to donate money to more hard-pressed candidates, most often to achieve elective party leadership posts or greater influence within the chamber. Baker uses data from the Federal Election Commission, congressional scholarship, and the journalistic record to determine the effects of these PACs on the political process. He finds that they tend to further decentralize party power in Congress; however, they also attract money from unconventional sources and disburse it more readily to challengers than does the average PAC. The author concludes with a discussion of possible reforms in this area.

Biersack, Robert, Paul S. Herrnson, and Clyde Wilcox, eds. *Risky Business: PAC Decisionmaking in Congressional Elections.* Armonk, NY: M. E. Sharpe, 1994.

This edited volume contains articles that provide an in-depth analysis of nineteen political action committees (PACs) and their organization and behavior during the 1992 congressional elections. The book comprises three sections in which PACs are grouped into general categories: opinion leaders, highly influential and powerful, and moderately influential. The editors highlight the similarities and differences among the various types, organizations, and sizes of PACs. Appendixes include details of PAC contributions and expenditures for seven congressional races before and including the 1992 election.

Clawson, Dan, Alan Neustadtl, and Denise Scott. *Money Talks: Corporate PACs and Political Influence.* New York: Basic Books, 1992.

The authors examine more than 300 political action committees (PACs) and include material collected through surveys of and interviews with corporate executives to evaluate the influence of corporate PACs on American politics. Clawson, Neustadtl, and Scott normatively oppose PAC activity because of its erosion of democratic practices. They attempt to address the pluralist counterargument that might be made against their claims.

Clawson, Dan, Alan Neustadtl, and Mark Weller. *Dollars and Votes: How Business Campaign Contributions Subvert Democracy.* Philadelphia: Temple University Press, 1998.

The authors draw heavily from their interviews with corporate government-relations officials about what they do and how they do it. They discuss loopholes in the system, the nature of gifts, the role of soft money in campaigns, political action committees (PACs), and how these processes subvert the democratic ideal.

Corrado, Anthony. *Creative Campaigning: PACs and the Presidential Selection Process.* Boulder, CO: Westview Press, 1992.

The author argues that the 1974 Federal Election Campaign Act failed because it produced a set of conflicting demands on presidential contenders. Candidates were encouraged to limit spending while simultaneously increasing the length of their campaigns. Corrado maintains that candidates were structurally forced to seek additional and creative funding sources, such as precandidacy political action committees (PACs). The author examines the evolution of organizational and financial constraints to explain the outcomes of the 1984, 1988, and 1992 presidential elections. He predicts similarly lengthy and costly campaigns to characterize the 1996 election.

Eismeier, Theodore J., and Philip H. Pollock III. *Business, Money, and the Rise of Corporate PACs in American Elections.* Westport, CT: Quorum Books, 1988.

The authors propose a model of the organizational and political behavior of corporate interests. They argue that corporate political action committees (PACs) are best understood as groups whose behavior is influenced by ideological, structural, and environmental forces. Eismeier and Pollock examine PACs and the politics of regulation. Next they focus on the political geography of corporate PACs. Finally, they consider PACs and the campaign environment. The authors argue that the future role of the political money of business will depend both on the course of public policy and on the parrying of the national parties.

Gais, Thomas L. *Improper Influence: Campaign Finance Law, Political Interest Groups, and the Problem of Equality.* Ann Arbor: University of Michigan Press, 1996.

The author argues that even though interest-group politics is regulated and constrained, much dissatisfaction continues with interest groups' role in campaign financing because current laws prevent many hard-to-organize citizen groups—but not business groups—from forming effective political action committees (PACs). Gais points out that many of the laws that regulate group involvement in elections ignore the difficulties of political mobilization and concludes that PACs and the campaign finance laws reflect a discrepancy between grassroots ideals and ways in which broadly based groups get organized.

Godwin, R. Kenneth. *One Billion Dollars of Influence: The Direct Marketing of Politics.* Chatham, NJ: Chatham House, 1988.

The author maintains that direct marketing techniques and mass mailings from political action committees (PACs), interest groups, and politicians have fundamentally transformed politics and political fundraising. Godwin examines the technological breakthroughs that allow for political mass mailings, criticisms of direct marketing, the content of the mailings, and the possible positive implications this has for democratic politics. Using samples of direct mailings, questionnaire responses from citizen action groups, and interviews with party leaders, PAC members, and interest groups, the author traces the evolution of this political technique and evaluates its significance.

Green, Mark J., and Michael Waldman. *Who Runs Congress?* 4th ed. New York: Dell, 1984.

The authors describe and document the negative influence of special-interest money in campaign finance. They blame excessive funding from political action committees (PACs) for concentrating power in the hands of corporations and draining it away from party and committee leaders in Congress, resulting in poor public policy and institutional paralysis. This scathing account of the seamy side of Congress catalogs illegal activities by individual members, questionable behavior on public policy questions, and the advantages members exploit in seeking reelection. In addition to decrying the contemporary functioning of Congress through anecdotal and statistical evidence, Green and Waldman offer some practical advice for citizen action and provide an appendix pointing to sources of information on Congress.

Handler, Edward, and John R. Mulkern. *Business in Politics: Campaign Strategies of Corporate Political Action Committees.* Lexington, MA: Lexington Books, 1982.

The authors examine the financial activities and internal organizational behavior of political action committees (PACs) during the 1978 and 1980 congressional elections. The authors find through a consideration of their expenditure patterns that PACs attempt to access as many incumbents as possible. In addition, PACs behave rationally when engaging in fundraising activities and seek not to alienate potential contributors with their policy stances. Handler and Mulkern also look at PACs' decision-making processes and evaluate the future influence of PACs on the electoral process.

Rozell, Mark J., and Clyde Wilcox. *Interest Groups in American Campaigns: The New Face of Electioneering.* Washington, DC: CQ Press, 1999.

The authors cover the growing influence that interest groups have on the electoral process. Using their research, interviews with interest group leaders, surveys, and coverage of campaign finance filings, Rozell and Wilcox offer their perspective on the roles that interest groups play in elections.

Sabato, Larry J. *PAC Power: Inside the World of Political Action Committees.* New York: W. W. Norton, 1984.

The author evaluates the issues behind the political debates over the role of political action committees (PACs) in electoral politics. Relying on a series of interviews with PAC members and party officials and a survey of 399 PACs, the author examines pre- and post-PAC political institutions, the internal machinations of PACs, and their decision-making processes. In addition, Sabato explores the role of PACs after the election, the relationships between political parties and PACs, and the potential ramifications PACs may have for the political system.

Stern, Philip M. *Still the Best Congress Money Can Buy.* Rev. ed. Washington, DC: Regnery Gateway, 1992.

In this revised edition Stern decries the influence of special interest money on campaigns and lawmaking and provides an action-oriented conclusion with suggestions for reform. Stern also explains how political action committees (PACs) operate, interviews current and former members of Congress, and discusses how present reform laws are easily skirted. Statistical anecdotal evidence supports his case. Stern concludes with a call for public financing to end a system he views as promoting legalized bribery. Appendixes present detailed information about each member of the House and Senate and a list of the 100 biggest PACs in the 1990 elections.

Reform

Adamany, David W., and George E. Agree. *Political Money: A Strategy for Campaign Financing in America.* Baltimore: Johns Hopkins University Press, 1975.

The authors examine the current state of campaign finance rules and propose a series of thoughtful and creative reforms. Accounting for the ramifications of the 1971 Federal Election Campaign Act and other federal reforms, the authors propose reforms blended from fundamentally different points of origin. They suggest encouraging volunteerism through a voucher system that would encourage participation in a more vigorous democratic politics and result in a flat and proportional grant system for financing political campaigns at different levels of government.

Kubiak, Greg D. *The Gilded Dome: The U.S. Senate and Campaign Finance Reform.* Norman: University of Oklahoma Press, 1994.

The author describes congressional attempts at campaign finance reform from 1985 to 1992. Reformers had to overcome both congressional self-interest and the power of special interests. Kubiak offers an account of the struggles of Senator David Boren (D-Okla.) to enact reform legislation and looks at the roles played by the media, lobbyists, and political party officials.

Magleby, David B., and Candice J. Nelson. *The Money Chase: Congressional Campaign Finance Reform.* Washington, DC: Brookings Institution, 1990.

The authors explore the role of money in congressional campaigns: where it comes from, how it is spent, and who oversees its use. Magleby and Nelson then discuss the likely partisan and institutional consequences of proposed reforms. They suggest a package of integrated reforms that recognizes the differences between the House and Senate and emphasizes bipartisanship. Magleby and Nelson evaluate reforms in the light of historical experience, the reported judgment of influential participants in the current system, and perceived political realities. Individual chapters address the role of political action committees, political parties, and the Federal Election Commission in campaign finance.

Mutch, Robert E. *Campaigns, Congress and Courts: The Making of Federal Campaign Finance Law.* New York: Praeger, 1988.

The author provides a detailed history of campaign finance regulation from 1904 to the 1980s. He discusses topics such as the development of and ideological debates over contribution and expenditure limits; focusing special attention on independent expenditures; the functioning of the Federal Election Commission; the politics of congressional passage of public financing in the 1970s; and the perennial conflict between business and labor.

7

Media Coverage

General

Adatto, Kiku. *Picture Perfect: The Art and Artifice of Public Image Making.* New York: Basic Books, 1993.

The author examines the rise in importance of the image in American society, from its inception in photographic stills to more advanced forms in film. She argues that the image is replacing the word as content in communication about human events, especially in the political arena. The epilogue reiterates findings of a previous consideration of television images in the 1972 and 1992 presidential campaigns.

Diamond, Edwin, and Robert A. Silverman. *White House to Your House: Media and Politics in Virtual America.* Cambridge, MA: MIT Press, 1995.

The authors trace the technological developments that have fundamentally transformed politics into a form of entertainment. They analyze political campaigns and candidates as they have harnessed the technological media available to them to garner political support, and the period of governance that transpires between elections (the perpetual campaign). Diamond and Silverman claim that individual technological access has created an active electorate that discusses and trades political information. The authors conclude that modern technology has "resuscitated a kind of Know-Nothing populism."

Kaid, Lynda L., and Dianne G. Bystrom. *The Electronic Election: Perspectives on the 1996 Campaign Communication.* Mahwah, NJ: L. Erlbaum Associates, 1999.

This edited volume presents a collection of articles that focus on electronic communication in the 1996 campaign. The articles examine topics such as advertising, convention appearances, Internet sites, communication through the news, and debates. The first part of the volume examines media coverage and use in the campaign. The second part of the volume looks at messages from the candidates to the voters.

Lichter, S. Robert, and Richard E. Noyes. *Good Intentions Make Bad News: Why Americans Hate Campaign Journalism.* 2d ed. Lanham, MD: Rowman and Littlefield, 1995.

The authors bring together important findings from a large body of data about national political news accumulated from 1987 through 1995. Most of this material consists of content analyses of 1987–1988 and 1991–1992 election news coverage on the network newscasts. These analyses monitor and code candidate appearances on political news shows. They also track CNN and PBS broadcast coverage and print accounts from the *New York Times, Washington Post,* and *Wall Street Journal.* Lichter and Noyes collect and analyze the candidates' general election speeches and campaign advertisements. The authors argue that journalists' efforts to intervene more actively in the campaign process produced unintended consequences that proved detrimental to both journalism and the electoral system.

Mickelson, Sig. *From Whistle Stop to Sound Bite: Four Decades of Politics and Television.* New York: Praeger, 1989.

The author examines the evolution of political campaigns and traces those trends that paralleled or were caused by the influence of television on campaign method. This shift toward televised campaigning has required candidates to use new talents, decreased the influence of party organization, and increased the importance of advertising agencies and consultants to the process of electioneering.

Mondak, Jeffery J. *Nothing to Read: Newspapers and Elections in a Social Experiment.* Ann Arbor: University of Michigan Press, 1995.

The author centers his discussion on the intersection of media and politics. The Pittsburgh newspaper strike during the 1992 general election season provides a unique context in which to assess the significance of local newspapers for electoral behavior. The author examines how voters reacted when this vital source of information was no longer available. He compares the reactions of Pittsburgh voters with those of voters in Cleveland, who did have access to newspapers during this time span. Mondak employs a quasi-experimental design to test his hypotheses. He explores the connection between local newspapers and political knowledge and the effect newspapers have on voting behavior. The author concludes that local newspapers, and the media in general, are important to voting behavior, but that when deprived of these resources, voters will seek other sources of political information.

Patterson, Thomas E. *Out of Order.* New York: Alfred A. Knopf, 1993.

The author's thesis is that the United States cannot have a sensible political campaign as long as the campaign is built around the news media. Patterson asks how the presidential selection system has come to be centered on the news media, explains why such a process cannot serve the nation's needs, and suggests what might be done to put campaigning on a sound footing. The author concludes that attempts to convince the press to behave differently can have only a marginal influence on the quality of the campaign.

Robinson, Michael J., and Austin Ranney, ed. *The Mass Media in Campaign '84: Articles from Public Opinion Magazine.* Washington, DC: American Enterprise Institute for Public Policy Research, 1985.

This collection of articles, originally published in *Public Opinion,* challenge many widely held views about the media's role in the electoral system. Some of the findings include: paid political advertisements had almost no effect on the 1984 Democratic presidential primaries; candidates who spent the most on primary campaigning usually lost; network news showed almost no political bias in covering campaign issues; less is spent per voter on campaigns in the United States than in most other democracies; and the American people have not turned against the media in the 1980s.

Wyckoff, Gene. *The Image Candidates: American Politics in the Age of Television.* New York: Macmillan, 1968.

The author examines how television has affected electoral politics. Wyckoff offers a discussion of party loyalty, campaign issues, and candidate images, and how the three affect voting. He explains how television affects these factors, thus indirectly influencing voting behavior. Wyckoff chronicles the adventures of an image specialist who worked on the 1960 Richard Nixon campaign. He presents a case study of candidate image in New York City in 1961. The author examines television coverage bias of the primaries there, parallel newspaper coverage, the postprimary campaign, and the outcome of the mayoral race. He chronicles the adventures of image specialists whose candidates are competing for the 1964 Republican nomination. Wyckoff concludes with a broad overview of the concept of an image candidate, an evaluation of television's role in building that image, and a look ahead to image candidacy in the 1968 election campaign and beyond.

Presidential Campaigns

Arterton, F. Christopher. *Media Politics: The News Strategies of Presidential Campaigns.* Lexington, MA: Lexington Books, 1984.

The author examines how the news media shape political campaign behavior and the consequences of that behavior for the outcome of presidential elections. Using interviews conducted in 1976 and 1980 with presidential campaign managers, press secretaries, pollsters, and advertising managers, Arterton analyzes the relationship and interplay between political campaigns and what the media report. By elaborating on how presidential campaigns are conducted, the author hopes journalists will reevaluate their approaches to covering elections.

Barber, James D. *The Pulse of Politics: Electing Presidents in the Media Age.* New York: Norton, 1980.

The author argues that conflict, conscience, and conciliation are cyclical themes that dominate presidential elections and politics between 1900 and 1980. Barber evaluates the campaigns of twelve twentieth-century presidents in terms of the cyclical themes noted above.

Blume, Keith. *The Presidential Election Show: Campaign '84 and Beyond on the Nightly News.* South Hadley, MA: Bergin and Garvey, 1985.

The author offers an in-depth explanation of the role that television plays in shaping the political course of the nation. Blume demonstrates the responsibility of television journalists in creating and contributing to the images and perceptions of the candidates. Blume begins by establishing the connections among presidential politics, television, and democracy. He reviews the 1984 presidential campaign up to Labor Day of that year; the campaign as portrayed on and influenced by the nightly news from Labor Day to October 5, 1984; the debates; the subsequent media analysis; and the last days of the election campaign. Blume looks back at the role that television played in helping to form opinions and perceptions during the presidential race. He concludes that television is increasingly the crucial factor in politics and calls for reforms.

Crouse, Timothy. *The Boys on the Bus: Riding with the Campaign Press Corps.* New York: Random House, 1973.

The author examines the role of the campaign press corps and, in particular, its role in the 1972 presidential campaign. Crouse presents much of the book as a series of reminiscences of the campaign trail. He begins with a brief history of the role of the press in presidential campaigns and how the campaign press corps evolved. Crouse profiles the major players in the press corps in 1972 and discusses the newsweeklies and television coverage. He describes how the press covered the Richard Nixon campaign, ranging from press treatment of the candidate in previous campaigns to Nixon's antagonistic relationship with the press and, ultimately, Watergate. Crouse deals with coverage of the George McGovern campaign, including the effect of Hunter S. Thompson's "gonzo journalism" on the press corps and the campaign, the Thomas Eagleton affair, and incorrect press predictions of the election.

Dautrich, Kenneth, and Thomas H. Harley. *How the News Media Fail American Voters: Causes, Consequences, and Remedies.* New York: Columbia University Press, 1999.

The authors present an evaluation of the institutional performance of the news media in its coverage of the 1996 presidential elections. They discuss how the electorate used the news media throughout the campaign and how it evaluated the new media's performance. They also discuss the perceptions of political bias in electoral coverage and the consequences of poor media performance.

Dover, E. D. *Presidential Elections in the Television Age, 1960–1992.* Westport, CT: Praeger, 1994.

The author examines the influence of television media on the outcome of presidential elections from the 1960 contest between John F. Kennedy and Richard Nixon to the 1992 contest between George Bush and Bill Clinton. Dover evaluates and offers a typology of the elections based on the strength and position of the incumbent. He concludes that television plays a variety of roles and presents several influences on election outcomes, including enhancement of leading candidates, acceleration of the defeat of weaker ones, and increased importance of the position of vice president as a platform from which to launch a nomination bid. Dover also cites the failure of television to provide much-needed candidate information to the electorate.

Gilbert, Robert E. *Television and Presidential Politics.* North Quincy, MA: Christopher Publishing House, 1972.

The author analyzes the use of television in political campaigning beginning with the 1952 contest between Dwight D. Eisenhower and Adlai Stevenson. Gilbert pays attention not only to television's use as a campaign instrument but also to other influences that the medium has exerted in political life. Gilbert argues that television has been a significant nationalizing force in politics. A major portion of the book addresses television's role in each presidential campaign from 1952 to 1968. The author examines television's effects on campaign costs, on the presidential office, and on the exercise of presidential power.

Gold, Vic. *PR as in President.* Garden City, NY: Doubleday, 1977.

The author examines the use, misuse, and manipulation of the media and public relations in the 1976 presidential campaign. He examines the preelection campaign of 1974 and 1975 and follows the campaign from primaries to conventions to debates and through the general election campaign. Gold examines the use of television, spin, the press, and image building in the modern campaign.

Harvey, Lisa St. C. *Stolen Thunder: The Cultural Roots of Political Communication.* New York: Peter Lang, 1994.

Although political communication and public opinion research have established the importance of emotion in determining voter behavior, little attention has been paid to the cultural understructure of the media environment in which both public life and political emotion take place. Using a combination of historical, critical, and anthropological techniques, the author explores that intellectual terrain. Harvey focuses on two complementary case studies—the 1988 presidential election and the George Bush administration's "War on Drugs"—to probe the underpinnings of political vision. The author suggests that in the age of television presidential elections are important primarily as public rituals.

Hofstetter, C. Richard. *Bias in the News: Network Television Coverage of the 1972 Election Campaign.* Columbus, OH: State University Press, 1976.

The author describes and evaluates the coverage of the 1972 presidential election campaign by the three major television networks. Hofstetter focuses on weekday evening news broadcasts from July 10 to November 6, 1972, a seventeen-week period of the most intensive election campaigning. He aims to identify and explain discernible patterns of campaign news coverage. Furthermore, he aims to show how these patterns or policies of treatment relate to the candidates, issues, parties, and campaign activities; how they relate to each of the networks; and how they persist or vary as the campaign progresses. The author covers bias in news programming, issue coverage, ratings, themes, and sources in news coverage.

Kerbel, Matthew R. *Edited for Television: CNN, ABC, and the 1992 Presidential Campaign.* Boulder, CO: Westview Press, 1994.

The author offers a year-long examination of the content of two networks' regularly scheduled evening news broadcasts about the 1992 presidential election. He supplements this with forty-four interviews with members of each network's election news unit. Kerbel examines what the election looked like on the two networks, including thematic content, analytical nature, portrayal of the individuals, institutions, and their relationships. Kerbel compares traditional broadcast coverage with its cable counterpart. Using elections as a case study, Kerbel examines how television covers events and assesses the mixture of organizational, procedural, and personal factors that help explain why television coverage looks the way it does.

Knappman, Edward W., Evan Drossman, and Robert Newman. *Campaign '72: Press Opinion from New Hampshire to November.* New York: Facts on File, 1972.

The authors examine why the American people elected Richard Nixon in 1972. Nearly 700 opinions on the issues, personalities, and results of the campaign have been reprinted in this survey of editorials from 117 newspapers covering every significant development from the first primary in New Hampshire to the final balloting in November. Each chapter is introduced by a brief, objective summary giving the factual background necessary for a full understanding of the editorials. All editorials are reprinted in full-text, exactly as they appeared in the cooperating newspapers.

Lavrakas, Paul J., and Jack K. Holley, eds. *Polling and Presidential Election Coverage.* Newbury Park, CA: Sage, 1990.

The editors of this volume collected a series of essays they think can improve the way the news media use election polls and other survey information. A pedagogical work, the book seeks to provide members of the media with some essential understanding of the polling information that they report and the effects that it has on voters and broadcast consumers. A variety of statistical and analytical methods are employed to make accessible the linkages between what polls actually report, how they are misinterpreted, and how public opinion is shaped by the information the media disseminates.

Lavrakas, Paul J., Michael W. Traugott, and Peter V. Miller, eds. *Presidential Polls and the News Media.* Boulder, CO: Westview Press, 1995.

This volume examines how the media use election polls. The thirteen chapters address how information gathered via election surveys is used. The authors also look at the use of focus groups, exit polls, and media polls in the 1992 election and the public's reaction to those polls.

Linsky, Martin, ed. *Television and the Presidential Elections: Self-Interest and the Public Interest.* Lexington, MA: Lexington Books, 1983.

This edited volume covers the proceedings of the Conference on Television and the Presidential Elections attended in 1981 by all three major networks, plus the BBC, CNN, and PBS. The conference agenda focused on current laws and regulations that guided media coverage of presidential elections and network policies that governed their behavior in the same process. The four primary themes of the conference are profits, votes, and the public interest; whether there is an adversarial relationship between the media and politicians; form and content of broadcast; and regulatory issues.

Mickelson, Sig. *The Electric Mirror: Politics in an Age of Television.* New York: Dodd, Mead, 1972.

The author examines television's influence on the political scene. Mickelson begins in 1952, with Dwight Eisenhower's presidential campaign, examining how the new medium was successfully used for political gain for the first time. Mickelson follows the evolution of the political advertisement, polls, projections, debates, and convention coverage. He also examines how television changed the nature of the campaign, often dictating new strategies, tactics, and even scheduled stops or photo opportunities. The author considers soaring campaign costs and concludes with a forecast for the future.

Owen, Diana M. *Media Messages in American Presidential Elections.* Westport, CT: Greenwood, 1991.

The author examines the importance of media messages to voters in the 1984 and 1988 presidential elections and studies how voters use those messages when selecting candidates based on campaign issues. She develops an audience-based model to pinpoint the direct effects mass media have on voter preferences. The media under consideration include televised advertisements, television and newspaper news, public opinion polls, and televised presidential debates. The author contends that the electorate's lack of gratification as campaign media consumers results from the media giving their audience what they think it wants.

Patterson, Thomas E. *The Mass Media Election: How Americans Choose Their President.* New York: Praeger, 1980.

The author analyzes the media's role and voter attention in presidential elections in Erie, Pennsylvania, and Los Angeles. Patterson, who conducted a panel survey in both cities, looks at the contents of three television networks, four newspapers, and *Time* and *Newsweek* to determine the role of the media. The author shows the relationship between the voter and the media during the campaign.

Perry, James M. *Us and Them: How the Press Covered the 1972 Election.* New York: Crown, 1973.

The author, a reporter for the *National Observer*, examines how the press covered the 1972 presidential election. He discusses press coverage of all the presidential candidates, the primaries, the conventions, and the campaign. Perry concludes by giving an assessment of how well the press covered the candidates and the issues.

Plissner, Martin. *The Control Room: How Television Calls the Shots in Presidential Elections.* New York: Free Press, 1999.

The author argues that the men and women who call the shots at the networks do have an agenda. Their goals are to get the largest possible viewership at the lowest possible cost and to score a competitive edge over their television rivals.

Reinsch, J. Leonard. *Getting Elected: From Radio and Roosevelt to Television and Reagan.* New York: Hippocrene Books, 1988.

The author examines the media's role particularly that of radio and television, in presidential elections. The first five chapters detail the author's inception into politics in the mid 1940s and the power that radio had to influence voters. The next section shows the shift in influence and importance from radio to television and chronicles campaign use of these media in elections from 1952 to 1984. Other sections focus on television's role in the caucuses, primaries, the convention, debates, and the general election campaign. The final section looks ahead to the 1988 campaign and deals with the issues of money, debates, and the influence of new technologies and innovations, such as cable television, videocassette recorders, and satellite broadcasting.

Rubin, Richard L. *Press, Party, and Presidency.* New York: Norton, 1981.

The author maintains that the structure, organization, and agenda of parties in combination with the speed, depth, and breadth of media transformation have directly shaped the character of the presidency. Rubin employs an historical approach to support these claims, analyzing how technological developments in the field of mass communications have shaped the campaigns, office, and duties of the presidency.

Schram, Martin. *The Great American Video Game: Presidential Politics in the Television Age.* New York: William Morrow, 1987.

The author examines the disparity between political reality and the televised portrayal of politics in presidential campaigns during the 1980s. He explores the decisions made in candidate headquarters and the effects on voters' decisions. In addition, Schram discusses how the television media (that is, producers, anchors, correspondents, and the network) filter information and how their selection of newsworthy events shapes the public perception of presidential candidates. Finally,

Schram studies the voter as consumer of televised information to determine the most influential information for selecting candidates.

Shields, Mark. *On the Campaign Trail: Wise and Witty Dispatches from the Front Lines of the 1984 Presidential Race.* Chapel Hill, NC: Algonquin Books, 1985.

The author offers a collection of his columns and broadcasts during the 1984 presidential campaign season. Shields covers all the major events of the campaign from the first primary in New Hampshire through the conventions, debates, and election day. He describes the political scene, charts the course of the campaign, gives the reader a feel for the mood of the electorate, examines campaign strategy and tactics, and makes some predictions. The book includes cartoons from ten of the nation's leading political cartoonists.

Stempel, Guido H., III, and John W. Windhauser., eds. *The Media in the 1984 and 1988 Presidential Campaigns.* Westport, CT: Greenwood, 1991.

This edited work examines various roles played by the media in covering the 1984 and 1988 presidential campaigns. The essays cover a variety of topics, including the media as a political actor; newspaper, newsmagazine, and television news coverage of the campaign; and editorials and editorial endorsements.

Tannenbaum, Percy H., and Leslie J. Kostrich. *Turned-On TV, Turned-Off Voters: Policy Options for Election Projections.* Beverly Hills: Sage, 1983.

The authors examine national election forecasting, and how the media affect voting behavior in time zones still open after polls close elsewhere. Tannenbaum and Kostrich look at the effects of the ordering on presidential voting, turnout, and even local elections. They lay out criteria for evaluating both the current early-return system and alternative systems, such as uniform poll closings or delayed release of election results. Tannenbaum and Kostrich also discuss curbs on media projections of or reporting of results and evaluate potential state-level actions.

Weaver, David H., Doris A. Graber, Maxwell E. McCombs, and C. H. Eyal. *Media Agenda-Setting in a Presidential Election: Issues, Images, and Interest.* New York: Praeger, 1981.

The authors explore the agenda-setting role of mass communication. They continue and expand on work by other scholars exploring issue orientation among voters, while broadening the inquiry into two new domains: candidate images and interest in politics. They provide an introduction and theoretical overview for the idea of media agenda setting. The authors include a review of major findings of many earlier studies and a discussion of many of the chief issues and developments in agenda-setting research. They examine the role of newspapers and television in setting interest, issue, and image agendas throughout the election year. They broaden the focus of media agenda-setting beyond its customary concentration on issues and extend the time period for agenda-setting effects from a few weeks or months to an entire election year.

Congressional Campaigns

Clarke, Peter, and Susan H. Evans. *Covering Campaigns: Journalism in Congressional Elections.* Stanford: Stanford University Press, 1983.

The authors provide a detailed analysis of press coverage of congressional campaigns, using data gathered in eighty-two districts in 1978. They interviewed political reporters and their editors in each district and analyzed the content of the news stories and editorials they produced during the campaign to ascertain the nature of the coverage. Clark and Evans examine endorsement policies, reporter assignments, and the struggle to achieve balanced content. Their study yields further evidence of the lopsided advantages enjoyed by incumbents in both coverage and endorsements. The authors conclude by presenting practical suggestions for improved coverage offered by journalists, candidates, and campaign managers.

Smith, Judith G., ed. *Political Brokers: People, Organizations, Money, and Power.* New York: Liveright, 1972.

This edited volume offers ten case studies previously published in the *National Journal* as part of its campaign coverage. Nine of the studies describe political groups active in the 1970 congressional campaign. The groups, identified as being among the most important in national politics, are the Americans for Democratic Action, Americans for Constitutional Action, the American Medical Political Action Committee, the Committee on Political Education of the AFL-CIO, the Business-Industry Political Action Committee, the National Committee for an Effective Congress, the National Republican Congressional Committee, the Ripon Society, and the Democratic National Committee. The tenth study discusses Common Cause, which was the subject of the first report of the *National Journal*'s 1972 campaign coverage. The studies describe the history, source of contributions, campaign activity, and claims of success of each of the identified power groups.

Vermeer, Jan P., ed. *Campaigns in the News: Mass Media and Congressional Elections.* New York: Greenwood Press, 1987.

The ten studies in this edited volume portray the relationship between the press and congressional campaigns using patterns of news coverage in congressional elections. Contributors also discuss the content of campaign materials, voter knowledge, ethics, and ideology. Together the studies make a strong case that the media cannot continue to be treated as external to the political system but instead must be seen as influential actors within that system.

8

Political Parties

General

Archer, J. Clark, and Peter J. Taylor. *Section and Party: A Political Geography of American Presidential Elections from Andrew Jackson to Ronald Reagan*. New York: Wiley, 1981.

Prompted by geographic shifts in partisan support as evidenced by the 1980 presidential election, the authors provide a systematic, quantitative analysis of geographic voting trends from 1789 through 1980. They examine the rise of political parties within a Federalist context, the emergence of geographic partisan cleavages as conflict grew between the North and the South, and the linkages that develop between partisanship and geographic sections in the post–Civil War era. Appendixes provide methodological detail of factor analysis and factor pattern matrices.

Bailey, Thomas A. *Democrats vs. Republicans: The Continuing Clash*. Des Moines, IA: Meredith Books, 1968.

This book provides a brief history of political parties at the national level, with particular attention paid to successive presidential elections. The author traces the differences between the Democrats and their opponents from the days of Thomas Jefferson to the late 1960s. Bailey delves into the differences between the parties, focusing on differing adherents, techniques, goals, and means to those goals. The author demonstrates how and why these divergences developed and how and why they continued. The stress is on recent trends and developments. An appendix provides presidential election data from 1828 to 1964.

Beck, Paul A. *Party Politics in America*. 8th ed. New York: Longman, 1997.

The author offers a comprehensive textbook about political parties and party systems. He focuses on party organization, the party in the electorate, and the party in government, examining the conflicting and dynamic relationships between these aspects of the party as they interact in the electoral process. Beck analyzes recent data on presidential and congressional voting and examines campaign finance reports and results from elections though 1994. The author provides information on political parties through the beginning of the 1996 presidential election campaign.

Bibby, John F. *Politics, Parties, and Elections in America.* 4th ed. Chicago: Nelson-Hall, 1999.

This book on party politics touches on a variety of issues. Bibby examines the role of political parties in organizing the legislative agenda, in generating voter turnout in elections, and in the competition between candidates for party nominations in primaries. He also discusses party influence in policy making and examines characteristics of the party system, including its ambiguous membership, unprogrammatic nature, and decentralized structure. The author identifies the successive eras of party government that have followed critical realignments.

Bibby, John F., and L. Sandy Maisel. *Two Parties—Or More? The American Party System.* Boulder, CO: Westview Press, 1998.

The authors discuss the role of third parties in politics at the national and state level. They discuss the barriers and problems that third parties encounter in the political system. They also discuss the public's demand for alternatives and the future of the two-party system.

Brady, David W. *Critical Elections and Congressional Policy Making.* Stanford: Stanford University Press, 1988.

The author examines the effects of critical elections on policy outputs in Congress by looking at three important historical periods: the realignments associated with the Civil War, the 1890s, and the New Deal. Brady analyzes how these elections affected the party composition of Congress, its committee structure, and the strength of party caucuses. In each period under study the elections that sent legislators to Washington were national in focus and the newly elected majority party had the comprehensive policy goals and the requisite unity to pass them into law. Brady argues that at these critical junctures the political parties provided an integrative mechanism to link the electorate to the party in government and overcome structural and dispositional incentives toward legislative individualism, incrementalism, and decentralization.

Broder, David S. *The Party's Over.* New York: Harper and Row, 1971.

The author analyzes the decline of the two-party system, urges a return to responsible party government, and warns of the consequences should the national parties fall into further decay. Broder indicts the parties for their lack of a disciplining sense of direction and principle or program during most of the 1950s and 1960s. He also links party breakdown to the perceived breakdown of American society as a whole. Broder makes several suggestions for reforming the political system, including direct election of the president, expansion of the role of party caucuses in congressional elections, and letting party caucuses rather than the seniority system determine congressional committee appointments.

Chambers, William N., and Walter D. Burnham, eds. *The American Party System: Stages of Political Development.* 2d ed. New York: Oxford University Press, 1975.

The authors offer a systematic study of what political parties are and how they got that way. This edited volume strives to illuminate problems of political party development and action. Historical issues addressed include party development and the American mainstream, the first American party system, political development and the second party system, and party politics and the Union and Confederate war efforts. Other party-related topics include the nationalization of electoral forces, the community-society continuum, social development, party competition, policy choice, the Constitution, and the overall political process. This second edition concludes with an updated chapter on politics and the party system in the 1970s.

Cotter, Cornelius P., ed. *Practical Politics in the United States.* Boston: Allyn and Bacon, 1969.

This edited volume examines parties from multiple vantage points: as auspices for candidacy for public office, as contributors toward dividing the public into majority and minority groupings for electoral purposes, and as expressions of forces of localism and nationalism in a federal system. The first section of the book addresses the development of parties, propositions concerning their appropriate functioning, and their efficacy. The second section reviews party organization at the state, city, and suburban levels. The third section deals with campaigning for state and national legislative office, as seen from the vantage points of the campaigner and the campaign manager. The fourth section describes the development of national convention politics, the selection of delegates who determine the presidential nominee, the conduct of national conventions, and campaign financing. The final section offers a basis for comparative analysis by looking at campaigning in Britain and Scandinavia. The book concludes with an evaluation of contemporary American parties.

Cotter, Cornelius P., and Bernard C. Hennessy. *Politics without Power: The National Party Committees.* Chicago: Atherton Press, 1964.

The authors examine what the national party committees are, who the members are, where the committees are located in relation to other politically oriented organizations, what they do, and what modest steps might be taken to make better use of them. Cotter and Hennessy begin with the historical development and organization of the national party committees. The authors then discuss the role of the national party chairpersons. Cotter and Hennessy examine conventions and campaign organizations and discuss organization functions such as public relations, research, fundraising, and patronage. They consider the interactions among the committees, other groups, and the government itself. The authors examine both the Republican National Committee and the Democratic Advisory Council.

David, Paul T. *Party Strength in the United States, 1872–1970.* Charlottesville: University Press of Virginia, 1972.

The author gives summaries of votes for president, governor, and Congress from 1892 through 1970. He explains and evaluates various types of indexes for measuring party strength. David analyzes national, regional, and state voting trends. He notes the shifting alliances during four time periods and concludes among other things that party realignment generally "works down from the top—from presidential voting to voting for other offices of high visibility and clear partisan identification, and only later to the lower offices, where election nevertheless occurs on a partisan basis." David believes the Republican Party was not dominant after 1896.

Fishel, Jeff, ed. *Parties and Elections in an Anti-Party Age: American Politics and the Crisis of Confidence.* Bloomington: Indiana University Press, 1978.

This edited volume examines the party and electoral systems in the context of growing anti-party sentiment among voters. The book begins with an overview of political parties and elections and continues with a discussion of politics and the legacy of discontent. Later it examines trends in public support for the system, responsible party government, and the parties' role in politics. The volume then takes on elections as instruments of popular control, examining voters, voting, and links between voters and decision makers. The third major section deals with parties as instruments of popular control, focusing on presidential nominations and elections, parties in government, and the effects of media, money, and campaign organization. The volume concludes with a reexamination of the two-party system and a rethinking of the role of political parties in the future of American politics.

Green, John C., and Daniel M. Shea, eds. *The State of the Parties: The Changing Role of Contemporary American Politics.* 3d ed. Lanham, MD: Rowman and Littlefield, 1999.

While this edited volume primarily discusses the state of parties and the two-party system in general, it also presents articles that focus specifically on changes in political party activities. Articles examine the role of national party committees, party strength, state party finance, and sources of activism. Other, more general articles examine party policy, value, activities, and culture.

Greenstein, Fred I., and Frank B. Feigert. *The American Party System and the American People.* 3d ed. Englewood Cliffs, NJ: Prentice-Hall, 1985.

The authors focus on the relationship between the electorate and political parties. They assess this relationship in terms of how political parties reinforce or fail to reinforce governmental and regime stability, democracy and democratic principles, and policy-making processes. Following a brief consideration of the citizen base of the electorate and the general role of parties in democratic political systems, Greenstein and Feigert evaluate parties on local, state, and national levels. Policy making is a primary focus throughout these considerations.

Gurin, Patricia, Shirley Hatchett, and James S. Jackson. *Hope and Indepen-dence: Blacks' Response to Electoral and Party Politics.* New York: Russell Sage Foundation, 1989.

The authors examine the social psychological relationship and reaction African Americans have to the party system, national politics, and candidates. The authors use Jesse Jackson's 1984 presidential bid to interpret the meaning of African Ameri-can political independence and activity. The authors also address keys to African American mobilization, including structural advantages, organizational experience, group cohesiveness, political beliefs, and shared psychological predispositions. The study is based primarily on a set of telephone surveys of African Americans con-ducted in 1984.

Hadley, Charles D., and Lewis Bowman, eds. *Party Activists in Southern Pol-itics: Mirrors and Makers of Change.* Knoxville: University of Tennessee Press, 1998.

This edited work includes chapters on sociodemographic, psychological, and political factors that influence partisanship and the two-party system in the South. Contributors analyze factors such as race, religion, gender, ideology, migration, party politics, and political issues. Chapters focus on the changing nature of party activists in the South, including Alabama, Arkansas, Florida, Georgia, Louisiana, Mississippi, North and South Carolina, Tennessee, Texas, and Virginia.

Herrnson, Paul S. *Party Campaigning in the 1980s.* Cambridge, MA: Harvard University Press, 1988.

The author provides an account of how the national parties have been able to adapt and survive in the modern political environment. Herrnson analyzes data drawn from a survey of nearly 500 congressional candidates; a study of campaign finance records; and interviews with campaign advisers, party officials, political action committee executives, and journalists. Herrnson finds evidence of stronger party organizations that have found innovative ways to affect the electoral process and increase party responsibility. He places contemporary developments in an his-torical context and describes in detail the new and highly organized national parties. The author also examines party role in congressional elections from the candidates' perspective and the national perspective.

Jacobson, Gary C. *The Electoral Origins of Divided Government: Competition in U.S. House Elections, 1946–1988.* Boulder, CO: Westview Press, 1990.

The author analyzes structural and political explanations for the Democrats' con-tinued dominance of Congress and the Republican lock on the White House. He con-cludes that divided party control reflects popular preferences. Using data gathered from an array of sources, Jacobson finds that none of the standard structural expla-nations for divided government, such as incumbency advantages, declining swing rations, gerrymandering, and campaign finance, withstand serious scrutiny. In trac-ing the evolution of competition in postwar House elections, Jacobson finds a substantial decline in the importance of party cues to voters. As individual candidates and campaigns have become more important in winning elections, the weakness of Republican candidates has prevented the party from winning more seats.

Jensen, Richard J. *Grass Roots Politics: Parties, Issues, and Voters, 1854–1983.* Westport, CT: Greenwood Press, 1983.

The author examines the grassroots level of electoral politics. He examines voter realignments, dealignment, and reactions from 1880 to 1980 and discusses the sources of these changes. Jensen focuses on race, ethnicity, class, and religion. He also addresses the political party, highlighting the differences between nineteenth-century and twentieth-century party organization. The author explores the big-city machine, the one-party South, crusades in both centuries, pressure groups, third parties, and special interests. The last section of the book contains thirty-eight documents related to grassroots politics. Topics covered include voter fraud, corruption, campaign finance, rhetoric, populism, the media, strategies and tactics, woman's suffrage, reforms, lobbyists, nonvoters, liberalism, and conservatism.

Jewell, Malcolm E., and David M. Olson. *Political Parties and Elections in American States.* 3d ed. Chicago: Dorsey Press, 1988.

The authors compare the political party and state election systems. They consider distinct characteristics of state political systems and national factors influencing state politics. The authors focus on the following elements in the context of state-level politics: two-party competition, state political party organization, the nominating process, the general elections, voting behavior, parties in state legislatures, and state parties in the context of national elections. They conclude with speculation on the future of state politics given the trend toward nationalization of politics. The authors emphasize that differences between and among states persist despite these nationalizing trends.

Kessel, John H. *Presidential Parties.* Homewood, IL: Dorsey Press, 1984.

The author uses knowledge about the most important elements of electoral, legislative, nominative, and executive politics to understand political parties, particularly as they function during presidential election years. He explains citizen response by examining their attitudes and behavior. The author argues that why something happens can sometimes be explained by internal structure, sometimes by external structure, and sometimes by both. When something happens is explained by the temporal pattern of the acting unit. Regardless, understanding the nature of the whole requires understanding the nature of the component parts. The author uses multiple methodologies, including probit analysis, other statistical techniques, and historical case studies.

Key, Valdimer O. *Politics, Parties, and Pressure Groups.* 5th ed. New York: Crowell, 1964.

The author examines politics, parties, and pressure groups. He examines the inner workings, roles, and techniques of pressure groups, including agrarian groups, workers, business, and other organizations. Key discusses party contests from 1896 to 1960 and looks at the nature and function of parties. He also examines sectionalism, urbanism, third parties, and parties at the state level. Key discusses party structure and procedure, including organization, the party machine as interest group, nominations, and national conventions. He also examines the relationship between the party and the electorate. He discusses campaign techniques, campaign finance, presidential and congressional elections, participation, registration, ballots, and elections. Key also discusses the party's role in government, focusing on party leadership in legislation and administration as politics.

Klinkner, Philip A. *The Losing Parties: Out-Party National Committees, 1956–1993.* New Haven: Yale University Press, 1994.

The author examines how the defeat of one of the two major political parties affects its postelectoral behavior by analyzing the out-parties in elections between 1956 and 1993. He assesses and evaluates three traditional theories of party behavior—rational organization, agenda-driven, and party culture—in terms of their responses to electoral defeat. Using detailed historical data, party documents, contemporary media accounts, secondary documents, and interviews with party activists, Klinkner examines what factors account for party behavior following defeat, their theoretical implications, and the patterns that emerge over time. The author concludes that defeated parties behave in accordance with their own particular party cultures.

Ladd, Everett C., Jr., and Charles D. Hadley. *Transformations of the American Party System: Political Coalitions from the New Deal to the 1970s.* 2d ed. New York: Norton, 1978.

The authors examine the reordering that societal change has imposed on political life since the New Deal. They focus mainly on the changes in parties within the broader context of changes in the social order. Ladd and Hadley examine the formation and extension of the New Deal and its first renderings in the South. Next the authors examine how postindustrialism affected the settings in which the party system operates and the coalitions that resulted. They then examine the 1976 elections in detail and discuss the ways electoral politics has changed since the New Deal. They conclude by recounting how the transformations in the party system affect contemporary politics.

Lipset, Seymour M., ed. *Party Coalitions in the 1980s.* San Francisco: Institute for Contemporary Studies, 1981.

This edited volume is partly an update of Lipset's 1978 *Emerging Coalitions in American Politics* and partly a new endeavor. Many of the essays in this book discuss the future prospects of the party system and are based to a large extent on interpretations of the politics of the 1970s and of the 1980 election. Political scientists wrote most of the chapters. A few chapters are examinations of the campaigns by political pollsters for the presidential candidates. The final section comprises the writings of six political intellectuals, representing clearly defined places on the political and ideological spectra. Their statements analyze recent events and trends in terms of their value preferences.

Maisel, L. Sandy, ed. *The Parties Respond: Changes in the American Parties and Campaigns.* 3d ed. Boulder, CO: Westview Press, 1998.

This edited volume brings together fifteen original studies on various aspects of partisan politics. The opening essay provides a broad historical overview of the development of political parties, furnishing the context for subsequent chapters that examine the resilience of these modern institutions as they adapt to changing political settings. Among the topics addressed are party organization, the party's role in the electorate, the influence of the party in the electoral arena, and the party in government. Special attention is given to issues of coalition building, campaign finance, candidate recruitment, and agenda setting in Congress. The volume concludes with two perspectives on the future of partisanship and is current through the aftermath of the 1996 election campaign.

Mayhew, David R. *Placing Parties in American Politics: Organization, Electoral Settings, and Government Activity in the Twentieth Century.* Princeton: Princeton University Press, 1986.

The author discusses the structure within parties—a what, why, when, where, and so-what treatment of the party structure at the local level in the twentieth century. Mayhew examines traditional patronage organizations, although other structural forms are also considered. Occasionally the author goes beyond the local level to examine state and national politics. Mayhew examines different forms of party organization on a state-by-state basis and the background and implications of party organization. Appendixes illustrate candidate activity in primaries and expenditure and revenue data for 1942.

Miller, Warren E., and M. Kent Jennings. *Parties in Transition: A Longitudinal Study of Party Elites and Party Supporters.* New York: Russell Sage Foundation, 1986.

The authors evaluate institutional stability in light of attempts to instigate reform and the dynamic changes in the composition, preferences, and goals of the actors, participants, candidates, and electorate in presidential campaigns from 1972 to 1980. The authors maintain that the analysis of elite, party, and issue changes over time can provide insights into the structural and institutional changes that accompany or parallel those shifts. Using survey data, they demonstrate the linkages between party elites and the mass constituency during electoral cycles.

Moreland, Laurence W., Tod A. Baker, and Robert P. Steed, eds. *Contemporary Southern Political Attitudes and Behavior.* New York: Praeger, 1982.

This edited volume, framed within the context of the debate over continued southern distinctiveness, presents new research exploring three aspects of contemporary southern political attitudes and behavior. Taken together the essays provide information pertinent to understanding the extent of southern assimilation into national cultural, social, and political patterns. The first section focuses on the nature of ideological and issue concerns in the region. Chapters in the second section examine the contemporary party system in the South to help ascertain whether the larger societal changes of the past three and a half decades have brought the region fully into the national party system. The final section investigates the relationships between mass electorates and elected or appointed government elites.

Phillips, Kevin P. *Mediacracy: American Parties and Politics in the Communications Age.* Garden City, NY: Doubleday, 1975.

The author discusses the enormous changes that have overtaken society and politics in the late 1960s and early 1970s and sets forth their implications. He examines the communications revolution and how it has affected the political system. Phillips argues that communications have replaced party organizations as the key to political success and that communications have come to dominate everyday life. The author documents the rise of the communications revolution and examines new patterns in politics and the new role of the political party. Phillips looks ahead to the future of politics in what he calls a mediacracy.

Polsby, Nelson W. *Consequences of Party Reform.* New York: Oxford University Press, 1983.

Observing what he believes to be a trend of presidential populism, the author explores the immediate effects and long-term consequences of party reforms. He attempts to demonstrate how changing institutional rules transform the incentive structure, which, in turn, changes political behavior and leads to more reform. Polsby begins by examining partisan delegate selection processes and party finance reform and follows with a discussion of their ramifications, of which the most serious is the declining emphasis on qualifications for presidential candidates. He also considers broader outcomes of reform. Polsby concludes with a revised suggestion for how institutions and organizations should approach reforms and calculate the possible consequences of reforms before implementing them.

Pomper, Gerald M., ed. *Party Renewal in America: Theory and Practice.* New York: Praeger, 1980.

This book focuses on political parties in general, with discussions of party renewal, the party caucus-convention system, and parties' roles in elections, using California and Minnesota as examples.

Rapoport, Ronald B., Alan I. Abramowitz, and John McGlennon, eds. *The Life of the Parties: Activists in Presidential Politics.* Lexington: University Press of Kentucky, 1986.

This edited volume contains articles that highlight various perspectives on the role of party activists in the presidential nominating process in the postreform era. Using survey data collected from delegates attending eleven state party conventions in 1980, the authors demonstrate that postreform activists behave differently from those involved in the prereform period. They maintain that contemporary activists possess highly complex motivational and belief systems, hold rigid positions congruent with party ideology, and seek electoral success in conjunction with their views. The result is a partisan politics of compromise and coalition-formation.

Reiter, Howard L. *Parties and Elections in Corporate America.* 2d ed. New York: Longman, 1993.

The author examines the function of political parties in the larger context of politics, who benefits from their existence and operation, and whether the United States would be better off without parties. He bases his investigation on the premise that the political system is fundamentally flawed, that our party system is a major component of this flawed politics, and that other systems would better serve the needs of the voting public. The author questions the efficacy of voting, the fairness of pluralism, and the sincerity of officeholders and candidates. By placing political parties in a broad social and economic perspective, Reiter demonstrates that the present political system serves those who control power in corporate America rather than the population at large.

Schlesinger, Joseph A. *Political Parties and the Winning of Office.* Ann Arbor: University of Michigan Press, 1991.

The author develops a general theory of party organization that is designed to aid in our understanding of parties and their activities. Using political parties as the primary reference point, the author discusses party mobilization, structure, and activity in his consideration of party organization. Three major variables contribute to the determination of a party's structure: the obtaining of key resources, the principal output of goods, and the ways participants are compensated. Schlesinger intends to produce a theory of parties that travels well to other cases and can be used in a comparative perspective.

Steed, Robert P., John A. Clark, Lewis Bowman, and Charles D. Hadley, eds. *Party Organization and Activism in the American South.* Tuscaloosa: University of Alabama Press, 1998.

The editors use data from local party organizations in eleven southern states to examine the structure and function of political parties in the region and the prospects for a revitalization of grassroots party activism there. They present and analyze data on the characteristics of local party activists, party recruitment and retention of activists, intraparty factionalism, and the effects of parties' external environments.

Steed, Robert P., Laurence W. Moreland, and Tod A. Baker, eds. *Party Politics in the South.* New York: Praeger Publishers, 1980.

This edited volume examines how the South has opened up participation and developed more factional and party competitiveness. The chapters center around three main subthemes: intraparty politics and the Democratic primary, interparty politics and two-party competition, and blacks and women as new participants in southern politics. The chapters rely on aggregate data analysis and survey research. The volume's general conclusion is that major changes in electoral politics have affected the region at large. These changes attended the collapse of conditions that had supported pre-1948 electoral practices in the South. They also have expanded the diversity of the individual states, a diversity that always existed but was not fully recognized in the face of characteristic and controlling uniformities when the region was dominated by one-party, rural-based, and racially constricted politics.

Alignment

Burnham, Walter D. *Critical Elections and the Mainsprings of American Politics.* New York: Norton, 1970.

The author attempts to breach the technological and cultural limits placed on the study of electoral behavior by examining elections over time and providing an historical context against which critical elections can be evaluated. Topics of particular interest include critical realignments, depoliticization, electoral change, and party decomposition. An appendix provides statistical information on electoral politics in five states from 1880 to 1968.

———. *The Current Crisis in American Politics.* New York: Oxford University Press, 1982.

In this collection of essays written between 1964 and 1981, Burnham examines the evolution of party systems in mass electorates through critical realignments. Using historical and comparative methodologies, he details the decline in importance of party to voters and cites a variety of factors that have contributed to this. Burnham notes in particular the increasing advantages of incumbency enjoyed by members of Congress. He devotes a chapter to insulation and responsiveness in congressional elections. Another essay explores shifting patterns of congressional voting participation through an historical overview of turmoil in congressional elections and comparison with contemporary participation levels in Europe.

Campbell, Bruce A., and Richard J. Trilling, eds. *Realignment in American Politics: Toward a Theory.* Austin: University of Texas Press, 1980.

This edited volume is devoted to the phenomenon of voter realignment—its causes, effects, and translation into public policy. The editors have assembled a collection of articles that attempt to provide a panoramic view of realignment in terms of a general theory and in relation to the American electorate. The book is divided into four general areas of interest: current issues in the study of realignment, changes in the mass behavior of the electorate, changes in the behavior of elites, and the effects of realignment on policy decision and implementation.

Clubb, Jerome M., William H. Flanigan, and Nancy H. Zingale. *Partisan Realignment: Voters, Parties, and Government in American History.* Beverly Hills, CA: 1980.

The authors seek to explain partisanship and political leadership in terms of realignment. They blend existing research with their own analysis of electoral and other data to present a model for understanding successive party systems in politics. Instead of a traditional reliance on the voting behavior of mass publics, Clubb, Flanigan, and Zingale reach beyond the voters to include elite behavior, control of government, and policy formation as explanations of partisan realignment. An epilogue focuses on the events of the past twenty years and documents the continuing decay of the New Deal realignment.

Glaser, James M. *Race, Campaign Politics, and the Realignment in the South.* New Haven: Yale University Press, 1996.

The author examines the choices offered to southern voters in congressional elections. He attempts to uncover why Republican success in presidential elections in the South has been so slow in translating to lower-level electoral success. Glaser investigates elections from 1952 to 1992. He observes that issues of group conflict and race continue to affect congressional politics in the South. He offers that southern Democrats have prolonged realignment and have controlled local elections by constructing biracial coalitions. His analysis gives insight into why Democrats were successful in Republican-dominated presidential election years.

Huckfeldt, Robert, and Carol W. Kohfeld. *Race and the Decline of Class in American Politics.* Urbana: University of Illinois Press, 1989.

The authors argue that the politics of race often prove to be incompatible with the politics of class. Race frequently serves as a wedge that disrupts lower-class coalitions, thereby driving out class from political arrangements. Huckfeldt and Kohfeld focus on the post–World War II period. They analyze how race affects volatility in party coalitions, postmaterialist politics, populism, and party dynamics. They examine prospects for heterogeneity within races and political parties. They also consider the interdependence of class and race and the authors conclude with a discussion of race, class, and the future of American politics. Huckfeldt and Kohfeld recommend that a significant portion of the African American community should shift to the Republican Party to reduce the incentives for racial polarization in politics and to reap the benefits inherent in bipartisanship.

Ladd, Everett C., Jr. *Where Have All the Voters Gone? The Fracturing of America's Political Parties.* 2d ed. New York: Norton, 1982.

In this second edition, Ladd expands his argument that the electorate is in a continued state of dealignment. Most of the earlier chapters remain as originally published. These chapters develop the dealignment argument by examining the problems faced by the Republicans and Democrats. The author follows with an evaluation of the structural constraints on the party system that would make it difficult to effectively reform and return parties to a central position in electoral politics. The new chapters discuss how the Reagan revolution reflects the process of dealignment.

Lawrence, David G. *The Collapse of the Democratic Presidential Majority: Realignment, Dealignment, and Electoral Change from Franklin Roosevelt to Bill Clinton.* Boulder, CO: Westview Press, 1996.

The author makes the case that a distinct sequence of events explains the pattern of recent Democratic presidential failures. He establishes that there is a pattern to explain. He argues that a mini-realignment, based around class and race, deprived the Democrats of their presidential majority and created a system of partisan balance. A second mini-realignment produced a Republican presidential majority. This realignment was caused by ideological failure on the part of the Democrats between 1968 and 1980 and the capture of economic issues by the Republicans. Finally, the author applies the basic logic of the argument to an analysis of the 1992 election.

Lipset, Seymour M., and Stein Rokkan, eds. *Party Systems and Voters Alignment.* New York: Free Press, 1967.

This edited volume brings together findings on electoral research in various countries. Lipset and Rokkan examine cleavage structures, party systems, and voter alignments in English-speaking democracies, continental Europe, Scandinavia, and in emerging nations in Asia, Africa, and Latin America. The analyses collected here bear on a series of central issues: the genesis of the systems of contrasts and cleavages within the national community, conditions for the development of a stable system of cleavage and oppositions in national political life, and the behavior of the mass of citizens within the resultant party systems. All the analyses share an important historical perspective. The introductory chapter, written by the editors, is considered a seminal work in the area of elections, parties, and cleavages.

Moakley, Maureen, ed. *Party Realignment and State Politics.* Columbus: Ohio State University Press, 1992.

This edited volume is the joint effort of a group of political scientists involved with research on the role of party systems in the political process. The central question asked is to what extent individual states have experienced a realignment of their political party systems. This comparative study charts shifts in the party systems of fourteen economically, politically, and regionally diverse American states: Alabama, Arizona, California, Colorado, Florida, Iowa, Kansas, New Jersey, New York, Ohio, Rhode Island, Texas, Virginia, and Wisconsin. Using statewide survey data, the studies track trends in the voters' party affiliation and voter registration. The studies also examine trends in voting behavior in the states, charting patterns in national, state, and local electoral contests. The authors also consider how leadership roles and important issues on the state's agenda have altered the fortunes of the party system. Finally, they consider prospects for the future.

Petrocik, John R. *Party Coalitions: Realignment and the Decline of the New Deal Party System.* Chicago: University of Chicago Press, 1981.

The author approaches the question of realignment from the perspective that the theories concerning realignment are highly disorganized and inchoate. Petrocik thinks that a fundamental reconceptualization of the term *realignment* is necessary for it to have meaning within the historical context of American politics and current indicators of political change. He attempts to explain the realignment shift in electoral politics and why our political system has been transformed since the New Deal era.

Shafer, Byron E., ed. *The End of Realignment? Interpreting American Electoral Eras.* Madison: University of Wisconsin Press, 1991.

This edited volume addresses many issues surrounding the realignment approach to electoral politics and attempts to frame the debate in terms of structure, history, and explanatory strength. Although a variety of perspectives are brought to bear on the subject of realignment, all the authors represented in this volume agree that the singular focus on electoral realignment is short-sighted and skews our understanding of electoral shifts.

Sinclair, Barbara. *Congressional Realignment, 1925–1978.* Austin: University of Texas Press, 1982.

The author provides an extended look at changes in the political agenda, changes in policy outputs, and changes in congressional alignments from 1925 to 1978. Sinclair examines the sources of these changes, their nature, and their consequences. She uses Aage Clausen's five policy domains to classify roll call votes from the period under study and then uses this information to identify changes in agenda and alignments. Sinclair considers shifting alignments within the body as a whole, intraparty changes, and the influence of region.

Sundquist, James L. *Dynamics of the Party System.* Rev. ed. Washington, DC: Brookings Institution, 1983.

The author uses an historical and theoretical perspective to examine the processes that reshape the two-party system from time to time. From an examination of three major transformations of the two-party system, realignments in the 1850s, 1890s, and 1930s, and several minor realignments, Sundquist constructs a theory of the realignment process, which he then applies in analyzing recent trends in the party system. He covers developments in the party system, including the rise of the New Right, the Ronald Reagan revolution, and the 1982 midterm election. The author finds that disintegration of the party system will more likely be stemmed and reversed than continue unabated.

Swansbrough, Robert H., and David M. Brodsky, eds. *The South's New Politics: Realignment and Dealignment.* Columbia: University of South Carolina Press, 1988.

This edited volume attempts to explain in general and specific terms the apparent partisan electorate shift that has occurred in the South from 1948 through the

Ronald Reagan revolution. The collected essays focus on the changes in southern politics from a variety of perspectives, including partisan conversion, new voter mobilization, demographic changes, and the decline of party importance in the South. In addition to the general theoretical issues concerned with southern politics, the book maps changes in the electorate of twelve southern states using aggregate state electoral data and survey data. The book also analyzes trends in southern politics on a more general and regional level.

Democratic

Brenner, Lenni. *The Lesser Evil.* Secaucus, NJ: Lyle Stuart, 1988.

The author examines the Democratic Party, arguing that the party often wins because the voters are voting against the Republicans. Brenner starts at the beginnings of the Democratic Party, with Thomas Jefferson, demythologizing the heroes and laying out the factual history of the 200-year-old party. He then describes the constant aspects of the present party, its congressional contingent, its finances, its local presence, its popular base, and the reforms it has instituted since the 1968 election. Finally the author takes up the 1988 campaign and looks toward the future of the party.

Campbell, James E. *Cheap Seats: The Democratic Party's Advantage in U.S. House Elections.* Columbus: Ohio State University Press, 1996.

The author examines the congressional election system to demonstrate how the system systematically advantaged the Democratic Party. In doing so Campbell touches on the historical evolution of a Democratic advantage, voters, parties, candidates, bias in the electoral system, the changing price of a seat in Congress, and finally the 1994 collapse of what Campbell terms the *Democratic Dynasty.* His analysis explains the era of Democratic House majorities and contributes to the growing debate on the fairness and efficacy of the electoral system. The author concludes with proposals and prospects for reform. Appendixes examine the effects of candidate advantages on the vote, a carryover effect of partisan bias through incumbency, wasted votes, and alternative estimates of bias.

Chambers, William N. *The Democrats, 1789–1964: A Short History of a Popular Party.* Princeton: Van Nostrand, 1964.

The author provides an historical overview and analysis of the Democratic Party from 1789 to 1964. Chambers examines the evolution of the Democrats from the party's Jeffersonian roots through Lyndon B. Johnson and how the party's activities and platforms have shifted over time. In addition, the author provides sixteen sets of primary documents related to the Democratic Party.

Crotty, William J. *Decisions for the Democrats: Reforming the Party Structure.* Baltimore: Johns Hopkins University Press, 1979.

The author examines the period in American politics between the 1968 Democratic National Convention and the 1972 George McGovern candidacy when the

Democratic Party experimented with reform unequalled in the nation's history. Crotty narrates the reform movement and its generative forces, contributions, and problems. The book primarily focuses on the serious attempts at major institutional change put forward by the McGovern-Fraser Commission on Party Structure and Delegate Selection and the O'Hara Commission on Rules. The author concludes with a reassessment of the reform movement and a look to the future of reform in the political process.

Goldman, Ralph M. *The Democratic Party in American Politics.* New York: Macmillan, 1966.

The author examines the Democratic Party's role in electoral politics. He places it in the more general context of mass politics by examining the grassroots support and organizational building blocks of the Democratic Party. He looks at state parties and sectional parties, followed by the national party's emergence as a dominant force in American politics. Goldman examines the renaissance of the party's presidential wing, the congressional Democrats, the contemporary presidential party, and emerging tendencies and future dilemmas.

Mayer, William G. *The Divided Democrats: Ideological Unity, Party Reform, and Presidential Elections.* Boulder, CO: Westview Press, 1996.

The author examines how the machinery of the party system has evolved in the making of presidential nominations, and in particular how that affects the Democratic Party. Mayer's assumption is that the two major parties are not more or less equivalent organizations simply located at different ends of the political spectrum, but rather differently constituted political parties. Thus the party reforms of 1969 and 1970 affected the parties differently, hurting the Democrats more than the Republicans. Mayer shows that the Democrats also are less ideologically cohesive than the Republicans are, but that because of this quality the Democrats are a more successful logrolling coalition. The author also argues that this wide spread on the issues hurts a Democrat's chances to attain the White House.

Rubin, Richard L. *Party Dynamics: The Democratic Coalition and the Politics of Change.* New York: Oxford University Press, 1976.

The author examines the contesting forces at work in the Democratic Party since the end of World War II. He examines strategic manipulations of party activists and the role of important groups of voters in the mass electorate. Rubin focuses on the decline in support among traditionally Democratic groups, which erodes the coalition that formerly supported presidential dominance. He analyzes how suburbanization has affected important urban groups such as Catholics and organized labor, the role of African American migration in the shift of electoral support, and the changing interrelationships of political party candidacy and party loyalty. The author links the effects of shifting partisan loyalties to intraparty struggle between old and new activists. Rubin analyzes activist conflict among Democrats as it converts into mass primary election conflict. He relates the overall effect of a step-level increase in the scope and intensity of competition among rank-and-file Democrats to significant changes in the political orientation of the electorate as a whole.

Republican

Aistrup, Joseph A. *The Southern Strategy Revisited: Republican Top-Down Advancement in the South.* Lexington: University of Kentucky Press, 1996.

The author examines why the Republicans have made such great progress at the statewide and national levels, while at the same time making little headway at the local level. Although the election results of 1994 suggest a top-down ripple effect from national politics is beginning to translate into substantial Republican subnational gains, these gains have taken more than thirty years to arrive. Using a pool time-series design, the author argues that explanations for the national-subnational difference can be found by examining the interaction between the ideological strategies promoted by Republican candidates, which lure voters to vote Republican, and the Republicans' top-down party development methods.

Brennan, Mary C. *Turning Right in the Sixties: The Conservative Capture of the GOP.* Chapel Hill: University of North Carolina Press, 1995.

The author discusses the rise of conservatives in the Republican Party in the 1960s. Brennan discusses the 1960 and 1964 presidential elections in particular, examining the struggles within the Republican Party and how they were related to the political climate of the 1960s.

Cosman, Bernard, and Robert J. Huckshorn, eds. *Republican Politics, the 1964 Campaign, and Its Aftermath for the Party.* New York: Praeger, 1968.

This edited volume places the Barry Goldwater phenomenon of 1964 in the context of ongoing party politics and probes the consequences of the election for both the party and the two-party system. Cosman and Huckshorn focus on electoral behavior, congressional leadership, party professionals, party operations, and regional politics. The various authors examine the bitter political infighting between Goldwater forces and party regulars, the rebuilding process in Congress and the Republican National Committee, the party's new financial sources, the future of conservative ideology in the party, and the newly emerging party in the South.

Jones, Charles O. *The Republican Party in American Politics.* New York: Macmillan, 1965.

The author offers an historical and analytical account of the Republican Party and its organization, leaders, supporters, problems, and work. He posits that the Republicans serve as a minority opposition party in America's two-party system and have done so since 1932. Jones also examines the Republican Party's role in light of the two primary functions of a political party: a vehicle for selecting those who will work in government and a vehicle for resolving the problems of society and state in a particular manner. The two parts of the book focus on the electoral role of Republicans (organizing, nominating, and electing) and the policy-making role of the Party (in Congress and the White House). The author concludes with an assessment of the Republican Party's future role in politics.

Mayer, George H. *The Republican Party, 1854–1966.* 2d ed. New York: Oxford University Press, 1967.

The author documents the history of the Republican Party. He discusses electoral politics, issues, personalities, and party dynamics. Mayer starts with the golden age of politics under Andrew Jackson and the birth of the new Republican Party. He covers the growth of the party through the nineteenth century, focusing on the secession crisis, the Civil War, reconstruction, and expansion. He then includes chapters on tariffs and silver, Theodore Roosevelt and the Progressive Movement, the Bull Moose Movement, the League of Nations debate, and the descent into the Great Depression. Mayer chronicles the long years of Republican frustration during World War II and the Franklin D. Roosevelt era. He discusses the rise of new issues and new leaders at the outset of the Cold War, and the post–Dwight D. Eisenhower frustration of the Republicans.

Thimmesch, Nick. *The Condition of Republicanism.* New York: Norton, 1968.

The author examines the history of the Republican Party, following its rise in 1860, its dominance of politics through 1932, its opposition to the Democratic New Deal, and its revival in the post–World War II era. Thimmesch, a political reporter, credits the party's resurgence to the emergence of problem-solving nonpoliticians and the increasing power of the independent voter. He argues that in the coming 1968 election the Republicans have the advantage in potentially attaining the nation's leadership roles. He examines the party's future leaders, such as Richard M. Nixon, Nelson Rockefeller, George Romney, Charles Percy, Ronald Reagan, and John Lindsay. The author concludes with a look to the future, and examines the prospects for success of a post–1968 Republican Party.

Third Parties

Canfield, James L. *A Case of Third Party Activism: The George Wallace Campaign Worker and the American Independent Party.* Lanham, MD: University Press of America, 1984.

The author employs interview and survey data to evaluate the behavior of third party political activists, specifically those working for the 1968 George Wallace presidential campaign. Canfield examines the current theories of third party politics. He analyzes the social and political backgrounds, the motivations, and the attitudes of Wallace activists towards traditional parties. Canfield evaluates their views on political events and issues and compares them with those of traditional party supporters. An appendix provides the interview schedule the author used for this project.

Mazmanian, Daniel A. *Third Parties in Presidential Elections.* Washington, DC: Brookings Institution, 1974.

The author explains George Wallace's 1968 presidential campaign as the result of intense public concern with Vietnam and race relations. He outlines the careers of various nineteenth- and twentieth-century third parties. Mazmanian asserts that third parties have had little impact on policy formation.

Rosenstone, Steven J., Roy L. Behr, and Edward H. Lazarus. *Third Parties in America: Citizen Response to Major Party Failure.* 2d ed. Princeton: Princeton University Press, 1996.

The authors examine the roles of third parties and candidates in presidential elections from 1840 to 1992. They identify constraints that have supported the two-party system over time and develop a theory that explains why voters support third parties. Third parties receive support because of major party decline, attractive and viable third party candidates, and surges of new and independent voters. Using historical, aggregate political, social, and economic data, and survey data, the authors offer a systemic and structural explanation for the cyclical support of third party presidential candidates over time. The final chapter uses the authors' theory to account for the phenomenal success of Ross Perot's 1992 candidacy and to put it in historical perspective.

Smallwood, Frank. *The Other Candidates: Third Parties in Presidential Elections.* Hanover, NH: University Press of New England, 1983.

The author discusses the structural constraints imposed on third party candidates in a supposedly open two-party system and examines third party candidates' historical impact on presidential elections before 1980. The author also provides full-text interviews conducted with independent candidate John Anderson and third party candidates who ran for president in the 1980 elections in at least two states.

Stedman, Murray S., Jr., and Susan W. Stedman. *Discontent at the Polls: A Study of Farmer and Labor Parties, 1827–1948.* New York: Columbia University Press, 1950.

The authors examine the functions performed by farmer and labor parties. They discuss the parties' roles as vehicles for the expression of political discontent and issues that the major parties initially ignored. Stedman and Stedman discuss how the farmer and labor parties performed those functions and the economic, geographical, and psychological conditions in which they took place. The authors discuss the parties' platforms and their records at the polls.

9

Electoral System

General

Bullock, Charles S., III, and Loch K. Johnson. *Runoff Elections in the United States.* Chapel Hill: University of North Carolina Press, 1992.

The authors examine the phenomenon of runoff elections and evaluate their effectiveness and fairness in relation to the Condorcet paradox and approval voting critiques. Bullock and Johnson examine the circumstances in which runoff elections are likely to occur and test myths about the outcomes of runoffs based on incumbency, voter sympathy, gender, and race. The authors then focus on how a dual-party system affects the relationship between race and elections, especially in the South. The book concludes with an evaluation of the runoff process and the prospects for its future as a viable political mechanism.

Clubb, Jerome M., and Howard W. Allen, eds. *Electoral Change and Stability in American Political History.* New York: Free Press, 1971.

The essays reprinted in this volume introduce the study of electoral history, with a particular focus on structure, continuity, and realignment. Many of these seminal essays have helped to define the arena for research and debate among students of American electoral patterns. Some of these works address the entire sweep of the nation's electoral history, while others focus on particular geographical areas, time periods, or problems. They use a variety of methodologies, ranging from highly sophisticated methods to simple arithmetic manipulations.

Clubb, Jerome M., William H. Flanigan, and Nancy H. Zingale, eds. *Analyzing Electoral History: A Guide to the Study of American Voter Behavior.* Beverly Hills: Sage, 1981.

The essays in this edited volume address methodological and conceptual issues and problems in the analysis of electoral history. The first section focuses on using

159

both computer-readable and printed data sources to find data on elections. The second section focuses on interpreting electoral history. Aggregate units of analysis, demographic and compositional change, estimation of voter participation, and voter fraud and data validity are examined in detail. The final section looks at analyzing quantitative data on electoral behavior. It addresses issues such as summarizing quantitative data, relationships among variables, and group data and individual behavior.

Cox, Gary W. *Making Votes Count: Strategic Coordination in the World's Electoral Systems*. New York: Cambridge University Press, 1997.

The author employs a unified game-theoretical model to study strategic coordination. Cox relies primarily on constituency-level rather than national aggregate data in testing propositions about the effects of electoral laws. He analyzes different forms of strategic voting, including single-member, single-ballot systems, multimember districts, and single-member, dual-ballot systems. Cox also examines the effects of cleavage structures, number of parties, and the makeup of constituencies. He uses data from seventy-seven democracies.

Ginsberg, Benjamin. *The Consequences of Consent: Elections, Citizen Control and Popular Acquiescence*. Redding, MA: Addison-Wesley, 1982.

The author expands the literature on electoral studies by focusing on the institution of the election. Ginsberg asks why individuals choose to participate in elections, why individuals choose elections over alternative political instruments, and what implications the answers to these questions have for democratic institutions. He maintains that asking these questions exposes the foundations of political democracy for analysis in terms of consent and rule.

Maisel, L. Sandy, and Joseph Cooper, eds. *The Impact of the Electoral Process*. Beverly Hills: Sage, 1977.

The editors examine how the electoral process affects the functioning of the political system. The authors of the nine articles discuss the decline of political parties, the delegate selection for the 1976 Democratic convention, the platform and caucuses of the 1976 Democratic convention, trends in party voting in the House from 1887 to 1969, welfare and civil liberties in House party voting, the media's role in presidential selection, referenda voting in Oklahoma between 1907 and 1974, and the policy impact of elected women officials. The authors argue that elections affect policy making.

Penniman, Howard R. *The American Political Process*. Princeton: Van Nostrand, 1962.

The author describes and analyzes the essence of the U.S. electoral system. Penniman examines the composition and views of the electorate and the nature and operation of interest groups. He briefly considers the nature and operation of the party system and its consequences for the way governmental decisions are made.

Penniman examines the nature of the nomination and election processes as they apply to the presidency on the one hand and to all other political offices on the other.

Pomper, Gerald M. *Elections in America*. New York: Dodd, Mead, 1977.

The author covers voting behavior, electoral studies, party platforms, the history of African American suffrage, party change, and the role of elections in the American political system. Pomper demonstrates that the vote is an important means to achieving popular demands, not necessarily directly, but instead indirectly.

Reichley, A. James, ed. *Elections American Style*. Washington, DC: Brookings Institution, 1987.

This edited volume comprehensively examines electoral procedures, institutions, and reforms from the local level up to the presidential. The authors evaluate political reform and conclude that reforms often are carelessly conceived and poorly designed by policy makers. The papers included in this volume were presented at a Brookings Institution conference on electoral politics and cover an array of topics that include the federal electoral system, the presidential selection process, voter participation, sources of political corruption, and the role of political parties. The book focuses on and offers pragmatic solutions to the problems of our electoral system.

Wayne, Stephen J., and Clyde Wilcox, eds. *The Quest for the National Office: Readings on Elections*. New York: St. Martin's, 1992.

The articles in this collection examine how the electoral system works, exploring tensions among its different elements. The editors offer an historical overview of the electoral system. The editors cover campaign finance, the general political environment, presidential nominations, nominating conventions, campaign strategy and tactics, mass media, the vote and its meaning, and electoral reforms. Each chapter focuses primarily on presidential elections but also includes at least one reading about congressional elections.

Representation

Amy, Douglas J. *Real Choices/New Voices: The Case for Proportional Representation Elections in the United States*. New York: Columbia University Press, 1993.

The author makes a detailed argument against maintaining the current single-member plurality (SMP) system by which the legislative seats are filled in the United States. Amy details the shortcomings of the SMP in the first seven chapters: low voter turnout, centrist candidates, two-party monopoly, wasted votes, issueless campaigns, underrepresentation of minorities and women, and gerrymandering. He also examines the strengths and deficiencies of a proportional representation (PR) system. Amy outlines proposed PR systems, examines their feasibility, and concludes by advocating implementation of a PR system to ensure a more democratic, fair, and equal system of representative selection.

Baker, Gordon E. *The Reapportionment Revolution: Representation, Political Power, and the Supreme Court.* New York: Random House, 1966.

The author evaluates the implications of increased suburbanization and the 1960s Supreme Court decisions on enfranchisement have on the political theory and practice of democratic representation. He first assesses Supreme Court decisions handed down between 1962 and 1964 against the background of the political thought of the founding period. He examines representation at the state and national levels and as a function of rural and urban political conflict. The author concludes with an evaluation of the Supreme Court's one man, one vote decision and the increased role of the judiciary in electoral politics.

Graham, Gene. *One Man, One Vote: Baker vs. Carr and the American Levelers.* Boston: Little, Brown, 1972.

The author discusses *Baker v. Carr,* which led to the one man, one vote rule. Graham fully sketches out the details of the case, including background, litigants, and outcome. He examines the roles of reformers and members of the establishment in the processes that led to and followed the landmark Supreme Court decision. The author discusses the consequences of the case for voting rights, culture, and politics.

Grofman, Bernard, Lisa Handley, and Richard G. Niemi. *Minority Representation and the Quest for Voting Equality.* New York: Cambridge University Press, 1992.

The authors evaluate two traditional but opposing positions by which scholars, politicians, and the courts explain minority underrepresentation: a de facto systemic and structural argument that emphasizes access constraints and a socioeconomic explanation that emphasizes the failure of minorities to mobilize and form cross-racial coalitions. The authors focus on the Voting Rights Act of 1965 and its subsequent amendments and revisions, review contradictory court decisions, trace the evolution of district vote dilution, develop a model by which racially polarized voting can be measured and observed, and evaluate single-member districts in light of alternative proposals.

Lublin, David. *The Paradox of Representation: Racial Gerrymandering and Minority Interests in Congress.* Princeton: Princeton University Press, 1997.

The author analyzes evidence that exposes the central paradox of racial representation: that racial redistricting remains vital to the election of African Americans and Latinos, but makes Congress less likely to adopt policies favored by African Americans. Lublin uses data on representatives elected to Congress between 1972 and 1994 to examine the link between the racial composition of a congressional district and its representative's race and ideology. Lublin argues that specially drawn districts must exist to ensure the election of African Americans and Latinos. He shows that a small number of minorities in a district can lead to the election of a representative attentive to their interests. He finds that when African Americans and Latinos make up 40 percent of the district, they have a strong liberalizing influence on representatives of both parties; when they make up 55 percent, the district is certain to elect a minority representative. Lublin shows that concentrating minority populations into a small number of districts decreases the liberal influence in the remaining areas. Thus a handful of minority representatives, almost invariably Democrats, win elections, but so do a greater number of Republicans. The author proposes that establishing a balance between majority-minority districts and creating districts where the majority population would be slightly more dispersed, making up 40 percent of a total district, would allow African Americans to exercise more influence over their representatives.

Moreland, Laurence W., Robert P. Steed, and Tod A. Baker, eds. *Blacks in Southern Politics.* New York: Praeger, 1987.

This edited volume examines race in southern politics. The first part of the book summarizes some of the main elements of race and southern politics before the passage of the landmark 1965 Voting Rights Act. The chapters in the second part present material on various aspects of contemporary African American involvement in southern politics, including voter registration, African American party activists, the role of African American churches and political organizations, racial polarization, regional congruence, and representation. The third part of the book examines how Jesse Jackson's 1984 presidential campaign affected southern politics. The final part of the book explores continuing questions in African American politics, including election of African Americans to city councils and the influence of race in runoff primaries.

Rule, Wilma, and Joseph F. Zimmerman, eds. *United States Electoral Systems: Their Impact on Women and Minorities.* New York: Greenwood Press, 1992.

This edited volume considers the impact of electoral systems on African American and Latino men and women and Anglo women. The essay authors explore preconditions for electoral success and current underrepresentation of women and minorities in Congress. They also consider electing state legislatures and judges. Rule and Zimmerman examine institutional opportunities and barriers, demography, culture, redistricting, alternative systems, and major electoral shakeups. They discuss the electing of local leaders. They analyze proportional representation, cumulative and limited voting, and city council, county, and at-large elections. They discuss options for increasing the representation of women and minorities.

Stone, Walter J. *Republic at Risk: Self-Interest in American Politics.* Pacific Grove, CA: Brooks/Cole, 1990.

The author offers a concise approach to the study of representative government, focusing on theory and critique. Stone discusses the need to enhance the democratic, representative, and participatory nature of politics and government. He studies the current system of government, exposing major theoretical and conceptual underpinnings of government and democracy to analysis from a contemporary perspective.

He focuses especially on the concept of self-interest as it applies to citizens and elites in politics.

Swain, Carol M. *Black Faces, Black Interests: The Representation of African Americans in Congress.* Cambridge, MA: Harvard University Press, 1993.

The author examines the representation of African American interests in Congress. She argues that representation cannot simply be equated with the number of African Americans in Congress. Swain seeks to determine whether white politicians can represent African American interests and whether African American representatives are limited to serving predominantly African American districts. She finds that African American representation is not limited to the ability of the courts and state legislatures to draw majority African American congressional districts. White representatives support several issues important to African Americans, while African American representatives have an opportunity to succeed in nonmajority African American districts without "selling out." Swain finds that significant problems remain, however, both in African American communities and in Congress, where the Black Caucus is small and the pursuit of legislative careers often weakens ties to constituency concerns.

Laws

Jones, Mark P. *Electoral Laws and the Survival of Presidential Democracies.* Notre Dame, IN: University of Notre Dame Press, 1995.

The author argues that electoral laws are linked to the longevity of democracy. Jones focuses on the most feasible mechanism for facilitating the proper functioning of democratic presidential systems: electoral law reform. Jones reviews the relevant literature and a set of empirical analyses of Latin American presidential systems. He maintains that certain electoral laws are more compatible with a successful democratic presidential system than others.

Rae, Douglas W. *Political Consequences of Electoral Laws.* Rev. ed. New Haven: Yale University Press, 1971.

The author analyzes the relationship between electoral laws and political party systems on a cross-national scale. Rae examines the political consequences of electoral laws and analyzes proportional representation and other specific types of electoral formulas, district magnitude, party competition, and ballot structure.

Reitman, Alan, and Robert B. Davidson. *The Election Process: Voting Laws and Procedures.* 2d ed. Dobbs Ferry, NY: Oceana, 1972.

The authors explain election laws and procedures. They discuss voter qualifications, voter disqualifications, registration procedures, absentee voting, and procedural reform. They examine malapportionment, the electoral college, campaign expenditures, corrupt practices, and obstacles to minor parties.

Smith, Constance E. *Voting and Election Laws.* New York: Oceana, 1960.

The author examines voting and election laws and discusses the right to vote, including constitutional and state provisions. Smith discusses the registration process, focusing on why registration is necessary, different kinds of registration systems, and the administration of a registration system. She examines election administration and the polling process and discusses civilian and military absentee voting. Appendixes include literacy requirements, poll tax requirements, registration and transfer requirements, and civilian absentee voting provisions for each state.

Redistricting and Reapportionment

Balinski, Michel L., and H. Peyton Young. *Fair Representation: Meeting the Ideal of One Man, One Vote.* New Haven: Yale University Press, 1982.

The authors discuss how to divide legislative seats fairly according to the populations of federal states or party votes. They aim to establish a solid, logical foundation for choosing among the available methods of apportioning power in representative systems. Balinski and Young consider methods proposed by Thomas Jefferson, Alexander Hamilton, and Daniel Webster, among others. They examine the paradoxes of apportionment, bias, methods, and quotas. Balinski and Young consider choices for both federal systems and proportional representation systems.

Butler, David, and Bruce E. Cain. *Congressional Redistricting: Comparative and Theoretical Perspectives.* New York: Macmillan, 1992.

The authors analyze the myths and realities surrounding congressional redistricting, as they discuss how lines are drawn, the political consequences of the process, and the possibilities for improving the system. They begin by attacking the subject from a broad historical perspective, looking at the phenomenon of redistricting from the nation's founding up through 1990. Butler and Cain examine the phases of the line-drawing process and the data that are used. They theorize that conflicting principles guide those creating new boundaries. The authors explore how the process has unfolded in the states, how other nations deal with redistricting, and the various pathways to reform.

Congressional Quarterly. *Jigsaw Politics: Shaping the House after the 1990 Census.* Washington, DC: Congressional Quarterly, 1990.

Political writers briefly profile each of the fifty states, discussing recent political developments in each state and assessing its redistricting outlook. An opening overview provides a thorough treatment of the history of congressional redistricting, its current forms, and the roles of political parties and incumbency. The authors provide electoral maps in effect for the 1990 campaign cycle for all fifty states. The maps furnish a baseline from which to explore potential changes resulting from a state's loss or gain in congressional representation and/or the redrawing of existing district lines.

Dixon, Robert G., Jr. *Democratic Representation: Reapportionment in Law and Politics*. New York: Oxford University Press, 1968.

The author examines whether the right involved in reapportionment cases is (1) the individual voter's personal claim to a fractional participation in his or her legislative district equal to that of a voter in another district or (2) a claim of the aggregate voters of a district to fair representation. Dixon shows that the Supreme Court's adoption of the first way of treating the issue has resulted in some over-simplification of the problem of representation, some rigidities of standards in judging the validity of apportionment plans, and some puzzling problems of how to avoid the simplistic one-man, one-vote formula in elections that are not representative in the legislative sense. The author provides a view of the strategies of counsel, the important role performed by the solicitor general as *amicus curiae,* and the practical workings of the reformed practice of apportionment in various states.

Hacker, Andrew. *Congressional Districting: The Issue of Equal Representation.* Rev. ed. Westport, CT: Greenwood Press, 1986.

The author provides an informative analysis of the 1962 Supreme Court decision in *Baker v. Carr* that required state redistricting for more equal representation. Hacker assesses how increased equality of representation will affect Congress by examining the constitutional history of congressional districting, the way states have responded, the disproportional representation that necessitated jurisdictional action, and the consequences of inequality in the House.

Hamilton, Howard D., ed. *Legislative Apportionment; Key to Power.* Houston, TX: Harper Press, 1964.

This edited volume examines the reapportionment struggle and how it relates to issues of democratic representation. The book begins by placing the struggle in historical context, examining the origins of the controversy. Next it details the reapportionment battle in the courts, focusing on three landmark decisions: *Fergus v. Marks, Colegrove v. Green,* and *Baker v. Carr.* The book's subsequent section looks at the effect *Baker v. Carr* had on the political scene. Next the book examines how to reapportion given the court's decisions, and gives several competing recommendations. In the final section the book analyzes apportionment standards in light of the 1964 Supreme Court decisions. An appendix gives a state-by-state summary of legislative apportionment as of May 1964.

McKay, Robert B. *Reapportionment: The Law and Politics of Equal Representation.* New York: Twentieth Century Fund, 1965.

The author appraises representative government in the United States from the perspective of state legislative apportionment and congressional districting. Given that the equal population principle has become established constitutional doctrine for state legislative representation and congressional districting, McKay examines the political theory that supports the legislative aspects of representative government in the United States. He reviews a series of cases in which the equal population principle was developed. McKay assesses possible future choices and the potential consequences of electing one alternative rather than another. The author finds that there is room for local diversity among state legislative apportionment formulas.

Polsby, Nelson W., ed. *Reapportionment in the 1970s.* Berkeley: University of California Press, 1971.

This edited volume examines the issue of reapportionment. The book concludes that reapportionment has important effects on political institutions and, through these institutions, on public policies that affect the lives of American citizens. Issues examined in this volume include the role of the courts and the Supreme Court, reapportionment and democracy, gerrymandering, and the effects of malapportionment on the states and on Congress. The volume concludes with a reexamination of both the theory and practice of drawing districts to determine congressional representation.

Rush, Mark E. *Does Redistricting Make a Difference? Partisan Representation and Electoral Behavior.* Baltimore: Johns Hopkins University Press, 1993.

The author develops an argument based on the differences among partisan and racial groups targeted in the process of redistricting. Rush maintains that the two types of groups have been conflated and that each requires a separate set of tools to study them. He finds that partisan-based gerrymandering is impossible to prove and indicts political scientists for ignoring the differences between groups, thereby exacerbating the public's negative views on redistricting.

Schwab, Larry M. *The Impact of Congressional Reapportionment and Redistricting.* Lanham, MD: University Press of America, 1988.

The author studies the effects of reapportionment and redistricting on the House between 1963 and 1984. Schwab analyzes how reapportionment affected the distribution of seats on political parties, reelection of incumbents, power structure, policy making, and House membership. Schwab finds that an increase of seats in suburbia and some sunbelt cities resulted in a power shift from rural representatives to metropolitan representatives.

Voting Rights

Claude, Richard P. *The Supreme Court and the Electoral Process.* Baltimore: Johns Hopkins University Press, 1970.

The author examines the relationship between the Supreme Court and the electoral system. Claude begins with a process-oriented and political introduction to the entire field of elections-related litigation. The next ten chapters are topically and historically differentiated. He offers a primer on the constitutionally based right to vote. He traces racial discrimination and voting cases in the late nineteenth and early twentieth centuries, and examines federal legislation at mid-century and Supreme Court rulings of the 1960s. He gives accounts of the one-person, one-vote rulings of the

1960s and explores Supreme Court litigation relating to congressional districting and presidential elections. The author concludes with a discussion of the nationalization of the electoral process and its relation to the courts.

Garrow, David J. *Protest at Selma: Martin Luther King Jr. and the Voting Rights Act of 1965.* New Haven: Yale University Press, 1978.

The author discusses voting rights and protest. Garrow tells the story of how southern African Americans won equal voting rights, and particularly how the three-month protest wave in Selma, Alabama, effected that change. He focuses on how the protest strategy used by the Southern Christian Leadership Conference and its president, Dr. Martin Luther King Jr., influenced the emergence of the Voting Rights Act. Garrow also examines the roles of members of congress, constituents, and the news media in contributing to the process. He considers enforcement and effects of the Voting Rights Act from 1965 to 1976.

Grofman, Bernard, and Chandler Davidson, eds. *Controversies in Minority Voting: The Voting Rights Act in Perspective.* Washington, DC: Brookings Institution, 1992.

The editors have collected a set of essays that evaluate the aims, accomplishments, and consequences of the 1965 Voting Rights Act on the occasion of its twenty-fifth anniversary. The volume assesses the Voting Rights Act in normative, juridical, historical, and policy-oriented terms. The editors have collected articles that examine the history of voting rights legislation; the ramifications of the 1965 Voting Rights Act; the roles played by lawyers, politicians, and interest groups during its implementation; and whether the act promotes racial harmony or racial strife in politics. The Voting Rights Act is contextualized to examine its applicability, usefulness, and appropriateness in addressing current issues related to race.

Lawson, Steven F. *In Pursuit of Power: Southern Blacks and Electoral Politics, 1965–1982.* New York: Columbia University Press, 1985.

The author charts the efforts of civil rights forces from 1965 to 1982 to redress grievances through federal action. This examination of African American suffrage concentrates on the enforcement of the Voting Rights Act in the South. The author argues that the balance struck between full implementation of the African American franchise and conciliation of southern leaders helped determine whether the suffrage offered long strides or small steps toward racial equality

Rogers, Donald W., ed. *Voting and the Spirit of American Democracy: Essays on the History of Voting Rights in America.* Urbana: University of Illinois Press, 1992.

This collection of essays places the problem of voting in the context of the country's 380-year history. It consists of eight essays by distinguished historians and political scientists who examine crucial phases of the historical development of voting and voting rights from the founding of the British North American colonies to the present day. Among the topics discussed are political participation, constitutional politics, social movements and suffrage reforms, immigration, and the nature of citizenship as defined by race, class, national origin, and gender.

Thernstrom, Abigail M. *Whose Votes Count? Affirmative Action and Minority Voting Rights.* Cambridge, MA: Harvard University Press, 1987.

Concerned with the poor representation of African Americans among officeholders, the author attempts to establish parameters that would define when federal intervention is necessary to resolve the problems of local and state electoral inequalities. Thernstrom examines the Democrats' and Republicans' relationship to eroding caste inequality, the juridical battles, and alternative avenues of recourse available to minorities. The author concludes that minority voting rights remain a problem in American politics, but the prospects for overcoming these inequalities are better than they would have been without the 1965 Voting Rights Act.

Electoral College

Abbott, David W., and James P. Levine. *Wrong Winner: The Coming Debacle in the Electoral College.* New York: Praeger, 1991.

Writing from the predisposition that the electoral college is innately undemocratic in its unrepresentativeness, the authors argue that the United States is on the verge of a constitutional crisis. The authors use the constitutional arrangements by which presidents are elected, electoral history, and current political trends to highlight the shortcomings of the electoral college. Abbot and Levine identify the primary shortcoming of the electoral college as its capacity to produce either the wrong winner or no winner. They contend that the United States is on the verge of such an outcome.

Berns, Walter, ed. *After the People Vote: A Guide to the Electoral College.* Rev. ed. Washington, DC: AEI Press, 1992.

This edited volume analyzes and describes the electoral college and how it operates in the process of selecting the president. The book then evaluates three elections (1800, 1824, and 1876) in which the electoral college selected a president who was not popularly elected. The book examines criticisms and proposed reforms to the electoral college and the general electoral process. Appendixes provide constitutional provisions regarding the electoral college, precedents, party rules, and the projected allocation of electoral votes among states until the year 2000.

Best, Judith. *The Choice of the People? Debating the Electoral College.* Lanham, MD: Rowman and Littlefield, 1996.

The author examines the electoral college as a method of selecting the president. Best's thesis is that the electoral vote system is the very model of our federal system. If the federal principle is legitimate, then it is just as legitimate in the selection of the president as in the selection of the Congress. If it is not legitimate, then it should be abandoned throughout the U.S. Constitution. Based on this logic and the analysis she develops in the book, Best concludes that the electoral college has endured because it is a mirror of and the ultimate expression of the federal system. Best also provides a series of readings on the subject, including statements by Gouverneur Morris and Daniel Patrick Moynihan; excerpts from *The Federalist Papers* 39, 51, and 68; relevant sections of the U.S. Constitution; and a report of the Senate Judiciary Committee on direct popular election of the president and vice president.

Glennon, Michael J. *When No Majority Rules: The Electoral College and Presidential Succession.* Washington, DC: CQ Books, 1992.

In light of recent third party challenges for the presidency the author examines and evaluates the electoral college as the institution that selects the president. The possibility of constitutional crises emerge when no clear majority of electoral votes is awarded among three or more presidential candidate. After an initial discussion about the function of the electoral college over time, the author discusses its origins, its function today, the legislature's role in elections, the courts' role, and the legitimacy of the current electoral system. Appendixes include the U.S. Constitution, the U.S. code regulating elections, Supreme Court cases regarding the process, and House rules.

Hardaway, Robert M. *The Electoral College and the Constitution: The Case for Preserving Federalism.* Westport, CT: Praeger, 1994.

The author presents an in-depth historical and analytical discussion of the electoral college. Hardaway examines how the electoral college fits into the electoral process and how it operates. He also discusses the origins of the electoral college in the Constitutional Convention, its institutional evolution as the electoral process has been refined, and how it has affected the outcomes of presidential races. The author concludes by evaluating the proposed reforms that accompany each election cycle and suggests that the electoral college be preserved as an institutional of the American federalist system of governance.

Longley, Lawrence D., and Neal R. Peirce. *The Electoral Primer.* New Haven: Yale University Press, 1996.

The authors provide a basic and clearly written introduction to why the electoral college was created and how it works. They discuss how popular votes do not equal electoral votes. Longley and Peirce explain the strange quirks of the electoral college and the significance of its consequences.

Peirce, Neal R., and Lawrence D. Longley. *The People's President: The Electoral College in American History and the Direct Vote Alternative.* Rev. ed. New Haven: Yale University Press, 1981.

The authors examine how the president is elected. They illustrate the discussion with an analysis of the 1976 and 1980 elections. Peirce and Longley examine the historical development of the system, including the birth of the electoral college; the first elections (in 1792 and 1796); and the conundrum presented by the 1800 election, which led to the adoption of the Twelfth Amendment. Peirce and Longley discuss years of controversy, including the elections of 1924, 1876, 1888, 1916, 1948, 1960, and

1968; then they return to 1976 and 1980. Following the historical explication the authors offer a discussion of the mechanics of the present system, the major reform efforts of the past two centuries, and the decade of electoral reform politics from 1969 to 1979. They compare the direct vote plan with the status quo electoral college system.

Sayre, Wallace S., and Judith H. Parris. *Voting for President: The Electoral College and the American Political System.* Washington, DC: Brookings Institution, 1970.

The authors examine the method used to elect the president and alternative systems of election. They begin with a summary of the debate over the electoral college system. Sayre and Parris discuss the historical setting and the present status of the system. They outline four major proposals for reform: the direct-vote plan, the automatic plan, the district plan, and the proportional plan. The authors examine each plan, focusing on the old problems it would help solve and the new problems it would create. Sayre and Parris conclude that the electoral vote system with the winner-take-all, state general ticket, is the best of the methods examined.

Yunker, John H., and Lawrence D. Longley. *Electoral College, Its Biases Newly Measured for 1960s and 1970s.* Beverly Hills: Sage, 1976.

The authors use a voting power approach to estimate the biases of the electoral college and other major reform plans. They derive new estimates for the 1960s and 1970s reapportionment. Yunker and Longley develop several methods of determining voting power. Some approaches use voter turnout data and other approaches are based on alternative definitions of pivotal voting power. A technical appendix deals with mathematical questions raised by different selection methods.

Reform

American Enterprise Institute for Public Policy Research. *Direct Election of the President.* Washington, DC: AEI Press, 1977.

This concise volume covers the proposal for a direct election of the president. The work reviews the historical development of the electoral vote system, the framers' intent, the rise and growth of political parties, and the Twelfth Amendment. The book includes criticisms of the direct election proposal and electoral vote systems.

Bickel, Alexander M. *Reform and Continuity: The Electoral College, the Convention, and the Party System.* New York: Harper and Row, 1971.

The author examines the electoral system and argues that, while reform may be necessary, radical changes in the system are not needed. Bickel examines the history, flaws, and effectiveness of three major elements of the system: the electoral college, the party convention, and the two-party system with its degree of accommodation for small third parties. The author primarily uses the 1968 presidential election to illustrate the faults and merits of the system. Appendixes cover constitutional provisions concerning the electoral college and proposals for changing them, a proposal for a national presidential primary election, antidiscrimination standards to be incorporated into rules of state Democratic parties, and a call for the 1968 Democratic National Convention.

Breckenridge, Adam C. *Electing the President.* Lanham, MD: University Press of America, 1982.

The author addresses the discussion about whether the electoral college needs to be replaced with a different system. The alternative programs for presidential selection that are under consideration include the Maine District Plan, the national popular vote plan, and other alternative proposals that have emerged during the 1970s. The author also evaluates the implications this debate has for constitutional stability and other political institutions.

Crotty, William J., ed. *Paths to Political Reform.* Lexington, MA: D. C. Heath, 1980.

This edited volume examines political reforms in a wide range of contexts. The first section examines the electorate, the public mood, the role of parties and issues, and how changes in all these aspects of the political system affect reform prospects. Crotty looks at efforts to reform the electoral college. Next the volume examines issues and institutions in contemporary reform, focusing on parties, primaries, Congress, and campaign financing. Finally, the general problems with reforms are discussed.

————. *Political Reform and the American Experiment.* New York: Thomas Y. Crowell, 1977.

The author examines the problems that lead to political reforms and the political mechanisms that enable these reform efforts. Crotty first discusses the ramifications of each problem. He then develops background information on the issue and presents several potential alternative approaches to resolving some of the dimensions implicit in the question. The author examines problems, including registration and voting, campaign financing, and the reform of political institutions. He concludes with a discussion of the reform cycle, including the unanticipated consequences of reform, the role of the courts and Congress, and federal funding and regulation.

Dummett, Michael. *Principles of Electoral Reform.* New York: Oxford University Press, 1997.

The author examines the issues involved in electoral reform. He examines the constituency principle that parliaments should exclusively comprise those elected to represent the constituencies. This principle is observed in many democracies, including Britain and the United States. If it is abandoned, Dummett argues, other and possibly better systems of representation may be more plausible. He then examines proportional representation and its alternatives. He looks at the advantages and disadvantages of the German constitution's method of evading the constituency principle dilemma. The author also considers other electoral system components, such as the single transferable vote and multimember constituencies.

Keech, William R., ed. *Winner Take All: Report of the Twentieth Century Fund Task Force on Reform of the Presidential Election Process.* New York: Holmes and Meier, 1978.

This special task force report examines the potential for reform in the current presidential election system. The report focuses on the electoral college and the various proposed alternatives to it in the context of the needs of the American political system. Task force members who defend the current system acknowledge its defects but maintain that the existing system is worth preserving because it embodies certain important values. Opponents argue that these values do not compensate for the failure of the current system to guarantee that the candidate with the most popular votes nationwide will be elected to the presidency. The members ultimately propose to preserve the values cited by the electoral college supporters while making virtually certain that the candidate who receives the largest number of popular votes will be elected president—the goal of direct election supporters.

Longley, Lawrence D., and Alan G. Braun. *The Politics of Electoral College Reform.* 2d ed. New Haven: Yale University Press, 1975.

The authors argue that the direct popular vote method for electing the president reflects the will of the electorate. They examine the electoral college and prospects for proposed reforms. Longley and Braun show the gerrymandering of the one-man, one-vote principle of the electoral college and demonstrate that proposed proportional and districting plans are biased. The authors show that the direct vote plan does not create the biases and distortions inherent in other alternative proposals for a method of electing the president.

Zeidenstein, Harvey G. *Direct Election of the President.* Lexington, MA: Lexington Books, 1973.

The author examines the argument that direct election of the president will have dire and dysfunctional consequences for the nation in general and for liberal groups in particular. Zeidenstein presents the charges against the electoral college as it currently operates, along with rebuttals against these charges. He outlines the case for direct election and other proposals for reform and analyzes the predicted dysfunctional consequences of direct election. He summarizes the conclusions drawn from his analysis and recommends change in the electoral system.

Term Limits

Benjamin, Gerald, and Michael J. Malbin, eds. *Limiting Legislative Terms.* Washington, DC: CQ Press, 1992.

This edited volume brings together twelve studies by legislative scholars on the issue of term limits. After establishing a general framework for analysis of the issue, contributors examine the history and political theory of term limits, campaigns for and against limiting legislative terms, and the likely effects of these limits on political careers and legislative institutions. Much of the analysis draws from the effects of similar provisions on elective offices in the states. Two extensive appendixes provide data on turnover and reelection rates in various legislative bodies, the texts of term limit initiatives, and the legal and political rationales advanced by supporters and opponents.

Coyne, James K., and John H. Fund. *Cleaning House: America's Campaign for Term Limits.* Washington, DC: Regnery Gateway, 1992.

The authors present the case for term limitations for members of Congress. They begin by detailing abuses in the operation of Congress and deficiencies in the current electoral system that promote legislative careerism. Coyne and Fund then discuss the historical, constitutional, and partisan aspects of the term limits initiative and rebut common objections. An appendix summarizes activity on this issue in all fifty states.

Jones, Charles O. *Every Second Year: Congressional Behavior and the Two-Year Term.* Washington, DC: Brookings Institution, 1967.

The author addresses the continuing debate over the length of terms for members of the House. Jones assesses current positions, examines alternative programs for reform, and considers the possibility of reform in the near future. The effects of the two-year term on representatives' ability to govern and the reasons behind the failure of previous reform attempts are thoroughly addressed. The author concludes that the two-year term will probably endure and should continue to do so.

Kamber, Victor. *Giving Up on Democracy: Why Term Limits Are Bad for America.* Washington DC: Regnery, 1995.

The author makes a case for increasing democratic, grassroots citizen participation rather than imposing limits on congressional terms of office. Drawing on a variety of information sources, Kamber traces the term limits movement from its inception through the 1994 midterm elections and criticizes it heavily for its antidemocratic tendencies. An appendix includes a list of sources and suggestions for increasing citizen awareness, participation, and mobilization.

Sorensen, Theodore C. *A Different Kind of Presidency: A Proposal for Breaking the Political Deadlock.* New York: Harper and Row, 1984.

The author argues that the presidency should be depoliticized by restricting presidents to only one term. Sorensen has tried to write a nonpartisan proposal for a one-term presidency. His main argument is that such a presidency would be more effective and stem the decline of the office.

Will, George F. *Restoration: Congress, Term Limits, and the Recovery of Deliberative Democracy.* New York: Free Press, 1992.

The conservative columnist describes his journey to the conviction that a constitutional change to limit legislative terms is essential to strengthening democracy.

In four essays, Will revisits some of the ideas and controversies that shaped the United States in the founding era, including a debate over term limitation; he presents evidence of congressional behavior to buttress his argument that careerism in Congress has replaced an ethic of representation. The author calls for a reassertion of congressional supremacy, a revival of the democratic tradition unique to the United States, and a return to deliberative democracy. He uses anecdotal and statistical evidence, along with citations of philosophical sources undergirding his beliefs.

10

Voting Participation

General

Abramson, Paul R., John H. Aldrich, and David W. Rohde. *Change and Continuity in the 1980 Elections.* Rev. ed. Washington, DC: CQ Press, 1983.

Using Survey Research Center data and a synthesis of scholarly literature, the authors undertake a collective analysis of the 1980 elections, seeking to explain why voters elected Ronald Reagan and why they gave the Republicans a majority in the Senate and more seats in the House. This revised edition covers the presidential election, voting behavior, the congressional elections, and how the 1980 election affects the future of politics. Abramson, Aldrich, and Rohde also discuss the results of the 1982 midterm elections and their likely influence on the next presidential election. In a section on Congress, the authors examine the effects of candidate decisions on electoral outcomes and the way voters make choices in congressional elections.

————. *Change and Continuity in the 1984 Elections.* Washington, DC: CQ Press, 1986.

The authors present a collective analysis of the 1984 elections. They examine the 1984 campaign cycle in depth by itself and in the context of more than thirty years of election studies. The authors divide their analysis into four parts: the presidential election, voting behavior, the congressional elections, and the importance of the 1984 elections for the future of politics. In the section on Congress, the authors explore the causes for limited Republican success in federal legislative races and the consequences of this limited success for policy making. They focus on candidate resources and their effect on electoral outcomes and on the way voters make choices in congressional elections.

————. *Change and Continuity in the 1988 Elections.* Washington, DC: CQ Press, 1990.

Using National Election Studies data, the authors construct a social-scientific evaluation of the 1988 presidential election and place it in the context of elections from the previous forty years. Of particular interest to the authors are the shifts in the electorate that represent dealignment and realignment and that manifest in split-ticket voting and divided government. The book comprises four sections that cover the 1988 presidential contest, the voting behavior of the electorate, the 1988 congressional elections, and the implications of the outcome of the 1988 elections.

————. *Change and Continuity in the 1996 Elections.* Washington, DC: CQ Press, 1998.

Using National Election Study data, the authors examine concepts of voting behavior through in-depth analysis of the 1996 presidential and congressional contests. They cover the 1996 presidential contest, the voting behavior of the electorate in 1996, and the 1996 congressional elections. They explore the implications of Clinton's reelection victory and the Republican congressional victory on the party system.

Alvarez, R. Michael. *Information and Elections.* Ann Arbor: University of Michigan Press, 1997.

The author shows that a tremendous amount of information has been made available to voters in recent elections and that voters learn about candidates during presidential campaigns. Using a rational choice framework, Alvarez explores how imperfect information affects the decisions voters make about presidential candidates. The author begins the study with the assumption that voters do not have the incentive or the inclination to be well informed. Candidates themselves have incentives to provide ambiguous information. And yet a tremendous amount of information is made available, as the author demonstrates by employing survey data from five presidential elections. Using sophisticated statistical modeling, Alvarez presents results that show that large amounts of informative media coverage helps inform voters. He also uncovers evidence that voters penalize ambiguous candidates. Voters are also unlikely to vote for candidates about whom they know little.

Bone, Hugh A., and Austin Ranney. *Politics and Voters.* 5th ed. New York: McGraw-Hill, 1985.

In this fifth edition, the authors include new data (from the 1972 and 1976 elections) against which they check their previous assumptions about political behavior. Bone and Ranney focus on the individual voter as the primary unit of analysis and discuss at length the intersection between how individuals process information and how they act on that information. In the second portion of the book the authors primarily discuss the organizations and institutions of electoral politics. They relate party and interest group composition, organization, and activities to the selection of candidates for public office.

Brams, Steven J., and Peter C. Fishburn. *Approval Voting*. Boston: Birkhauser, 1983.

The authors evaluate the electoral procedure of approval voting in which each voter votes for each of the candidates that he or she prefers; the candidate that receives the most votes, or receives the highest rate of approval, wins the election. Brams and Fishburn contend that approval voting is better than typical electoral procedures and the book defends this proposition. Using rigorous theoretical analysis and case studies, the authors focus primarily on the linkages between the institutional constraints and actual voter preferences.

Broh, C. Anthony. *Toward a Theory of Issue Voting*. Beverly Hills: Sage, 1973.

The author specifies several conditions under which issue voting is likely to take place. Broh tests three different voting behavior models using data from the 1964 presidential election. The first model suggests that issue voting did take place in the 1964 presidential election. The second model suggests that more issue voting took place by voters with high levels of political conceptualization. The third model suggests that more issue voting took place only among people who perceived a difference between the two parties on issues. Misperceivers show a constant correlation of issue attitudes and voting preferences for all four levels of conceptualization of politics. These models are complementary rather than contradictory.

Busch, Andrew. *Horses in Midstream: U.S. Midterm Elections and Their Consequences, 1894–1998*. Pittsburgh: University of Pittsburgh Press, 1999.

The author argues that midterm elections play a role in American politics that is more important and systematic than is generally acknowledged. Busch argues that midterm elections serve as an integral part of the system of checks and balances, providing both negative and positive institutional checks in American politics. He also discusses how midterm elections have contributed to realignments, presidential politics, and the development of issues and agendas.

Campbell, Angus, Philip E. Converse, Warren E. Miller, and Donald E. Stokes. *The American Voter*. New York: Wiley, 1960.

This book issues from a research program on the electorate initiated by the Survey Research Center. Using national surveys conducted during the 1952 and 1956 presidential election years and supplemental materials from additional election studies between 1948 and 1958, the authors examine the behavior of the mass electorate within the context of a larger political system. The book's first major emphasis is on political attitudes and the vote. The authors examine perceptions of parties and candidates, partisan choice, and voter turnout. Next they turn to the political context, focusing on party identification, political preference, public policy, attitude structure, ideology, issue concepts, partisan change, and election laws. Next the authors examine the social and economic context, and specifically memberships in social groups, the role played by class, economic antecedents of political behavior, population movement, agrarian political behavior, and personality factors. The book concludes with a reexamination of the electoral decision in the context of the political system.

—————. *Elections and the Political Order.* New York: Wiley, 1966.

This book emphasizes the collective processes of politics. A successor to the authors' pioneering work, *The American Voter,* it shifts the attention from the voter to the full electorate and from the individual choice to the collective decision. Using recent developments in survey research and drawing on the findings of a national survey from 1948 to 1960, the authors make an effort to reveal the character of the collective vote to expand our understanding of the part played by elections in the functioning of the total political system. They develop a model of electoral change and explore aspects of party systems, comparative political behavior, and historical and institutional analysis.

Campbell, Angus, Gerald Gurin, and Warren E. Miller. *The Voter Decides.* Evanston, IL: Row, Peterson, 1954.

This classic study examines the 1952 election. The authors analyze the motivations behind voting behavior, including party identification, issue orientation, and candidate orientation. They discuss the differences and interactions of the motivating factors.

Campbell, Bruce A. *The American Electorate: Attitudes and Action.* New York: Holt, Rinehart and Winston, 1979.

The author uses presidential election studies data from 1952 to 1976 to address three areas of individual and aggregate political behavior: political socialization, public opinion, and political participation. Campbell provides an empirical framework that emphasizes attitudes with which these three topics can be integrated and evaluated. Campbell's normative interpretation of the findings concerns the role the electorate should take in American politics. The author concludes with a section that discusses the electorate's role in public policy–making processes.

Cantor, Robert D. *Voting Behavior and Presidential Elections.* Itasca, IL: F. E. Peacock, 1975.

The author examines trends and transformations in the process of electing presidents and in the character of the electorate. Cantor develops a theory and classification of presidential elections and examines the strength of party identification. He discusses voting patterns, campaign tactics and techniques, and candidate positions on issues.

Christian, Spencer. *Electing Our Government: Everything You Need to Know to Make Your Vote Really Count.* New York: St. Martin's, 1996.

The author offers a guide to the political process at the local, state, and national levels. He explains the structure and functions of government, how the average citizen can make government more responsive, and how to broaden one's role as a citizen. Christian offers historical perspectives, insights into the thinking of the Founding Fathers, and little-known facts about our political leaders—all centered on a framework provided by our quadrennial contests for president. He includes brief summaries of each presidential election, along with state-by-state political profiles and information on upcoming gubernatorial and senatorial elections.

Crotty, William J., ed. *Political Participation and American Democracy.* New York: Greenwood Press, 1991.

This edited volume concerns itself with the political involvement of citizens in self-government. The book begins with an overview of the literature on political participation. Subsequent chapters cover theories of turnout, nonvoting, mobilization, legal-institutional factors and voting participation, discrimination and participation, voting for judges, and participation and political knowledge.

Dunham, Pat. *Electoral Behavior in the United States.* Englewood Cliffs, NJ: Prentice-Hall, 1991.

The author examines state, congressional, and presidential elections, focusing on the role elections play in a democracy. He explores the roles of public opinion, political parties, political participation, and the mass media and realignment. Dunham examines presidential elections from 1960 to 1988. He provides an introduction to political behavior as it relates to elections.

Edsall, Thomas B., and Mary D. Edsall. *Chain Reaction: The Impact of Race, Rights, and Taxes on American Politics.* New York: Norton, 1991.

The authors focus on three volatile issues that drive politics today: race, rights, and taxes. Edsall and Edsall argue that these issues have come to intersect with an entire range of domestic issues, from welfare policy to suburban zoning practices. In an explosive chain reaction, a new conservative voting majority has replaced the once-dominant Democratic presidential coalition, and a new polarization has pitted major segments of society against one another. The authors trace the history of American politics and these issues to uncover how this massive power shift occurred.

Elliott, Euel W. *Issues and Elections: Presidential Voting in Contemporary America: A Revisionist View.* Boulder, CO: Westview Press, 1989.

The author maintains that electoral behavior must be viewed as a dynamic process rather than as a series of snapshots of aggregate individual voting behavior and electoral outcomes. Elliott develops a model by which the linkages between individual behavior and election outcomes can be isolated by focusing on issue-oriented conditions. Elliott contends that in order to determine electoral outcomes, issues must be highly salient to the individual, parties must be equipped to effectively address the issues, and issues must explain electoral shifts over time. The author concludes that, if issue-saliency is the determining factor affecting electoral outcomes, rarely do elections result in a mandate for a particular politician's policy agenda.

Gimpel, James G. *National Elections and the Autonomy of American State Party Systems.* Pittsburgh: University of Pittsburgh Press, 1996.

The author seeks to understand political behavior in the western United States. Gimpel begins by studying electoral behavior in state politics, then focuses on the associations of state and national party electorates. He evaluates the implications of the state political alignments and explores how differences between state and national politics influence the political behavior of voters, candidates, and state party organizations. Gimpel contends that the lack of electoral coherence in the West is the pattern for understanding what is happening in the rest of America. He asserts that cohesive state and local organizations are largely a thing of the past, even in the industrial East and Midwest. Electoral foundations for traditional party politics have given way to a less reliable, more candidate-centered, locally autonomous system.

Granberg, Donald, and Soren Holmberg. *The Political System Matters: Social Psychology and Voting Behavior in Sweden and the United States.* New York: Cambridge University Press, 1988.

The authors use long-term cross-sectional and panel national surveys of electorates in Sweden and the United States to examine how the political system affects the political behavior of individuals. They examine the interaction of political context with social psychological processes. Their interdisciplinary and comparative study considers topics such as ideological perception of abstract and concrete issues at the party and individual level; the polarization, interrelation, and transitivity of attitudes; the relationship between intention and behavior; and how behavior may be predicted.

Hill, David B., and Norman R. Luttbeg. *Trends in American Electoral Behavior.* Itasca, IL: F. E. Peacock, 1980.

The authors examine change in electoral behavior as evidenced in presidential and congressional elections from 1952 to 1978. They present their model of voter behavior, reviewing findings and theory within the historical context of their development by electoral researchers. Hill and Luttbeg analyze the hypothesized decline of political parties, declining political participation, and declining political trust. They include a trend assessment at the conclusion of each chapter. The authors consider several additional trends at work in society, including increased levels of education, and enumerate their own conclusions about the extent of change in the electorate and its importance. They believe stability is more characteristic of the behavior of the electorate than is change.

Jacobson, Gary C., and Samuel Kernell. *Strategy and Choice in Congressional Elections.* New Haven: Yale University Press, 1981.

Jacobson and Kernell explain the link between national political conditions and individual-level voting decisions through the mediating influence of politically active elites whose behavior (candidate recruitment and financing) tends to structure the vote choice. The authors consider other theories of congressional elections before exploring in detail the forward-looking strategic calculations of challengers, incumbents, and contributors to determine if cumulative elite decisions affect aggregate election returns. The authors test their theory against competing theories by looking at the 1980 election results. They conclude with a discussion of the implications of their theory for a representative democracy.

Kelley, Stanley, Jr. *Interpreting Elections.* Princeton: Princeton University Press, 1983.

The author examines the implications, consequences, and significance of the act of voting in elections. Kelley's interpretation of voting is informed by the academic study of voting, the ideas and attitudes of campaign organizers, and political philosophy. He uses opinion survey data to develop a theory of voting and examines the issues and outcomes associated with the 1964, 1972, and 1978 elections, and the concept of political mandates.

Key, Valdimer O., and Milton C. Cummings Jr. *The Responsible Electorate: Rationality in Presidential Voting, 1936–1960.* Cambridge, MA: Harvard University Press, 1966.

This posthumous volume continues the optimistic outlook for American democracy developed previously by the authors. Key and Cummings believe that the electorate is responsible, rational, and interested in policy making, representative accountability, and government performance. By classifying voters into three categories (standpatters, switchers, and new voters), the authors examine the correlates between presidential vote, the type of voter, and the issues shared by the electorate and candidates. The authors find that policy preference is a guiding force behind voter choice. Using data from the 1936 to 1960 elections, the authors conclude that the individual voter is rational, as are the democratic institutions created by the electorate.

Kleppner, Paul. *The Third Electoral System 1853–1892: Parties, Voters, and Political Cultures.* Chapel Hill: University of North Carolina Press, 1979.

The author analyzes mass voting behavior from 1853 to 1892. He focuses on the party and the electorate, describing and analyzing the social bases of mass partisan support. Kleppner discusses how changing demographics affect partisan politics, and the role of minor and third parties.

Lazarsfeld, Paul F., Bernard Berelson, and Hazel Gaudet. *The People's Choice: How the Voter Makes Up His Mind in a Presidential Campaign.* 3d ed. New York: Columbia University Press, 1968.

The authors study political behavior during the 1940 presidential campaign. The authors conducted interviews with 3,000 respondents at different stages over the course of the election. One panel of 600 respondents was kept under continual observation from May until November 1940. The other respondents were split into three control panels used at three different points in the study. The authors charted changes in voter behavior over time and the reasons for those changes. The authors find that personal contacts are more influential than are more formal means of communication. The preface to this edition comments on developments in the field that affected the way the data collected for this study could be analyzed. The authors also include the main results of these new mutual interaction analyses, a technique not available to them at the time of the original study.

Luttbeg, Norman R., and Michael M. Gant. *American Electoral Behavior: 1952–1992*. 2d ed. Itasca, IL: F. E. Peacock, 1995.

The authors provide a review of the scholarly literature within a text designed for undergraduate students. They include analyses of all presidential elections from 1952 to 1992, paying particular attention to behavior patterns. Luttbeg and Gant include a section on the meaning of party identification that focuses on the debate between traditional and revisionist interpretations. They also include a chapter on congressional elections, focusing especially on the House. They examine explanations about declining political participation and trust, and discussions of incumbency, partisanship, and change.

McLean, Iain. *Dealing in Votes: Interactions between Politicians and Voters in Britain and the USA*. Oxford: Martin Robertson, 1982.

The author examines different types of interactions between voters and politicians. He covers voting, and things other than voting that citizens do when they want to influence their government. McLean deals with politicians' responses, particularly why they deliver the policies that they do and why they play the game at all. McLean examines these interactions in two parallel contexts, Great Britain and the United States.

McWilliams, Wilson C. *Beyond the Politics of Disappointment? American Elections, 1980–1998*. 2d ed. New York: Seven Bridges Press, 1999.

The author chronicles and interprets presidential and national elections between 1980 and 1998. His evaluation is couched in terms of an ever-growing discontent with national politics and the programs offered by candidates and parties. Appendixes present the presidential vote for the 1980 to the 1996 elections.

Miller, Warren E., and J. Merrill Shanks. *The New American Voter*. Cambridge, MA: Harvard University Press, 1996.

The authors discuss evidence from recent presidential elections concerning a comprehensive set of explanations for individual citizens' electoral choices. Miller and Shanks seek to present an overall framework that can be used to assess and compare explanatory ideas based on different theoretical or conceptual foundations. They identify long- and short-term factors that influence voter decisions as to whether to vote and, if so, for whom to vote. They examine partisan identification. The authors interpret and compare the 1988 and 1992 elections specifically to test their earlier analysis.

Nie, Norman H., Sidney Verba, and John R. Petrocik. *The Changing American Voter*. Rev. ed. Cambridge, MA: Harvard University Press, 1979.

Drawing primarily on a series of surveys conducted by the University of Michigan's Survey Research Center from 1952 to 1972, the authors depict a changing and increasingly dissatisfied and disillusioned citizenry. They find that contemporary voters feel more and more alienated, not only from political parties, but also from the electoral process itself. They show that contemporary American voters are not only more aware of and sensitive to political issues but also far more likely to rely on their own issue position and to desert their party in making the voting decision. Tracing these changes both to the issues and to the entry of new voters into the electorate, the authors make a case that the electorate is undergoing a fundamental realignment, similar to that of the New Deal era. The authors present several alternative futures and indicate through a series of mock elections how the electorate might react in 1976 to various candidate choices.

Niemi, Richard G., and Herbert F. Weisberg, eds. *Classics in Voting Behavior.* Washington, DC: CQ Press, 1993.

The editors have collected a series of essays and articles that have proved to be some of the most seminal in the study of voting behavior and public opinion. They cover election turnout, ideology, determinants of voting behavior, congressional elections, party identification, and historical perspectives on the changing character of American electoral politics. Each section of the book includes a brief introductory essay on the topic at hand.

————, eds. *Controversies in Voting Behavior.* 2d ed. Washington, DC: CQ Press, 1984.

This edited volume enables the reader to make sense of a wide array of recent studies of voting and elections. This volume is the second edition of *Controversies in American Voting.* The new edition includes information on cases outside the United States to incorporate the changes presented by the growth of the comparative study of voting and elections into a major sub-field of political science. An introductory essay written by the editors precedes each article. The editors provide the background necessary for a full appreciation of the current work. Six major controversies are examined: election turnout, determinants of the vote, congressional elections, the ideological level of the electorate, the nature of partisanship, and the nature of partisan change.

Pomper, Gerald M. *Voter's Choice: Varieties of American Electoral Behavior.* New York: Dodd, Mead, 1975.

The author argues that the rationality of the electorate is set by the bounds of the public political debate. If the political leaders present clear-cut issue alternatives and information on which the voter can act rationally and responsibly, the voter will so act. If the public debate is muddled, the voter's response will be muddled. Pomper discusses dynamic models, the independent voter, class voting, sex roles in voting, the youth vote and generational change, racial divisions, issue voting, and variability in voter behavior.

————. *Voters, Elections, and Parties: The Practice of Democratic Theory.* New Brunswick, NJ: Transaction Books, 1988.

In this volume Pomper collects his previously published articles and essays on the topics of voters, elections, and political parties. His primary focus is the intersection between empirical findings and democratic theory. A new introductory essay evaluates the performance of the current electoral process as a democratic institution in juxtaposition with traditional democratic political philosophy. Each section, which focuses on one of the three main topics, is briefly introduced with a contextualized framework.

Popkin, Samuel L. *The Reasoning Voter: Communication and Persuasion in Presidential Campaigns.* 2d ed. Chicago: University of Chicago Press, 1994.

The author offers an insider's look at campaigns, media, and voters. He argues that voters make reasoned choices. Popkin analyzes three primary campaigns—Jimmy Carter in 1976; George Bush and Ronald Reagan in 1980; and Gary Hart, Walter Mondale, and Jesse Jackson in 1984—to arrive at a new model of how voters sort through commercials and sound bites to choose a candidate. He includes a chapter focusing on the 1992 presidential campaign, and how Bill Clinton defeated George Bush. Drawing on insights from economics and cognitive psychology, Popkin demonstrates that, as trivial as campaigns often appear, they provide voters with a surprising amount of information on a candidate's views and skills.

Potholm, Christian P., Richard E. Morgan, and Eric D. Potholm. *Just Do It: Political Participation in the 1990s.* Lanham, MD: University Press of America, 1993.

The authors examine the political process from both the inside and outside perspectives of a former politician from Maine and his academic coauthors. They discuss voters, issues, candidates, campaigns, polling, the media, and ballot measure campaigns. They examine strategies and tactics, and how citizens can participate in more ways than they realize. The authors call for participation and reflect on the primary author's personal participation over the last twenty-five years.

Rae, Douglas W., and Theodore J. Eismeier, eds. *Public Policy and Public Choice.* Beverly Hills: Sage, 1979.

The articles in this volume analyze the choices of citizens and politicians. Each article touches on the relationship between democratic political processes and public policy decisions. The first section of the book examines citizens' policy judgments, looking at both the evidence regarding issue voting and the positions, payments, and attitudes toward wealth redistribution. The second section deals with elections as referenda on government policy performance. These authors look at economic and fiscal effects on the popular vote for the president and other political consequences of fiscal choices. The third section examines institutional arrangements and policy decisions. These chapters present a theory of nominating convention conflict, examine rational allocation of congressional resources, and detail how institutional structure helps create of policy equilibrium.

Rifkin, Jeremy, and Carol G. Rifkin. *Voting Green: Your Complete Environmental Guide to Making Political Choices in the '90's.* New York: Doubleday, 1992.

The authors look at electoral politics through the lens of environmental politics. They present a sweeping political platform that touches on a wide variety of environmental issues, including global environmental security, clean air and water, health-ful food, safe workplaces, animal protection, preserving biodiversity, and the future direction of science and technology. They give a complete checklist of "green" posi-tions by which a voter can judge political candidates in the upcoming election. The authors provide a comprehensive congressional report card, with each member scored on their performance on nearly three hundred pieces of environmental legis-lation. They also provide a detailed analysis of the George Bush administration's per-formance on environmental issues.

Rose, Richard, ed. *Electoral Participation: A Comparative Analysis.* Beverly Hills: Sage, 1980.

The authors of the articles in this edited volume offer a comparative look at vot-ing behavior studies on European and U.S. elections. The two entries of particular interest to American electoral scholars concern the socioeconomic and cultural influ-ences on voting turnout in thirty democracies and electoral demobilization in the United States over time.

Rosenau, James N. *Citizenship between Elections: An Inquiry into the Mobiliz-able American.* New York: Free Press, 1974.

The author examines the interactive characteristics of citizen participation. In par-ticular, he looks at the interaction between mobilizers and mobilized citizens, ema-nating from stimuli from the mobilizers appealing for support. Rosenau employs data that contrast social backgrounds, perceptions, attitudes, and political activities of more than 3,000 citizens at two proximate yet different moments in history. Rosenau sys-tematically probes the data in an effort to delineate both the common and different experimental, attitudinal, perceptual, and behavioral sources of attentiveness and mobilizability. The author affirms mobilizability as a characteristic of some active cit-izens but fails to uncover its main sources. He also finds that citizenship between elec-tions comes from many interdependent variables rather than from a single factor.

Rosenstone, Steven J., and John M. Hansen. *Mobilization, Participation, and Democracy in America.* New York: Macmillan, 1993.

The authors argue that citizens participate in elections and government because they go to politics and because politics comes to them. They argue that mobilization is the key to determining participation in politics. The authors look at the personal attributes that inspire and enable individuals to become involved in politics, con-centrating on elements of the political system that pull people into politics. They examine citizen political participation in governmental politics using cross-sectional and time-series data. Rosenstone and Hansen assess the contributions of resources, interests, and strategic mobilization to public involvement. They use data from national surveys since 1952 to analyze popular attitudes toward parties and candi-dates. They explore the many facets of strategic electoral mobilization and show how the political environment affected the decline of citizen participation since the 1960s. The authors reflect on the meaning of political participation in a democratic society.

Scammon, Richard M., and Ben J. Wattenberg. *The Real Majority.* New York: Coward-McCann, 1970.

The authors examine elections and the electorate. They examine the electoral divisions over issues of civil rights, the Vietnam War, and the economy and argue that social issues have gained new potency. Scammon and Wattenberg consider how race, age, and wealth affect voting behavior. They also examine voter attitudes and the move to the center. The authors then apply their ideas to two contexts: the 1968 presidential contest and the state and local elections of 1969. They conclude by discussing how these ideas might affect the 1970 election.

Schlozman, Kay L., ed. *Elections in America.* Boston: Allen and Unwin, 1987.

This edited volume focuses on the various interpretations and meanings associated with the act of voting. All the authors see voting as a means to resolve pluralistic conflict in a resolute and peaceful manner. Each, however, brings a unique approach to this collection. Authors address voting as a democratic institution, as a republican form of leadership selection, as an institution of civic education, and as an institution by which the state can derive its legitimacy. The essays employ a variety of methodologies, theoretical dispositions, and issue foci.

Shaffer, William R. *Computer Simulations of Voting Behavior.* New York: Oxford University Press, 1972.

The author offers a study of the voter's decision-making process. Shaffer focuses on the acts, cognitions, and emotions that, when combined, constitute a coherent series of events leading to the voting decision. He examines several models designed to offer accounts of the process by which voters select their candidate of choice. The models he uses are classified into three theoretical levels of analysis: sociological, sociopsychological, and psychological. Using computer modeling, the author examines large, complex models. Shaffer evaluates the accuracy with which simulation models predict actual behavior.

Silbey, Joel H., Allan G. Bogue, and William H. Flanigan, eds. *The History of American Electoral Behavior.* Princeton: Princeton University Press, 1978.

This edited volume shows by concrete illustration how mathematical methods are being used to attack problems associated with popular voting behavior. The first section of the book focuses on electoral sequences in American history. Partisan realignment, third party alignments, and stability and change in voting patterns are examined here. The second section examines popular participation in elections. The effect of voting laws on participation in the South, the democratization of the party system, and party systems in the early national period are all discussed. The third section looks at the determinants of popular voting behavior, including political machines and progressivism, and discusses the retrieval of individual data from aggregate units. Finally, the editors analyze how popular voting behavior affects public policy.

Silbey, Joel H., and Samuel T. McSeveny, eds. *Voters, Parties, and Elections: Quantitative Essays in the History of American Popular Voting Behavior.* Lexington, MA: Xerox College Publishing, 1972.

This edited volume examines popular voting behavior over time. The first section of the book focuses on the historical structure of popular voting behavior. The second section defines popular voting behavior from 1800 to 1860. Next, the editors present an examination of stability and realignment from 1860 to 1896. The volume also deals with the Republican era of 1896 to 1928, and more recent voting behavior up to 1970. In each section of the book the authors ponder the overall trends for the era and the social, economic, and political factors that drive popular voting behavior.

Smith, Eric R.A.N. *The Unchanging American Voter.* Berkeley: University of California Press, 1989.

The author argues that changing conditions cannot improve the political awareness and sophistication of the voter. Smith evaluates the validity and reliability of the level of conceptualization index and various indexes of attitude consistency in relation to issue voting in a cross-temporal context. He builds a model that tests sophistication levels and concludes that since the 1950s only trivial changes have occurred in the political sophistication levels of the electorate.

Thompson, Kenneth W. *Cross-National Voting Behavior Research: An Example of Assisted Multivariate Analysis of Attribute Data.* Beverly Hills: Sage, 1970.

The author illustrates the utility of computer-based effect parameter analysis in the study of voting behavior from a cross-national perspective. Using this method on American and British elections and survey data from the 1950s and 1960s, Thompson concludes that status-dependence theory has relatively little power to explain voting behavior.

Tolchin, Susan J. *The Angry American: How Voter Rage Is Changing the Nation.* 2d ed. Boulder, CO: Westview Press, 1998.

The author focuses on the nature and role of anger in the political system. Tolchin examines the dilemma of voter rage in a democratic government. She explores the roots of antigovernment anger, examining psychological explanations, the roles of change and populism, and the legacy of violence and distrust. Tolchin discusses how economic uncertainty contributes to political anger. She considers values, hate, intolerance, the media, and language use as sources of cultural factors that affect political anger. She considers the problem of how to govern an angry mass public, including problems with electoral politics such as term limits, issue extremism, and the preference for any candidate other than a Washington insider. Finally, the author examines competing angers and political change.

Verba, Sidney, and Norman H. Nie. *Participation in America: Political Democracy and Social Equality.* New York: Harper and Row, 1972.

The authors consider two general political processes: citizens' participation in political life and governmental leaders' responsiveness to citizens' participation. Verba and Nie discuss several variables, including measures of various forms of participation, social status, political attitudes, voluntary association memberships, and both citizen and leader policy preferences, and how these variables affect participation and responsiveness. These variables form the building blocks with which the authors construct a theory of the causes and consequences of participation applicable to any nation.

Weisberg, Herbert F., ed. *Democracy's Feast: Elections in America.* Chatham, NJ: Chatham House, 1995.

This collection of articles focuses on the 1992 elections using surveys from the 1992 National Election Study. The articles examine the election outcome, voting behavior, and the congressional elections. The authors examine voter turnout, party identification, and group loyalty.

Weisberg, Herbert F., and Janet M. Box-Steffensmeier, eds. *Reelection 1996: How Americans Voted.* New York: Chatham House, 1999.

In this volume, a group of analysts at Ohio State University examine the election of Bill Clinton and the reelection of the Republican Congress in 1996. Using National Election Study data, they examine voter realignment, partisanship, candidate factors, ideology and issues, voter turnout, campaign finance, and media innovations.

White, John K. *The New Politics of Old Values.* 3d ed. Hanover, NH: University Press of New England, 1998.

The author reveals how values shape Americans' choices in the voting booth and in the marketplace. White pulls together a wide range of materials, including speeches, surveys, ballots, and ballads, to describe the nature of contemporary elections. He demonstrates the central role of shared values as the building blocks of leadership, and in particular as the basis of Ronald Reagan's remarkable voter appeal. In the first edition, the author predicted that future candidates beyond Ronald Reagan would have to pursue a strategy of focusing on values to win. In this edition, the author assesses the validity of that hypothesis by examining the George Bush and Michael Dukakis campaigns of 1988 and the American values articulated in Bill Clinton's race for the presidency.

Wilcox, Clyde. *The Latest American Revolution? The 1994 Elections and Their Implications for Governance.* New York: St. Martin's, 1994.

The author discusses the political developments that led to and resulted from the 1994 midterm elections. Wilcox examines the election results, dissecting the vote and explaining its meaning. He considers the possibilities of realignment and/or dealignment. Wilcox discusses the personnel changes in the House and Senate and how they affected government processes, institutional interaction, and public policy. He covers the new Republican agenda and the Contact with America. Appendixes contain the Contract with America, a list of governors of all fifty states, and Senate and House membership in the 104th Congress.

Wright, Gerald C. *Electoral Choice in America: Image, Party, and Incumbency in State and National Elections.* Chapel Hill: Institute for Research in Social Science, University of North Carolina, 1974.

The author moves beyond traditional sociological approaches that are overly deterministic in predicting voting behavior and develops a theoretical framework in which the voter operates as a decision maker. By doing so, Wright is able to examine the relationship between information processed by voters and the characteristics of different offices (president, governor, and senator). The author also explores the validity of the incumbency effect on subpresidential offices and the effects of the media's control of information on candidates and offices on the decision-making process.

Class

Kimball, Penn. *The Disconnected.* New York: Columbia University Press, 1972.

The author employs a variety of reporting methods to triangulate the facts about electoral participation by the urban poor. Kimball uses journalism, political science theory, and public opinion polling to examine the broad spectrum of the minority poor in the context of their past and present political participation. He verifies that their rates of voting registration and turnout are very low, and that this condition has stubbornly resisted conventional forms of political organization and activity. Kimball argues that the structure of the system discriminates most particularly against the poor. He focuses on African Americans and Puerto Ricans in New York, Newark, and Cleveland; Chicanos in Los Angeles and San Antonio; Indians in Arizona; and southern African Americans in New Orleans and Atlanta.

Koch, Jeffrey W. *Social Reference Groups and Political Life.* Lanham, MD: University Press of America, 1995.

The author argues that political science has failed to appreciate the role of social groups in structuring political thinking and behavior. Koch finds that social reference groups affect political life in a multitude of ways. Among other things, they help us understand how citizens deal with some of the most important decisions they must make with regard to politics. The author examines how group identifications shape candidate preferences, whether citizens' assessments of their group's economic well-being affect their political preferences, how citizens explain group economic outcomes, and how differently such explanations explain the ways these assessments affect political preferences. The author also looks at the effect of groups on shaping citizens' assessments of their own political abilities, on their willingness to engage in collective action, and on their ability to acquire information.

Ra, Jong O. *Labor at the Polls: Union Voting in Presidential Elections, 1952–1976.* Amherst: University of Massachusetts Press, 1978.

The author studies how labor union members and their families voted in seven presidential elections from 1952 to 1976, why they voted as they did, and the systematic implications. He crafts a theory of labor union voting behavior based on insights from plural levels of inference. Ra reconstructs the historical pattern of organizational involvement of labor unions and their leaders in party politics. He investigates how union membership affects political behavior. Ra then tests his model with data from the 1952, 1956, 1960, and 1964 presidential elections. He tests some additional hypotheses deduced from the theory using election data from 1968, 1972, and 1976. The author concludes with a discussion of the implications of his theory for the political system.

Shade, William L. *Social Change and the Electoral Process*. Gainesville: University of Florida Press, 1973.

The author reviews two dominant but problematic theories of electoral behavior and political change. Shade subsequently develops an alternative theory that attempts to resolve the problems he has identified. He tests the alternative theory by examining shifts in the electorate between each presidential election from 1860 to 1968. Shade then compares the results with trends in social, political, economic, intellectual, and technological spheres of society during this period.

Shienbaum, Kim E. *Beyond the Electoral Connection: A Reassessment of the Role of Voting in Contemporary American Politics*. Philadelphia: University of Pennsylvania Press, 1984.

The author offers a reinterpretation and reconceptualization of political behavior by attending to the problems of socioeconomic bias and noninstrumentality that characterize voters' preferences. Shienbaum argues that structural developments both inside and outside of electoral politics have made voting one of the least important political acts carried out by citizens.

Wolfinger, Raymond E., and Steven J. Rosenstone. *Who Votes?* New Haven: Yale University Press, 1980.

The authors describe and explain variations in turnout among different types of people. They classify types of voters by demographic characteristics, such as age, income, or place of residence, and some contextual variables, such as voter registration laws. Wolfinger and Rosenstone analyze survey data from studies conducted by the Census Bureau in 1972 and 1974. They find that education is the most important determinant of voting, followed by age. Being a college student and having a spouse affect turnout somewhat. The authors also find no relationship between the top incomes and voting. Other interpersonal surroundings associated with higher status occupations also do not seem to generate higher voting rates. The authors did not find free time to be an important resource for voting.

Age

Abramson, Paul R. *Generational Change in American Politics*. Lexington, MA: D. C. Heath, 1975.

The author recommends including generational differences in attitudes, values, and preferences among the structural factors that constrain and shape electoral politics.

Beginning with the working-class coalition that allowed the New Deal coalition to emerge, Abramson traces the declining importance of class-based participation and voting that transformed the Democratic coalition. The author maintains that what replaced class and race as forms of political and party identification resulted from generational changes in the electorate.

Borresen, C. Robert, and G. Michael Meacham. *The Youth Vote and the Study of Values.* Wichita, KS: Wichita State University, 1975.

The authors examine the youth vote in the 1960 elections. Borresen and Meacham compare the interests of college youth versus working youth, and youth voters versus youth nonvoters. Borresen and Meacham employ a standardized interest and attitude test, the Allport-Vernon-Lindzey Study of Values, to measure interest in politics among youth voters. They conclude that college students are more extreme in their political interest or disinterest than working youth. Voting college students scored highest, while nonvoting college students scored lowest on the Study of Values test. Nonvoting working youth scored about average on the scale, while voting working youth scored above average. The authors also examine their results in light of a study done in the early 1950s. They find that college students' voting patterns have become more extreme since the 1950s.

Economic

Berry, Thomas S. *On Measuring the Response of American Voters to Changes in Economic Conditions, 1792–1972.* Richmond, VA: Bostwick Press, 1972.

The author examines how economic conditions affected the voting choices of the electorate from 1792 to 1972. Berry finds that gross national product growth rates and other business conditions had no apparent bearing on presidential election results before 1828 but greatly affected them afterwards. Purely economic factors have furnished the key to nearly half the elections since 1828 when business was well above or below normal. The author also finds that the White House has its best opportunity for getting along with Congress after midterm elections when the nation is in good economic shape. Conversely, when the economy is faltering the voters will typically choose members of Congress who opposed the administration during the midterm election campaign.

Ferguson, Thomas, and Joel Rogers, eds. *The Hidden Election: Politics and Economics in the 1980 Presidential Campaign.* New York: Pantheon, 1981.

The editors have collected a series of essays that examine the linkages between political groups and economic interests in the 1980 presidential election. The essays examine the public record of the 1980 campaigns, the transformation of social and economic interests into political agendas and platforms, and the underlying sources of political conflict that emerged through the course of the campaign. The essays cover the political economy of the Ronald Reagan victory, the campaign as a public event, shifts in the electorate, the Federal Reserve, foreign policy issues and sources of domestic support for said policies, economic regulation and deregulation, policies concerning science and technology, and the implications of the 1980 election for the social welfare state.

Hibbs, Douglas A., Jr. *The American Political Economy: Macroeconomics and Electoral Politics.* Cambridge, MA: Harvard University Press, 1987.

The author examines the connections between public opinion and electoral behavior, and between macroeconomic policies and outcomes. Hibbs finds that macroeconomic policies are responsive to and constrained by the electorate's reactions to economic events. He gives an historical account of postwar macroeconomic performance. Hibbs then focuses on the electorate's reactions to economic outcomes. He shows that many citizens of modest means and status view rapidly rising prices as a significant problem. The author illustrates voter preferences and demands for other economic outcomes.

Kiewiet, D. Roderick. *Macroeconomics and Micropolitics: The Electoral Effects of Economic Issues.* Chicago: University of Chicago Press, 1983.

The author examines how economic events, crises, and concerns affect how the electorate votes for presidential and congressional candidates. Using advanced statistical analysis, the author tests four general hypotheses formulated in previous research on similar issues: (1) incumbents tend to be voted out of office during periods of economic downturn; (2) the electorate tends to evaluate policy differences between candidates and parties; (3) directly personal experiences tend to shape the decisions of the voter; and (4) voters tend to base their decisions on interpretations of the general state of the national economy. Appendixes include information on statistical methods, variable construction, and statistical tables.

Ethnic

Bailey, Harry A., Jr., and Ellis Katz, eds. *Ethnic Group Politics.* Columbus, OH: Charles E. Merrill, 1969.

The articles in this edited volume discuss the important role ethnicity plays in American politics. The first part of the book deals with the historical dimensions of the categories and identification of race, religion, and nationality. The second part is concerned with social and psychological forces that lead people of different groups to different patterns of political behavior. This section also attempts to document the differences in political behavior by the standard of voting in national elections. The third part examines to what extent people of different ethnic groups have been assimilated into the local urban political process. Finally, the fourth part deals with the extent to which ethnicity will continue to be an important variable in the explanation of political behavior.

Dawidowicz, Lucy S., and Leon J. Goldstein. *Politics in a Pluralist Democracy: Studies of Voting in the 1960 Election.* New York: Institute of Human Relations Press, 1963.

The authors attempt to fill a theoretical void in electoral behavior by attending to the variation of regional ethnic and religious minorities. They evaluate the 1960 presidential election by examining the electoral behavior of Irish Bostonians, the Italians of Providence, and Poles in Buffalo. They assess the effects of Protestant Fundamentalists in Tennessee, Ohio, and Illinois; German Catholics in Cincinnati; Jews in urban and suburban areas. They also compare Catholic and Protestant differences in Louisiana and Minnesota. Dawidowicz and Goldstein conclude that making broad generalizations about ethnic and religious groups is ill-founded.

De la Garaza, Rodolfo O., Martha Menchaca, and Louis DeSipio, eds. *Barrio Ballots: Latino Politics in the 1990 Elections.* Boulder, CO: Westview Press, 1994.

The authors use survey results and the results of the Latino Political Ethnography Project to explore political participation in Mexican American, Puerto Rican, and Cuban communities. They reject anthropological explanations of voting behavior and suggest new voter socialization strategies.

DeSipio, Louis. *Counting on the Latino Vote: Latinos as a New Electorate.* Charlottesville: University Press of Virginia, 1996.

The author examines how Latino populations have been and can be incorporated into society. He discusses earlier and current efforts at inclusion. He uses survey data to examine the impact Latinos would have if they began to vote commensurate with their numbers. DeSipio finds a portion of Latino nonvoters likely to participate under the proper circumstances and labels these potential voters the *new electorate*. Finally, the author provides new strategies for enabling Latinos who are not U.S. citizens to vote and discusses how and when politicians count on Latino votes. Appendixes list data sources and discuss estimating the size of the naturalization-eligible noncitizen population.

Fuchs, Lawrence H., ed. *American Ethnic Politics.* New York: Harper and Row, 1968.

The author attempts to explain why ethnicity has been so important in American politics and why American politics have been so important to ethnic groups. He presents a series of articles that deal with these issues and includes them in a second section. Among the scholars whose pieces appear in this volume are Elmer E. Cornwell Jr., Leon D. Epstein, Benton Johnson, Dwaine Marvick, Daniel P. Moynihan, Joseph Schafer, Harry M. Scoble, James Q. Wilson, and Raymond Wolfinger.

Levy, Mark R., and Michael S. Kramer. *The Ethnic Factor: How America's Minorities Decide Elections.* New York: Simon and Schuster, 1972.

The authors attempt to weigh data on ethnic voting and to assess their significance. Their targets include 65 million *ethnics*, their political backgrounds, the forces working on them, and their present and future political tendencies. Levy and Kramer present their findings about the outlook and voting habits of ethnic voters, including African Americans, Italians, Jews, Poles, Hispanic Americans, and the Irish. The authors emphasize the heavy Democratic vote among African Americans, Poles, and Italians. Jews continue to be the most liberal and issue-oriented of any of the groups analyzed. The Irish still vote Democratic two-to-one.

Parker, Frank R. *Black Votes Count: Political Empowerment in Mississippi after 1965.* Chapel Hill: University of North Carolina Press, 1990.

The author examines the plight of African American voting equality in Mississippi and the South since the Voting Rights Act of 1965. Parker examines Mississippi's strong resistance to African American enfranchisement through litigation struggles to block and increase access to political office for African Americans and to enforce and eliminate racially discriminatory districting practices. Parker assesses the effects of these political and juridical conflicts in terms of Mississippi state politics and national voting rights. The author concludes with a consideration of other racial impediments that face African Americans in Mississippi.

Rothenberg, Stuart, Eric Licht, and Frank Newport. *Ethnic Voters and National Issues: Coalitions in the 1980s.* Washington, DC: Free Congress Research and Education Foundation, 1982.

The authors examine social, economic, and foreign policy attitudes of five ethnic groups: Hispanics, Irish, Italians, Jews, and Poles. Rothenberg, Licht, and Newport provide an historical framework of ethnic voting patterns and statistical data collected from a series of surveys conducted in 1982. The authors suggest that the collected information and analysis can be used to incorporate ethnic voters into an ideological party system by framing issues in the appropriate manner.

Stanley, Harold W. *Voter Mobilization and the Politics of Race: The South and Universal Suffrage, 1952–1984.* New York: Praeger, 1987.

The author probes southern electoral expansion since the 1950s, an expansion far more white than black. The critical questions are why the expansion occurred and what difference it made. He examines the possible causes of southern electoral expansion, including racial attitudes, socioeconomic conditions, competition, attitudes, media usage, and registration requirements. He outlines consequences of electoral expansion, focusing on political implications and other more general considerations. The appendixes address methodological concerns, including the reliability of the National Election Studies data (1952–1984) used, data sources, the intricacies of logit analysis, and ways of remedying missing data.

Tate, Katherine. *From Protest to Politics: The New Black Voters in American Elections.* New York: Russell Sage Foundation, 1993.

The author examines the African American voter's role in the 1984 and 1988 presidential elections with a specific focus on contextual influences. The author finds that African American voters are traditionally liberal in their politics, tend to vote for Democrats, and that they tend to support viable African American candidates regardless of partisan affiliation. She also suggests that while the study of African American voting behavior is in its infancy, electoral politics may serve to further promote socioeconomic egalitarianism.

Demographic

Bartley, Numan V. *From Thurmond to Wallace: Political Tendencies in Georgia, 1948–1968*. Baltimore: Johns Hopkins University Press, 1970.

The author examines the effects of major political trends in the South on the politics of Georgia between 1948 and 1968. Increased African American participation, increasing voter participation, and representative equity are assessed in terms of Georgia's traditional voting tendencies. He evaluates differences between urban and rural politics, the Republican and Democratic parties' roles in Georgia, and the 1968 elections. Bartley concludes with a consideration of the general implications these trends have for southern politics.

Black, Earl, and Merle Black. *The Vital South: How Presidents Are Elected*. Cambridge, MA: Harvard University Press, 1992.

The authors evaluate the shift of southern voters' preferences to Republican presidential candidates and assess the possibility of a return of Democratic popularity to the region. They employ National Election Studies data on presidential elections from 1952 to 1988 and media exit polls from 1976 to 1988 to provide an in-depth analysis of southern politics. They examine southern politics compared to national presidential politics, within an historical context and in terms of electoral preference shifts.

Havard, William C. *The Louisiana Elections of 1960*. Baton Rouge: Louisiana State University Press, 1963.

The author interprets the gubernatorial and presidential elections in Louisiana in 1960 from the standpoint of the political ecology of the state. He shows how various factors have been distributed geographically within the state to create tendencies on the part of the electorate. He also attempts to show how these trends of the past impinged on the 1960 elections, and he discusses the meaning that the changes discerned in those elections may have had for the continuity of the traditional political system. Appendixes contain election data relevant to this study.

Gender

Baxter, Sandra, and Marjorie Lansing. *Women and Politics: The Invisible Majority*. Ann Arbor: University of Michigan Press, 1980.

The authors document the political standing of women in the last quarter century and suggest what the future may hold. They explore changes in the political attitudes and behavior of women from the 1950s through the 1980s and assess the implications of these shifts as women move from an ineffective political minority to a more activist numerical majority. They cover topics including the woman voter, attitudes, the African American woman voter, participatory politics, and how women view public policy, candidates, and parties. The authors engage in a comparative analysis, crossing boundaries and cultures. They conclude with an evaluation of the contemporary woman's political standing and discuss the outlook for the future of women in political life.

Smeal, Eleanor. *Why and How Women Will Elect the Next President*. New York: Harper and Row, 1984.

The author provides a wealth of information pertinent to the woman voter. She discusses gender gap issues and how they can be overcome through political organization by women. Other issues pertinent to women, such as reproductive rights, contraception, and the right to equal pay, and how these issues (should) affect women's selection of a president, are discussed. Furthermore, the author offers a guide to women interested in running for public office. An appendix includes a resource guide for organizations relevant to women's issues through which political mobilization can occur.

Religion

Flanigan, William H., and Nancy H. Zingale. *Political Behavior of the American Electorate*. 9th ed. Washington, DC: CQ Press, 1998.

The authors explore the ways that religious beliefs, income, and other demographic characteristics affect voting patterns. Incorporating data from the National Election Studies and other sources, the authors place recent voting trends, such as voter turnout and party loyalty, in an historical context of the past forty years.

Guth, James L., and John C. Green, eds. *The Bible and the Ballot Box: Religion and Politics in the 1988 Election*. Boulder, CO: Westview Press, 1991.

The editors have collected original research that focuses on the role played by religion during the 1988 presidential elections. The five parts of this work cover an array of topics on politics and religion, including the presidential campaigns of Pat Robertson and Jesse Jackson, the involvement of religious leaders in voter mobilization, the role of politico-religious activists, and activities of the religious voter. The editors conclude that religion continues to play an important role in politics despite the secular processes endemic to the institutions of government.

Lopatto, Paul. *Religion and the Presidential Election*. New York: Praeger, 1985.

The author examines the rise of the religious right in politics and the political system. Seeking to establish religion as a primary explanatory variable in presidential voting behavior, the author studies linkages between religion and voting in the six presidential elections between 1960 and 1980. After a consideration of the historical role of religion in politics, Lopatto explores the nature of religious cleavage in society to better understand the true relationship between religious belief and presidential preference. Using simulated election analysis, the author also explains how religious cleavages are mobilized, their long-term effects on politics, and how this increased activity may influence young voters.

Menendez, Albert J. *Religion at the Polls.* Philadelphia: Westminster Press, 1977.

The author looks at specific historical instances in which religion affected the tone, debate, and outcome of presidential elections. He considers the way religion shaped the cultural milieu. He discusses the influence of religion on congressional decisions and referendum elections. Menendez traces voting behavior over several elections across the country. He highlights the geography and demography of religious groups and follows the role of religion in elections throughout electoral history: religion and the presidency from 1789 to 1928, the Al Smith campaign, the John F. Kennedy campaign, and religion and politics from 1961 to publication. The author provides analyses of religious factors in the 1928 and 1960 presidential elections, political profiles of religious groups, and an examination of their representation and influence in Congress.

Prendergast, William B. *The Catholic Voter in American Politics: The Passing of the Democratic Monolith.* Washington, DC: Georgetown University Press, 1999.

The author examines the changing partisan attachment and voting patterns of Catholics. He analyzes Catholic voting patterns from the election of 1844 to 1998. Prendergast discusses how the Catholic population has changed, how the parties have changed, and how the political environment has changed.

Rozell, Mark J., and Clyde Wilcox, ed. *God at the Grass Roots: The Christian Right in the 1994 Elections.* Lanham, MD: Rowman and Littlefield, 1995.

This edited volume examines the Christian Right's role in the so-called Republican Revolution in general and in the 1994 congressional elections specifically. After a brief overview chapter examining the extent of that role, the book focuses how the Christian Right affected grassroots politics and elections in eleven states: California, Florida, Georgia, Iowa, Michigan, Minnesota, Oklahoma, Oregon, South Carolina, Texas, and Virginia. A final chapter projects the potential influence of the Christian Right on the 1996 elections.

———. *God at the Grass Roots, 1996: The Christian Right in the American Elections.* Lanham, MD: Rowman and Littlefield, 1997.

In this edited volume the authors discuss the Christian Right and the 1996 elections. They give an overview of the Christian Right in elections in South Carolina, Texas, Georgia, North Carolina, Florida, Virginia, Michigan, California, Oregon, Washington, Minnesota, Kansas, Maine, and West Virginia.

———. *Second Coming: The New Christian Right in Virginia Politics.* Baltimore: Johns Hopkins University Press, 1996.

The authors examine the relationship between the Christian Right and the Republican Party of Virginia. They describe the Virginia political structure in some detail, provide a brief political history, and discuss the state's political institutions that create special opportunities for Christian Right influence. The book focuses on context and the Christian Right as a party faction. The authors include in-depth case analyses of the 1992 and 1994 elections. They use a variety of data, including more than 100 in-depth interviews with Virginia Republicans and Christian Right leaders and activists.

Public Opinion

Buchanan, Bruce. *Renewing Presidential Politics: Campaigns, Media, and the Public Interest.* Lanham, MD: Rowman and Littlefield, 1996.

The author addresses five election-centered problems that flow from the reactive rather than proactive nature of democracy. Buchanan discusses why voters have not learned to signal clear expectations for positive and substantive campaigns. He argues that civic programming is weak and shows how the rival wants of the main actors do not favor effective civic programming. The author examines the less clearly understood social costs of retaining the political status quo against the perceived benefits of change. Buchanan argues that the media can correct for the imbalance of interests between candidate and voter. He focuses on the voter in discussing what might drive the rebalancing of interests. The author examines what it would take to effect changes in the habits of voters, and which changes would be most effective.

Cantril, Albert H. *The Opinion Connection: Polling, Politics, and the Press.* Washington, DC: CQ Press, 1991.

The author offers a broad-gauged, scholarly, but real-world examination of modern polling: the good and the bad, the new criticisms and the old, and the use and misuse of polling by news organizations. Cantril provides a concise guide to the elements in the design, conduct, and reporting of effective and enlightening polls. The author examines polling in its changing environment; reciprocal effects of polls, politics, and the press; quality of polls; polls and public trust; and polls serving democracy and the public purpose.

Dreyer, Edward C., and Walter A. Rosenbaum, eds. *Political Opinion and Electoral Behavior: Essays and Studies.* 2d ed. Belmont, CA: Wadsworth, 1970.

This edited volume analyzes how people perceive political life. The authors examine the process of opinion formation and expression as it occurs, not as it should occur. The first section of the volume examines the models and methods that make up the technology of public opinion research. A second section details the historical context of public opinion, focusing on political culture and socialization. A third section examines attitudes and behaviors of groups. A fourth section focuses on orientations and belief systems. A fifth section of the volume covers political campaigns and communication as public opinion context. Finally, the authors examine elections and the representation of constituency opinion.

Holbrook, Thomas M. *Do Campaigns Matter?* Thousand Oaks, CA: Sage, 1996.

The author attempts to determine whether campaigns matter by analyzing changes in public opinion during and across several presidential election campaigns. Holbrook argues that, although the national political and economic context of the election is very important, campaigns also play a crucial role in determining the outcomes of elections. He finds that campaign events, such as conventions and debates, primarily effect the changes in public opinion that occur during the campaign period. Using many different data sources from several presidential campaigns through 1992, Holbrook demonstrates that campaigns and national conditions jointly produce election outcomes.

McPhee, William N., and William A. Glaser, eds. *Public Opinion and Congressional Elections.* New York: Free Press, 1962.

This edited collection of essays analyzes problems in public opinion and mass behavior. Most of the authors attack problems in attitude consistency, the effect of varying community contexts, the use of computer models, and voting behavior. Specific topics covered include turnout, independent voters, coattails, political immunization, the influence of voluntary associations, and behavior in midterm elections. Appendixes discuss the candidates examined and the data samples, indexes, and questionnaires used in the overall project.

Neuman, W. Russell. *The Paradox of Mass Politics: Knowledge and Opinion in the American Electorate.* Cambridge, MA: Harvard University Press, 1986.

The author theorizes politics as a fluid process, emphasizing public opinion as process, the setting of the political agenda, the process by which nonissues become issues, and, at the individual level, the process by which nonpartisans become partisans. Neuman explores and critiques alternative theories. He demonstrates the link between sophistication and opinion. Subsequent chapters deal with political participation, political socialization, the role of the mass media, and democratic norms. Appendixes cover the concept and measurement of political sophistication and political conceptualization and the data sets used in the study.

Stockton, Ronald R., and Frank W. Wayman. *A Time of Turmoil: Values and Voting in the 1970s.* East Lansing: Michigan State University Press, 1983.

The authors trace the shifts in political values and opinions of voters between the 1972 and 1976 presidential elections. Employing a panel study in which 801 residents of Dearborn, Michigan, were interviewed several times, the authors argue that we are in a period of electoral disintegration rather than electoral realignment. Stockton and Wayman use advanced statistical methods to develop a model that explains shifts in public opinion as candidates campaigns and as issues change over time. They provide a sample questionnaire in an appendix.

Tobier, Arthur. *How McGovern Won the Presidency, and Why the Polls Were Wrong.* New York: Outerbridge and Lazard, Ballantine, 1972.

The author examines how and why public opinion polls taken during the course of a presidential election can be misleading or wrong. Tobier uses the 1972 election campaign as the primary case, examining why the polls—which predicted a George McGovern victory—were inconsistent with the election results. Tobier also examines the 1936 contest between Alf Landon and Franklin D. Roosevelt, and the 1948 contest between Harry Truman and Thomas E. Dewey. The author's general conclusion is that the polls can be wrong because they do not measure or take into account election strategy.

Party Identification

Carmines, Edward G., and James A. Stimson. *Issue Evolution: Race and the Transformation of American Politics.* Princeton: Princeton University Press, 1989

The authors examine the politics of race from Franklin D. Roosevelt to Ronald Reagan, examining executive, legislative, party, and grassroots actions and ideology regarding the issue. Carmines and Stimson propose a theory of issue evolution that explains normal partisan change. They illustrate the theory by examining how racial issues affect party identification. They argue that the evolution of new issues is the stimulus for partisan change and that the continuous replacement of the electorate is the mechanism by which such change is effected. The authors conclude that the issue of race has transformed the face of American politics.

Converse, Philip E. *The Dynamics of Party Support: Cohort-Analyzing Party Identification.* Beverly Hills: Sage, 1976.

The author performs a time-based cohort study to trace the evolution of partisan strength and changes in party identification of individuals as they age. His time-series analysis focuses primarily on the years between 1964 and 1975 and Converse uses these data to evaluate traditional theories of party identification and the strength of that identification.

Cosman, Bernard. *Five States for Goldwater; Continuity and Change in Southern Presidential Voting Patterns.* Tuscaloosa: University of Alabama Press, 1966.

The author discusses the elements of continuity and change in the presidential voting patterns of southern electorates. Cosman focuses on one dimension—presidential Republicanism—and in particular on the 1964 Barry Goldwater outcome, especially in the South. Cosman compares this outcome to earlier voting alignments.

Cummings, Milton C., Jr. *Congressmen and the Electorate: Elections for the U.S. House and President, 1920–1964.* New York: Free Press, 1966.

The author studies the elections for the House and the interrelationship between the vote for president and the vote for members of Congress in presidential election years. Cummings analyzes the general election results for president and for members of Congress in the twelve presidential election years between 1920 and 1964. He explores the similarities and differences between the congressional and presidential electoral support as polled by each of the major parties. Cummings examines factors associated with national-level split-ticket voting. He is concerned with some of the long-term trends in congressional partisan strength that have been manifesting themselves since 1920. The author argues that these trends have been reshaping the character of congressional electoral politics since the 1930s.

DeVries, Walter, and V. Lance Tarrance Jr. *The Ticket-Splitter: A New Force in American Politics.* Grand Rapids, MI: William B. Erdmans Publishing, 1972.

The authors reject the accepted methods of classifying voters and gauging the influence of partisanship. DeVries and Tarrance classify voters on the basis of how they cast their ballots. Ticket-splitters are identified as voters who have cast a ballot for candidates of more than one major party for important offices in the same election. The authors contrast ticket-splitters with independent voters, who identify themselves as independent. Whereas self-identified independent voters are less likely to vote than people who identify with a political party, ticket-splitters are found to be more likely to vote. Ticket-splitters base their decisions on their judgment of a candidate's ability, personality, and stand on the issues more than on partisan identification.

Fiorina, Morris P. *Retrospective Voting in American National Elections.* New Haven: Yale University Press, 1981.

The author examines the consequences for decisions of the distinction between retrospective and prospective voting. Fiorina assigns retrospective evaluations to a central position in his model of individual voting behavior. The culmination of these evaluations, he argues, is the basis of a long-term partisan predisposition known as party identification. The more recent evaluations are a large part of what are called the issues of the campaign. And both the long-term and recent evaluations contribute to the future consequences that ride on the election.

Keith, Bruce E., David B. Magleby, Candice J. Nelson, Elizabeth Orr, Mark C. Westlye, and Raymond E. Wolfinger, eds. *The Myth of the Independent Voter.* Berkeley: University of California Press, 1992.

The authors examine the partisan tendencies of self-proclaimed independent, or neutral, voters. Finding that approximately one-third of independent voters actually are neutral, the authors maintain that the strength of party identification is not declining as fast as other studies have demonstrated. They demonstrate that independents who lean toward one party or the other tend to vote reliably for that party. They examine party identification across age groups, educational backgrounds, race, and region over time.

Moreland, Laurence W., and Robert P. Steed, eds. *The 1996 Presidential Election in the South: Southern Party Systems in the 1990s.* Westport, CT: Praeger, 1998.

This edited volume, the fourth in a series of analyses of elections in the South, focuses on the setting and nominating process in the 1996 presidential election. The book includes individual chapters on Alabama, Georgia, Louisiana, Mississippi, South Carolina, Arkansas, Florida, North Carolina, Tennessee, Texas, and Virginia.

Moreland, Laurence W., Robert P. Steed, and Tod A. Baker, eds. *The 1988 Presidential Election in the South: Continuity amidst Change in Southern Party Politics.* New York: Praeger, 1991.

This is the second volume in a series of analyses on presidential elections in the South. The work looks at the 1988 elections in Alabama, Georgia, Louisiana, Mississippi, South Carolina, Arkansas, Florida, North Carolina, Tennessee, Texas, and Virginia.

Phillips, Kevin P. *The Emerging Republican Majority.* New Rochelle, NY: Arlington House, 1969.

The author studies the changing course of voting patterns. One thesis is that, because of the erosion of the southern Democrat tradition, the South is turning into an important presidential base for the Republican Party. Phillips also examines the extent of ethnic influences, the role of suburban voters, and regional variations in American politics. Using 143 charts and 47 maps to supplement his narration, the author argues for the national emergence of a Republican majority. Originally written before the 1968 election, the author points out that the 1968 contest verifies his hypotheses.

Pierce, John C., and John L. Sullivan, eds. *The Electorate Reconsidered.* Beverly Hills: Sage, 1980.

This edited volume reflects some major currents present in the study of the electorate. Chapters explore distinct elements of the public's political beliefs and behavior. The book opens with a brief overview of the electorate. Next the authors examine the structure of public opinion, including attitude stability and change, belief system organization, watershed years, and change in the public's thinking. The next section examines the sources of public opinion, ranging from perceptions of political leaders to socialization to personality. Next is a section on the substance of public opinion, focusing on public tolerance and the effects of and changes in race and gender roles. A final section examines party and candidate choice. These authors look at the nature of party identification, candidate preference under uncertainty, and contextual sources of voting behavior.

Steed, Robert P., Laurence W. Moreland, and Tod A. Baker, eds. *The 1984 Presidential Election in the South: Patterns of Southern Party Politics.* New York: Praeger, 1986.

The editors have collected a set of essays that examine the 1984 presidential election in eleven southern states. Each case study examines political developments in the state, the nomination process, and the general campaign within the state. Each case study also provides an in-depth analysis of the election results in the state and a contextualization of the 1984 election and its results within the recent political history of that state. The articles also deal with specific electoral contests within each state. The volume is bounded by a consideration of southern politics in general and an analysis of the 1984 elections in the South.

————, eds. *The 1992 Presidential Election in the South: Current Patterns of Southern Party and Electoral Politics.* Westport, CT: Praeger, 1994.

This volume continues a series of analyses of presidential elections in the South. The fourteen chapters examine the setting and nominating process, discuss the elections in each southern state, and present a conclusion. The states examined are Alabama, Georgia, Louisiana, Mississippi, South Carolina, Arkansas, Florida, North Carolina, Tennessee, Texas, and Virginia.

————, eds. *Southern Parties and Elections: Studies in Regional Political Change.* Tuscaloosa: University of Alabama Press, 1997.

This volume examines parties and elections in the South from the 1940s to the 1990s. The twelve articles cover topics such as voting rights, voter turnout, political activists, age and partisanship, primaries, and increasing liberalism among southern members of Congress.

Trilling, Richard J. *Party Image and Electoral Behavior.* New York: Wiley, 1976.

The author examines how party image affects voters' decisions at the polls. Trilling discusses the concept of party image as it has been developed in other political science publications. Trilling examines party images in three different ways: (1) through the development of a general index and its comparison with the standard partisanship index; (2) through the development of separate component indexes; and (3) via discussion of the substantive concerns of voters that constitute their party images. He examines party images among important political groups defined by class and race. In the last section, the author deals more specifically with theoretical propositions. He analyzes the ability of party images to transform party identifications and relates the properties of the party image concept to the dynamics of the party system.

Forecasting

Budge, Ian, and Dennis J. Farlie. *Explaining and Predicting Elections: Issue Effects and Party Strategies in Twenty-Three Democracies.* Boston: Allen and Unwin, 1983.

The authors adopt an issue-oriented approach in their study of twenty-three postwar democratic states and their elections. By focusing on changing political conditions and the electorates' responses to them, the authors develop a general theory of democratic electoral participation and outcome that goes beyond the traditional indicator of party identification. Budge and Farlie contend that a general understanding of how democratic institutions work contributes to the practical defense of democracy. Such understanding, particularly of elections, may provide strategic information to candidates, parties, and voters as they compete and participate in democratic elections.

Crespi, Irving. *Pre-Election Polling: Sources of Accuracy and Error.* New York: Russell Sage Foundation, 1988.

The author evaluates methods used in pre-election polling and outlines the areas in which it is accurate and inadequate for making predictions about electoral outcomes. After evaluating the design of the pre-election poll, the sample from which information is drawn, and its relationship to the actual voter, the author concludes that most of the error present in pre-election polls can be attributed to nonsampling measurement error.

Lichtman, Allan J. *The Keys to the White House, 1996: A Surefire Guide to Predicting the Next President.* Lanham, MD: Madison Books, 1996.

The author provides a guide to how to predict success in a presidential election. Each element or issue is considered a key. If enough keys turn against the incumbent party, then the candidate will lose. Among the keys Lichtman considers are the economy, social conditions, foreign affairs, political factors like a contested nomination or a third party candidate, and even candidate charisma. The author finds that the environment in which the candidate must run, which is often shaped by things out of the campaign's control, often determines the outcome. Only when these environmental forces are inconclusive can little things, like campaign mistakes or poor strategy, have an exaggerated impact. The book incorporates the experience of the 1992 campaign and indicates how the incumbent party should fare in the 1996 election.

Lichtman, Allan J., and Ken DeCell. *The Thirteen Keys to the Presidency.* Lanham, MD: Madison Books, 1990.

The authors argue that an extensive, in-depth examination of presidential elections since the 1850s produces a set of thirteen important factors that are relevant to each presidential election. This historical analysis of enduring principles produces reliable forecasts of presidential elections. Lichtman and DeCell maintain that despite massive economic and cultural changes, technological developments, and historical watersheds, a set of constant variables can be used to forecast electoral outcomes.

Rosenstone, Steven J. *Forecasting Presidential Elections.* New Haven: Yale University Press, 1983.

The author develops a theoretical model by which to forecast differences between election outcomes. After considering other mechanisms that are used to predict electoral outcomes, the author contextualizes voter preference in terms of issues, the electorate's position on these issues, the economic condition of the country, and whether or not the state is in a state of war or peace. Rosenstone then tests the model for how well it predicts presidential elections from 1948 to 1972, with special attention given to the 1976 and 1980 elections. The author concludes by evaluating the effectiveness of the model as a predictive tool and discussing its implications for future presidential and congressional elections.

Turnout

Avey, Michael J. *The Demobilization of American Voters: A Comprehensive Theory of Voter Turnout.* Westport, CT: Greenwood, 1989.

The author takes issue with traditional explanations of declining voter turnout, such as education levels, low socioeconomic status or political apathy. Avey posits a theory in which politicians, the political system, and elites are the causal elements that explain the behavior of nonvoters. His approach emphasizes the mobilization and demobilization of the electorate over time and examines the structural constraints and facilitators elites use to do both tasks effectively. Avey suggests that approximately 80 percent of eligible voters would participate if politicians would adopt policy stances that address the needs of traditionally ignored segments of the population.

Campbell, James E. *The Presidential Pulse of Congressional Elections.* Lexington: University Press of Kentucky, 1997.

The author examines explanations for midterm losses and looks at how presidential elections influence congressional elections. He examines congressional elections from 1862 to 1996. Campbell argues that in presidential election years, members of Congress ride coattails into office, but that in midterm election years this is not the case. He also addresses how the presidential pulse affects voting behavior, electoral accountability and change, split-ticket voting, and congressional party strength.

Chen, Kevin. *Political Alienation and Voting Turnout in the United States, 1960–1988.* San Francisco: Mellon Research University Press, 1992.

The author examines linkages between cynicism, apathy, and voter abstention. Chen elaborates on previous efforts to identify what political alienation means and how it should be measured. He argues that previous attempts to link declining turnout to rising political alienation foundered on weak theory, inadequate conceptualization, and poor measurement. Chen confirms the findings of political scientists who argue that alienation is multifaceted. He attributes declining turnout since the 1960s entirely to cohort replacement.

Doppelt, Jack C., and Ellen Shearer. *Nonvoters: America's No-Shows.* Thousand Oaks, CA: Sage, 1999.

The authors conducted a national survey and interviewed nonvoting Americans in relation to the 1996 presidential and congressional elections. They discuss their findings and the five clusters of nonvoters they label as doers, unpluggeds, irritables, don't knows, and alienated. Doppelt and Shearer analyze nonvoting in local, off-year, and presidential elections.

Ginsberg, Benjamin, and Martin Shefter. *Politics by Other Means: The Declining Importance of Elections in America.* New York: Basic Books, 1990.

The authors posit that politics has reached an era of postelectoral politics characterized by the simultaneous decline in voter participation and increased preoccupation with controversy, scandal, and ethics. Campaign strategy is now more oriented to sensationalized events than to political issues as politicians attempt to outmobilize one another's electorates. The authors examine the decline of electoral politics, the solidification of deadlock, partisan tactical movements, and how institutions and power operate to shape postelectoral politics.

Hadley, Arthur T. *The Empty Polling Booth.* Englewood Cliffs, NJ: Prentice-Hall, 1978.

Using survey data of and interviews with eligible voters in 1976, the author attempts to explain the trend of nonvoting in elections. Hadley examines the rise of nonvoting, its significance, its implications for a democratic polity, and theories that have previously attempted to explain it. After developing a six-fold typology of the nonvoter, the author concludes that nonvoters are demographically distributed as randomly as voters and that voters and nonvoters share more in common than previously thought. He offers some tentative conclusion, suggestions, and proposals in the final chapter. Appendixes present the technical operationalization of the nonvoter and the results of the original survey data.

Hyneman, Charles S., C. Richard Hofstetter, and Patrick R. O'Connor. *Voting in Indiana: A Century of Persistence and Change.* Bloomington: Indiana University Press, 1980.

The authors offer an account of how Hoosiers behave on election day. They confine the study to general elections and fix their attention mainly on voter turnout and the distribution of votes between Democratic and Republican candidates. They note the appearance of third parties but do not examine them in depth. They report tendencies of individuals in different parts of the state to seek nomination for office, but they do not include the decisions made by voters on primary election day. The authors' case study confines itself to particular behavioral experiences of Indiana voters. The authors place Indiana in context of the other forty-nine states. They then examine voter turnout, party competition, electoral success, third parties, party rivalry, partisan voters, and trends in party preferences. They examine subunits of the state, emphasizing the urban-rural cleavage in particular. They consider topics such as selectivity in voting, consistency of party support, determinants of electoral participation, and office seeking in Indiana.

Kleppner, Paul. *Who Voted? The Dynamics of Electoral Turnout, 1870–1980.* New York: Praeger, 1982.

The author analyzes longitudinal voter turnout and electoral participation patterns from 1870 to 1980. He focuses on distinct waves of high voter participation in congressional and presidential elections and the structural constraints that affected them. The author isolates social- and political-structural variables that predict voter turnout and uses those to explore the evolutionary and cyclical nature of voting behavior as citizen mobilization and demobilization.

Lang, Kurt, and Gladys E. Lang. *Voting and Nonvoting: Implications of Broadcasting Returns before Polls Are Closed.* Waltham, MA: Blaisdell, 1968.

In context of the 1960 and 1964 presidential elections, the authors evaluate how broadcasting early election returns affects the voter who has yet to cast his or her preference. Based on their analysis, Lang and Lang make policy recommendations regarding the release of the information. They examine the previous work and literature on this subject, consider the salience of the query, and assess the direct impact of the bandwagon and underdog effects that might result from early returns. They conclude with an assessment of the significance of the late voter.

Moos, Malcolm C. *Politics, Presidents, and Coattails.* New York: Greenwood Press, 1952.

The author examines voting behavior in congressional and presidential elections to identify the relationship between presidential and congressional tickets. Moos also discusses the nature of the two-party system, and examines the Republican Party's role in this system.

Piven, Frances F., and Richard A. Cloward. *Why Americans Don't Vote.* New York: Pantheon, 1988.

The authors discuss institutional arrangements that produce massive nonvoting by lower-class and working-class people. While Piven and Cloward agree that a multifaceted historical process is truly the cause of declining voter participation, they argue that the root contemporary cause is the distinctive system of voter registration procedures. Voter registration barriers not only restrict the suffrage, argue the authors but also transform the calculus of the political parties. These effects on parties in turn affect attitudes of nonvoters. To illustrate their argument the authors trace electoral mobilization and demobilization from the nineteenth century to the 1980s.

Sandoz, Ellis, and Cecil V. Crabb Jr., eds. *Election '84: Landslide without a Mandate?* New York: Mentor, 1984.

This edited volume examines the national and state elections in 1984. In particular, the authors examine the odd occurrence of a Republican landslide with relatively short coattails. They ask whether the Republican victory represents a mandate or simply a vote of confidence for a popular president. Along the way they examine the so-called Reagan phenomenon, election results, policy implications, economic issues and Reaganomics, the New Federalism and state elections, and how the Reagan victory will affect future politics.

Smith, Jeffrey A. *American Presidential Elections: Trust and the Rational Voter.* New York: Praeger, 1980.

The author argues that trust has been a consistent and rational criterion that voters use in turnout and candidate choice. To explain the decline of voter turnout since 1960, the author examines four models of voting behavior and offers an alternative to them that focuses on the rationality of the individual voter. From there, he evaluates the theoretical and empirical roles played by trust in the voter's decision-making process.

Smolka, Richard G. *Election Day Registration: The Minnesota and Wisconsin Experience in 1976.* Washington, DC: American Enterprise Institute for Public Policy Research, 1977.

The author analyzes registration procedures in Minnesota and Wisconsin on election day in 1976. Smolka finds that election-day registration probably contributed to a marginal increase in voter turnout but also encouraged many voters to wait until election day to register. Moreover, it caused long lines and confusion at many polling places, allowing hundreds of voters to vote in the wrong places and without adequate identification. The author finds little evidence that either party gained from election-day registration, except in Milwaukee. The potential for voter fraud, however, was great; the probability of detection was small; and the discovery of fraud could only occur too long after the election to affect the outcome.

Teixeira, Ruy A. *The Disappearing American Voter.* Washington, DC: Brookings Institution, 1992.

The author addresses the steadily decreasing voter turnout rates and empirically examines a series of questions related to this topic. The author examines the causes of the decline in a comparative context, analyzes the trend since 1960, discusses the ramifications of low voter turnout, and offers solutions to the problem. Teixeira insists that we correct the decrease in voter participation to maintain democratic legitimacy and to set the appropriate agendas reflective of the total population's interests.

Author Index

The author index lists authors mentioned in Part I, "Secondary Sources, Primary Sources, and Finding Tools."

Title Index

The title index lists titles mentioned in Part I, "Secondary Sources, Primary Sources, and Finding Tools."